Princely power
in the Dutch Republic

MANCHESTER
1824

Manchester University Press

STUDIES IN EARLY MODERN
EUROPEAN HISTORY

This series aims to publish
challenging and innovative research in all areas
of early modern continental history.
The editors are committed to encouraging work
that engages with current historiographical
debates, adopts an interdisciplinary
approach, or makes an original contribution
to our understanding of the period.

SERIES EDITORS
Joseph Bergin, William G. Naphy, Penny Roberts and Paolo Rossi

Already published in the series

Portrait of William Frederick of Nassau-Dietz, by Wybrand de Geest, dated 1632. The panel is part of a series of portraits, which originally hung at Honselaarsdijk, one of the palaces of Frederick Henry of Orange (1584–1647). Collection of the Rijksmuseum, Amsterdam.

Princely power
in the Dutch Republic

Patronage and William Frederick
of Nassau (1613–64)

GEERT H. JANSSEN
translated by J. C. GRAYSON

Manchester University Press

Manchester and New York

distributed exclusively in the USA by Palgrave Macmillan

Published by Manchester University Press
Oxford Road, Manchester M13 9NR, UK
and Room 400, 175 Fifth Avenue, New York, NY 10010, USA
www.manchesteruniversitypress.co.uk

Distributed exclusively in the USA by
Palgrave Macmillan, 175 Fifth Avenue, New York,
NY 10010, USA

Distributed exclusively in Canada by
UBC Press, University of British Columbia, 2029 West Mall,
Vancouver, BC, Canada V6T 1Z2

British Library Cataloguing-in-Publication Data
A catalogue record for this book is available from the British Library

Library of Congress Cataloging-in-Publication Data applied for

ISBN 978 0 7190 7758 6 *hardback*

First published 2008

17 16 15 14 13 12 11 10 09 08   10 9 8 7 6 5 4 3 2 1

The translation of this book was made possible by a generous grant from the Netherlands Organisation for Scientific Research (NWO)

Typeset in Perpetua with Albertus display
by Koinonia, Manchester
Printed in Great Britain
by Biddles Ltd, King's Lynn, Norfolk

Contents

CONTENTS

Preface

This book is a revised and slightly abbreviated version of *Creaturen van de macht. Patronage bij Willem Frederik van Nassau (1613–1664)*, published in Dutch by Amsterdam University Press in 2005. I am grateful to the Netherlands Organisation for Scientific Research (NWO), for generously funding the English translation.

The book came into being with the help of many people. I should like to thank former colleagues at Leiden, Oxford, St Andrews and Mainz for their continuing support and advice. Over the years, I received valuable suggestions from my supervisor Simon Groenveld, as well as from Paul Arblaster, Paul Hoftijzer, Jonathan Israel, Luuc Kooijmans, Hans Mol, Henk van Nierop and Andrew Spicer. I am also grateful to Joseph Bergin, Robert Evans, Willem Frijhoff, Robert Frost, Benjamin Kaplan, Sharon Kettering, Marika Keblusek and Andrew Pettegree for their encouragement and invitations to test out my ideas at their seminars and conferences. A special word of thanks goes to Chris Grayson who proved to be such a dedicated translator.

Cambridge, July 2008

Glossary

Binnenhof	Complex of government buildings in The Hague: seat of the States of Holland and the central institutions of the Republic (States-General, Council of State). The north-west side was occupied by the stadholder of Holland (stadholder's quarter).
Burgomaster	Mayor: highest magistrate in a town, elected from the *vroedschap*.
Council of State	Advisory body of the Generality (States-General), particularly in financial and military matters.
Delegated States	Standing committee of the States of Friesland.
Grietman	Key rural magistrate in the Friesian countryside.
Landdag	Diet: annual assembly of the States of Friesland.
Mindergetal	Preparatory committee of the States of Friesland.
Pensionary of Holland	High official of the States of Holland, chief representative of Holland in the States-General.
Regent	Common description for anyone in the Dutch Republic who held a political office on local, provincial or national level.
Stadholder	Holder of the highest office in one or more of the seven provinces that constituted the Dutch Republic.
States	The highest authority in a province, generally made up of representatives from the local nobility and the towns.
States-General	National assembly, consisting of representatives from the seven provinces of the Dutch Republic. Dealt with limited number of issues, including defence, foreign affairs and conflicts between provinces.
Union of Utrecht	Act of defence, agreed between the rebellious provinces in 1579. Later served as a constitution of the Dutch Republic.
Volmacht	Representative of one of the four quarters of the province of Friesland.
Vroedschap	Town council. Varied in size but usually consisted of about forty members.

Abbreviations

UA	Utrechts archief
UBL	Universiteitsbibliotheek Leiden
WF	William Frederick
WFG	Archiefdienst Westfriese gemeenten
WII	William II
WIII	William III

Note on references and manuscript sources

William Frederick often abbreviated names and titles in his diaries. For ease of reading these have been expanded in the English translation. 'S.H.' thus becomes 'His Highness' ('Sijne Hoocheyt').

Dates in the text are given as far as possible in the New or Gregorian Style, which was used in the western provinces of the Dutch Republic in the seventeenth century. This style was ten days in advance of the Old or Julian calendar, which was still in use in the eastern provinces and also in Friesland. As a precaution William Frederick often noted both dates in his diaries and correspondence. Where possible both Old and New Style dates have been given in the notes.

In 2003 the archives of the Friesian stadholders in The Hague (Royal House Archives) and Leeuwarden (Tresoar) were reinventoried and new numbering systems were applied. This new inventory can be searched on the internet using keywords, and has made using the stadholders' archives considerably easier. To avoid confusion and erroneous conversions, the references in this book are still given to the old inventory numbers. Both archives have concordances, which allow conversion to the new numbering.

Introduction

When William Frederick of Nassau started his diary in the new year of 1652, he did not choose a lapidary phrase, an edifying motto or even a religious adage. His first words were characteristically sober and down-to-earth:

> If anyone urges me to do something which suits me, and which I am inclined to do, I must make it appear as if I do not do it willingly, or cannot do it. For if it then comes about, those who urged it on me will be all the more obliged and bound to me, and I will be better able to use them at another moment, when I have need of their services. But all this with moderation and discretion.[1]

Over three hundred and fifty years later the social skills revealed by this seventeenth-century diary are still as recognisable as ever, for they describe an everyday aspect of human interaction: anyone who does a service to another may expect a reward at some time. This common mechanism of give and take, of services rendered and returned, is usually defined by scholars as patronage or clientage. William Frederick's remarks on the patronage customs of his own time, however, are exceptional, for few seventeenth-century men left such a detailed record of their social network, and of the strategies that they pursued in their relationships. The ways in which he and his contemporaries negotiated the consequences of patronage in their lives is the subject of this book.

A study of patronage in the early modern period is not a self-explanatory concept, for however familiar the words of a seventeenth-century diarist may seem, William Frederick's world was not ours. The very terms 'patronage' and 'clientage' were even unknown at the time, and their precise meaning and relevance have been hotly debated by historians and social scientists in the past decades.

Patronage

The American historian Sharon Kettering has once boldly defined the essence of patronage in just three words. 'Patronage studies', she wrote in her *Patrons, Brokers and Clients*, 'concern the realities of power'.[2] Kettering thus assigns only two basic characteristics to her subject: in the first place patronage always revolves around power and the ways in which it is acquired and exercised. Her second point is to stress that it is not so much the formal power relationship which deserves attention as its operation in practice. This means that clientage may be defined in terms of dependence. Patronage, according to this line of argument, is indirect control over the conduct of others.

This terse characterisation is apt in itself, but a rather challenging starting-point for a book. The 'reality of power', after all, is not a very practical definition of a research topic. Social scientists have therefore tried to formulate a more descriptive definition of patronage as well. They usually define clientage as a personal relationship between social unequals, in which the superior – the patron – grants certain favours to the inferior – the client – in exchange for his loyalty, dependence or support.[3] This comes down to saying that the patron controls certain scarce resources, such as money, offices, influence or protection, to which the client has no direct access. To be able to profit from the patron's resources the client can offer him his services and in exchange he is willing to bind himself to the patron by ties of obligation. With the patron's backing the client is thus able to increase his financial or 'social' income, but at the cost of losing some of his freedom of manoeuvre. In his turn the patron profits from this dependence, and can henceforth influence his client's conduct by drawing on the 'credit' granted, in the form of the promised service. This creates an unequal relationship of services rendered and returned, a sort of social credit and debit account.[4]

Because relations between patron and client are always founded on an exchange of services, at first sight they may resemble business transactions. The difference in practice is that patronage and clientage are rarely embodied in formal contracts, but rely more on unwritten rules, implicit expectations or tacit understandings. This makes it difficult for researchers to expose the ties and codes of patronage, for clientage involves putting people under an obligation; a kind of human behaviour which is rarely explictly recorded on paper.[5]

A multidisciplinary tradition

Research into patronage has a long history that draws on various disciplines, including political science, anthropology and art history. Such a wide range of interest is not surprising, for it is generally assumed that patronage is an everyday phenomenon that can be found in every society.[6] The common feature of these different traditions of research is to assume that patronage goes hand in hand with 'brokerage'. In practice patron and client do not always need to be connected directly, for in many cases intermediaries or agents serve as the link between them. These 'power brokers' pass on the services they have received from their own patrons to their clients, thus creating pyramid-like, vertical connections in an organisation or society.[7]

Until the 1970s, research into patronage and brokerage was largely the preserve of social scientists, who applied the concept chiefly to analyse social relationships in primitive or non-Western societies.[8] These studies, however, increasingly suggested that the manifestations of patronage in a given society were related to the degree of state formation. In this way research into clientage acquired a historical dimension. More specifically, it was suggested that the process of state building in medieval and early modern Europe had run in parallel with the use of specific forms of patronage.[9] As feudal systems of power declined, some scholars reasoned, clientage and brokerage could give a new structure to the developing early modern state and to the authority of its monarchs.[10]

Although much research was carried out in the 1970s and 1980s to test these assumptions, no truly coherent picture has emerged from the numerous French, German, and above all Anglo-American case studies. While historians such as Robert Harding, Sharon Kettering and Antoni Mączak were able to reveal ties of patronage between local regions and centres of royal power, cultural historians, among them Kristen Neuschel, doubted the usefulness of this detective work.[11] Neuschel claimed that historians had misunderstood the language of patronage that was commonly used in early modern Europe, and had therefore been led to exaggerate the extent of the dependence and loyalty involved.

These assumed qualities of the patron-client relationship had been addressed earlier by the French scholar Roland Mousnier. He argued that early modern ties of patronage could not be described in purely functionalistic terms. Mousnier introduced the concept of *fidélité*, to give certain enduring forms of clientage more emotional content. Many Anglo-American historians, for their part, have found Mousnier's model equally misleading, because his emphasis on 'eternal friendship and loyalty' underplays the opportunism of many clients and the power politics of the patron.[12] Similar discussions about terminology could be observed among social historians, who argued that in a society in which inequality was so fundamental, kinship and patronage continually overlapped, while early modern friendships were often based on clientelistic principles as well.[13]

When Ronald Asch made up the balance in 1991, he therefore concluded that clientage had been so pervasive in early modern Europe that 'proving the existence of patronage relationships in any given early modern social system is often doing no more than proving the obvious'.[14] Asch argued that historians ought not to try to 'prove' the existence of ties of patronage, but should instead investigate the various possible forms that clientage took. Those differences may depend on the degree of state formation, yet possibly on countless other environmental factors as well. Was it not likely that patronage displayed different characteristics in urban and rural, princely and bourgeois settings? Did certain forms of patronage perhaps develop more fully under conditions of political and economic stability, while others were able to profit from tension, conflict and war?[15] What, in other words, were the general factors that determined the forms, durability and degrees of mutual obligation in early modern patron-client relationships?

Dutch traditions

While historians of early modern France, Germany and England have been discussing these questions in the past few decades, scholars of the Dutch Republic have paid remarkably little attention to patronage issues.[16] The explanation for this silence seems to lie in the tendency to regard the Dutch Republic as a profoundly decentralised, relatively egalitarian and, above all, bourgeois society. This persistent image of the Dutch 'Golden Age' has little room for princely hegemony and hierarchical networks of clientage. In the older historiography, the few examples of patronage that were known were commonly dismissed as 'un-Dutch' excesses of corruption and nepotism, which became apparent above all during the assumed decline of Dutch culture in the eighteenth century.[17]

Although this cherished self-image slowly began to change in the past century, historians of the early modern Netherlands have long been reluctant to view the structures of Dutch political and social life in terms of clientage. At most, it has been claimed that patronage was of mere local importance, since a religiously and politically segmented society did not offer fertile soil for ramified or pyramidal systems of patronage.[18] However relevant this 'bottom-up' approach to Dutch early modern history may have been, it had in common with the older historiography that it tended to emphasise the atypical and exceptional character of Dutch political, religious and social arrangements. Yet perhaps it would be sensible to ask ourselves what form patronage assumed in this deviant republican polity, and how it compared with forms of clientage in other, monarchical states. This question becomes all the more relevant since the United Provinces were less republican and segmented than their name suggested. For example, it retained a remarkable monarchical and unifying element in the form of the stadholder's office. Officially the stadholder was no more than the highest office-holder of one or more of the seven provinces that constituted the Republic. But in practice these 'servants of the States' held several semi-sovereign powers, maintained a private court while they were drawn exclusively from the high noble houses of Orange and Nassau.[19]

There is ample evidence that the ambiguous position of the stadholder facilitated clientage practices and generated an informal power structure that was at odds with the formal republican system. Yet as J. L. Price concluded in his survey of the Dutch political system: 'Detailed studies of the workings of this patronage system are lacking and we have to make do with patchy anecdotal material'.[20] And even though there are now numerous indications that the stadholders operated a sophisticated system of clientage, we are not yet able to form a clear picture of exactly what such patronage involved.[21] The scope, intensity and degree of mutual dependence of these contacts have not yet been investigated. We hardly know how the seventeenth-century princes of Orange and counts of Nassau formed their clienteles, or what social and political implications such ties had for them and their dependants.[22]

Questions and starting-points

This study intends to address these questions by exploring the different forms that clientage took among the stadholders, and by identifying the various patronage roles that they could develop. In so doing, it will adopt a different approach to the question of patronage as well. Many of the clientage studies of the 1980s and 1990s shared a largely 'structuralist' approach, inspired by the social sciences. These historians examined the extent and the ramifications of given networks, which they often presented in the form of diagrams and tables. This approach has proven to be extremely helpful in showing the size and composition of early modern clientage networks, but it also suggested a sort of static uniformity that barely takes into account the dynamic character and diverse nature of human relationships. The use of such abstract paradigms often made the varying experiences of individual 'patrons', 'brokers' or 'clients' disappear behind a façade of numbers and network analyses.[23]

The aim is therefore not to provide a quantified analysis of clientage networks, but rather to explore the personal consequences and perceptions of patronage in seventeenth-century Dutch society. What did clientage precisely *mean* to those whom we commonly label as patrons, brokers or clients? First, how did such relationships come into being; was the initiative usually taken by a patron or a broker, or did the client usually volunteer his services? Did personal affection play any part in those circumstances, or was clientage inspired chiefly by pragmatic calculations of material advantage? How far were such choices influenced by family traditions or religious backgrounds? For example, did a patron generally take over the network of his predecessor, and did its confessional make-up match his own religious convictions? Finally, could political preferences or ideological considerations be the cause or rather the consequence of ties of clientage?

Finding the answers to questions of this sort will also be the starting point for our investigation into the practical implications of patronage. To what extent could the patron really influence his client's conduct, and vice-versa? Did patronage demand exclusive loyalty, or could a client serve several patrons at the same time? Did clientage also change people's view of themselves, of their family and society, and of those who were not part of their 'network'? In other words, did patronage create a form of social segregation, or did it instead generate feelings of solidarity and stability? And if so, how can we explain that some forms of early modern patronage proved durable while others were not? What factors determined the permanence, intensity, dependence and mutual obligation of these relationships?

In order to find an answer to questions like these, a series of well-documented case studies is indispensable. The seventeenth-century Dutch Republic offers only a few eligible candidates, among whom William Frederick of Nassau-Dietz (1613–64) clearly stands out. As count of Nassau he became stadholder of the province of Friesland from 1640, and ten years later acquired the same office in Groningen and Drenthe. The case of William Frederick is exceptional, not only because of his social standing as stadholder, but also because of the extraordinary wealth of archive sources he left. They make it possible to reconstruct his various networks as well as to examine the different roles he developed in these circuits.

It has often been remarked that the term patronage seems to be a catch-all for contacts of all kinds, and the existence of early modern clientage in itself is therefore not hard to demonstrate. That does not necessarily mean that historians should define the concept more narrowly, to allow them to distinguish it from other forms of relationship. It may be more rewarding to show just why patronage was so all-pervasive in early modern society, and why seventeenth-century men such as William Frederick do not appear to have drawn any essential distinction between their family ties, their friendships and their dealings as patron or client.[24] Many of his relationships had features of clientage, but precisely which features were most apparent in particular cases depended on specific circumstances. It is these defining factors that this book attempts to identify.[25]

Social spheres and social roles

It may be useful to introduce this approach in some greater detail. Historians usually assume that patronage develops in concentric circles of 'satellite' clients orbiting around their patron. Certain characteristics, such as the degree of dependence, mutual obligation and durability, would then be determined by the distance between client and patron.[26] Using William Frederick as an example, this study tries to make the case that such characteristics were influenced as much by the social *sphere* within which the relationship was formed as by the social *distance* between patron and client. Early modern patronage will therefore be presented as a response to the various environments in which these contacts took place. This also implies that clientage cannot be approached as a particular 'status' that could be 'attained'. Patronage was a continual process, which adjusted to change and took different forms in different social settings.

Once we approach patronage as a process of adaptation to change, we can presume that the patronage roles which people assumed also evolved. Many scholars in the past, however, tended to use the terms 'patron', 'client' or 'broker' as uniform, static categories; those involved must be placed in one or the other. Yet labels of this kind can do no more than indicate someone's position in a given situation; and a man or woman who was a patron in one social setting might well be a client in another. This is true at any rate of William Frederick. This book will argue that he in fact combined several different patronage identities: in his own household and in the provinces where he was stadholder, he acted as patron; but at the same time he played the part of a client at the court of his cousins, the princes of Orange in The Hague. William Frederick will therefore be presented in those different capacities in this book, to reveal the pitfalls that could beset such continual change in and switching between competing patronage roles.

The need to adjust his position applied in other circumstances as well. Clientage did not merely take on another form when William Frederick exchanged his own court for that of the prince in The Hague. In his position as patron he also distinguished distinctive roles, for in a sense the Dutch state system created two institutional spheres in which William Frederick could act as patron. His authority as stadholder (a public official) allowed him to appoint certain posts within the republican government, and to build up a 'public' clientele. Apart from that, in his capacity as count of Nassau (a private nobleman) William Frederick had similar opportunities for clientage in his household and domain lands. This 'private' patronage, however, was not connected to the republican state, nor was it restricted by public laws and regulations. In other words, because the conditions for patronage differed in 'public' and 'private' spheres, William Frederick could develop different patronage roles. In this study we will examine the practical consequences of this division between public and private patronage spheres by investigating William Frederick's responses to them. This means that a study of the different *spheres* of patronage becomes in fact an analysis of the various patronage *roles* that William Frederick found appropriate in them. This fluidity of patronage roles and the ways in which they developed in the course of his career will therefore be the central theme of this book.

A chronological approach offers the best way of following the transformation of William Frederick's various patronage identities. The remainder of this introduction will describe the rich but hermeneutically complex source material that he left, while the narrative proper occupies the remaining three parts. Part I, 'Patron in Friesland, 1640–1650' focuses on the period in which William Frederick became stadholder of Friesland (chapter 1) and began to build up his patronage, both as stadholder (chapter 2) and as count (chapter 3). It thus examines and compares the various ways in which he performed his role as patron in the public and private spheres. Part II, 'Client at the Orange Court, 1640–1650', turns its attention to William Frederick's position as a client of Frederick Henry and William II, sketching his various functions in the clienteles of the two princes (chapter 4), before analysing the consequences of the death of the latter (chapter 5). Part III, 'Without a Patron, 1650–1664', deals with the way in which William Frederick had to adjust and redefine his patronage roles after the death of William II (chapter 6), and finally describes the limits to which his various patronages were subject (chapter 7).

The language of patronage

On 13 December 1649 William Frederick noted in his diary a conversation he had had earlier that day with Alle van Burum, burgomaster of the Friesian capital Leeuwarden. Van Burum had told the stadholder that he would do well to stay on friendly terms with the judges in Friesland. 'He who has no friends there, has no patron' the burgomaster said, explaining the arbitrariness with which, in his opinion, the counsellors of the Court of Friesland rendered justice.[27] Van Burum's analysis is one of the few sources in which the central theme of this book is actually named, for although the terms 'patron' and 'client' were known in the seventeenth century, they have not left frequent traces in the archives.[28]

However rare the terminology as such may have been, the phenomenon of patronage appears only too familiar to contemporaries, for they frequently used a vocabulary in diaries and correspondence that display all the hallmarks of clientage. Such expressions as 'servant', 'lord', 'boss' and 'creature' were commonly applied by William Frederick and his circle to describe certain social contacts. It has even been argued that this language of patronage was the narrative discourse in which early modern people could imagine and represent themselves. Yet even if this assumption is correct, it is not always clear how far we should accept this early modern clientelistic discourse as an accurate description of real social relationships.

This question is one of the central themes of Kristen Neuschel's thought-provoking study *Word of Honor*. It attempted to prove that even though sixteenth-century nobles used such terms as 'servant' or 'creature', they cannot possibly have regarded themselves as clients. In Neuschel's opinion, patronage did not exist as a real concept in the sixteenth century: 'The possibility of *being* a client was a behavioral and psychological possibility that postdates sixteenth-century warrior society'.[29] Neuschel's flat rejection of the clientage model has failed to find general support among historians, but her provocative thesis did point out the shortcomings of many patronage studies. She rightly noticed that historians have often fallen into the easy habit of interpreting early modern language in a modern sense that confirms their ideas of, among other things, the process of state formation. The problem of reading early modern discourses has also been addressed by Sharon Kettering, but her conclusions were more nuanced. She believed that real dependence might indeed lurk behind the seventeenth-century rhetoric of loyalty and fidelity, but did not always do so. Kettering urged historians to analyse the various meanings of this early modern vocabulary of politeness and dependence with more precision.[30]

One way to do so, and to assess the reality of social dependence as well as the language used to express it, is to compare different types of source. This study will compare William Frederick's letters, which typically include many standard expressions of friendship and loyalty, with the more informal language of patronage he employed in his diaries, and finally with the way in which he dispensed and received favours in practice, and expected or had to perform services in return. This approach does not mean, however, that the vocabulary used in the diverse sources is always easy to characterise. William Frederick's detailed diaries, above all, are complicated sources and require a further introduction. In recent decades much attention has been paid to the form and function of early modern autobiographical texts and the risks that the use of these 'ego-documents' can entail.[31] Some historians have argued that we should see the rise and flourishing of autobiography in the early modern period in connection with the construction of a concept of personal identity. This has inspired much research into forms of individuality and perceptions of the self in sixteenth- and seventeenth-century texts. Although some scepticism is now felt about the general value of this approach, it is advisable not simply to accept William Frederick's diaries and correspondence as a mere record of his life, but to ask what function these texts fulfilled at the time.

Autobiographical sources

William Frederick kept day-by-day notes from 1643. This 'diary' was ostensibly published in 1995, but that is only true up to a point.[32] In the first place, because no more than a small part of his autobiographical notes appeared in print; the rest of this extensive collection is still only to be consulted in the Royal House Archives in The Hague. In the second place, the term 'diary' in itself is not appropriate, for it suggests a clearly defined and structured daily record. William Frederick's notes, which occupy hundreds of pages, are by no means so easy to categorise.[33]

Most of his notes were made in almanacs, simple books often used at the time to keep accounts or to jot down brief reminders. William Frederick did this more regularly than many other users, and had his almanacs interleaved with blank pages, giving ample room for a detailed diary.[34] It is not always clear exactly when he made these notes. In May 1651, for example, he recorded that he had not had time in the preceding few days to write 'in this book'; from which we can infer that he often made the entries on the day of the event. In that case, he would not have had much time for retrospection, though now and then he added some reflections. There are, on the other hand, no signs of censorship after the event.[35] What is remarkable is that William Frederick kept other autobiographical notes alongside the diaries, sometimes written down years after the event. From early 1647, for example, he kept a register of the occasions in his life when God had intervened to protect him from harm or adversity.[36] These notes fall more easily into a distinct group than do the daily diary entries, but even so they do not really follow a standard format. The simultaneous use and mixture of different genres in William Frederick's diary records was not uncommon. Scholars in recent decades have shown how difficult it is to allocate early modern autobiographical documents to neatly defined literary genres.[37]

The differences in the form of William Frederick's diary records reflect the different purposes they served for him. The recordkeeper never explicitly declared his intended readership, but his unflattering character sketches of his family members, his terse telegrammatic style and abbreviations all suggest that William Frederick's notes served a private function. Reports of his visits to brothels and taverns are equally unlikely to have been written as a lesson for posterity, let alone for an even wider public. Yet it is not probable that the author altogether ruled out the possibility that others might read them. Just as William Frederick kept and when necessary consulted the archives of his uncle, father and brother, so he may have expected his own descendants to preserve his diaries for consultation.[38] It is also certain that, even in his own lifetime, the outside world knew of William Frederick's habit of recordkeeping, and sometimes held it against him. In March 1645 the count himself noted that '[sir] Andla told Vegelin that I acted like Nero and wrote down in my almanac everything that people said to me, of which he disapproved, because his conscience reproached him with giving me his word and not keeping it'.[39]

In January 1651 William Frederick made a few brief notes which refer to the purposes of his various records and registers: 'To remind me of that which it is necessary for me to do during my life'.[40] These words implied two basic functions of his diarykeeping: as a practical *aide-memoire* and a personal justification to God. The former will perhaps receive most attention in a study of William Frederick's patronage practices, for his notes furnish an excellent record of whom he met, where and when. The almanacs give the impression of being a kind of ledger, but of social rather than financial capital. The count kept a meticulous, if not always structured, record of services rendered and received. 'N.B. Not to be forgotten, that Wydefelt did not thank me for giving an office to Ziercksma on his recommendation', reads a typical comment on 23 February 1647.[41] Notes of this sort helped the count to keep track of his social capital – 'my credit' – of which he drew up a balance sheet from time to time, for example at the beginning of each new year. The regularity of his references to his 'credit' illustrates the perspective from which William Frederick viewed his social contacts. Moreover, it is interesting that William Frederick did not present his 'credit' and 'reputation' as an individual asset; rather they were a patrimony, intimately related to that of his forebears and relatives.[42]

The detailed record of favours, services and courtesies exchanged was coupled with a more spiritual bookkeeping. Making these notes for William Frederick was also an exercise in justifying himself to God. This second function appears to have gained in importance in the 1650s, as his notes became more religious, above all more pietist, in tone. This may have been a result of the way in which he was certainly influenced by the ideas of the so-called 'Further Reformation', a popular pietist movement, whose recent publications were prominently represented in William Frederick's library.[43] By making connections between his own experiences and God's providence, events from his life seemed to have served as moral *exempla*.[44] In a sense, William Frederick's remarkable and frequent mentions of visits to brothels or bouts of drunkenness may also be regarded as a form of self-examination and a sign of his increasing pietist attitudes.[45]

The varied forms and functions of William Frederick's notes do not rule out the possibility that he may have been inspired by existing autobiographical traditions, or even borrowed texts from his reading. Some of the notes in his almanacs, for example, were modelled on a balance-sheet format that belonged to a familiar tradition of bookkeeeping. Besides the two copies of the *Essais* of Michel de Montaigne in his library, he must also have known of such famous autobiographies as the *Confessions* of Augustine of Hippo.[46] Unfortunately, because William Frederick never referred to such literary examples in his diary or his letters, we cannot determine if he had really read them, let alone to what extent he used them as a source of inspiration. As a well-educated count of Nassau he must have been familiar with the classical and biblical tradition, and he had studied for a time at the renowned University of Leiden. But even a careful humanistic and Reformed education did not make a man an intellectual. William Frederick's diaries reveal, on the whole, a more practical bent and down-to-earth interests. It was not Ovid or Cicero, but horse breeding and military tactics that were his favourite studies. This is not to say that William Frederick's humanist and noble education is of little relevance in examining his diaries. The way in which this frame of reference shaped and guided his writings can best be discussed in connection with his correspondence.[47]

Correspondence

For a study of patronage experiences and perceptions, William Frederick's correspondence is at least as important as his autobiographical writings. Several thousands of William Frederick's letters have survived and most of them have never been studied, let alone published. The great size of the archive may suggest that the correspondence is preserved intact, but that is certainly not the case. Some important and compromising letters would have been destroyed as soon as they were read. 'Yesterday I burned some letters which were from a good friend', William Frederick wrote in passing on 26 May 1648, while in December 1650 Anthony van Haersolte was able to assure the count 'that I immediately burned the letter, and pray Your Excellency to burn this one too after reading it'.[48]

Some of the evidence for William Frederick's dealings with clients and brokers was therefore lost in his lifetime, and the stadholder's archives may have been further combed after his death. Patronage was a matter of trust, for which the evidence was liable to be destroyed during periods of political unrest or changes of power. Moreover, personal contact was always preferable: 'the bearer of this letter', William Frederick wrote on a letter of November 1650 'would like to communicate the said matters to you secretly'. A few months later Dirck van Ruijven was only willing to give the count a report of a conversation 'by word of mouth'. In 1650 a nobleman hoped that in a certain delegation 'there would be someone who is one of Your Excellency's creatures', so that he could 'speak to him freely about everything, and tell him how things stand here'.[49] The scraps of written evidence left by such habits remind us that most patronage relations must have been built up and maintained on a basis of oral arrangements, and that by definition the surviving written sources cannot be pieced together to form a full picture of how William Frederick managed his networks.

William Frederick's surviving correspondence is varied in style. The letters he sent and received were clearly not written impromptu, but generally modelled on certain social or legal conventions that prescribed the appropriate form in which a letter must be cast, the language in which it must be phrased, and the arguments that could be used to put its case. An application for a position, there-fore, would be couched in a style very different from that of a newsletter, even when the same man wrote both. William Frederick himself invariably wrote to his family in French or German, but his letters to the Dutch authorities were always in Dutch, albeit with Germanisms. This stylistic variety sometimes makes it difficult to determine exactly what relationship lay behind a given profession of courtesy, loyalty and mutual service.[50] At any rate, a closing formula such as 'your very humble, most serviceable and lowly servant for always' does not necessarily imply that its author should be identified as William Frederick's client.

That does not mean that these formal courtesies were just empty words; expressions of trust and assurances of loyalty were a means of explicitly confirming the reputation of the addressee, and therefore particularly indispen-sable in keeping a patron-client relationship in repair. It has been asserted that the terms 'good friend' or 'agreeable friendship' can indicate a specific obligation of help and service.[51] Certainly there are times when William Frederick gives the impression of using this salutation rather selectively when he assumed mutual dependence or required a particular service. But it is hard to say how far others were alert to such possible signals; to prove it, one would have to compare the requests with the actual favours and services exchanged.[52]

This approach requires some further explanation, because the different sources at times appear contradictory. An example may illustrate this: in 1650, after William Frederick had been appointed to the stadholderships of Groningen and Drenthe, he described the election proceedings in several letters. The new stadholder made it appear that the nominations had been arranged entirely without his knowledge. He wrote that he had 'heard that he was being asked by those in Groningen to accept the stadholdership and captain-generalship of the said province'.[53] Remarkably, his diaries confirm this impression, suggesting that the local authorities invited him to accept the stadholdership 'from their own inclination and affection, without my intervention as pro forma'.[54] This reading, however, contradicts the version given by other sources. His secretary Philip Ernst Vegelin wrote that 'we had to spend notable sums and expressly sent the steward Wiedenfelt to Groningen'.[55] William Frederick's archives give further proof that he had in fact lobbied actively, even paying bribes. What could have led him to give in his private diaries an account of the nomination procedure that was so obviously at odds with the true story?

One possible explanation may be that William Frederick used his diary as a technique to justify his development as a patron and to make more sense of his own experiences. In so doing, he had a permanent tendency to attribute important events in his life to forces outside his control, specifically to the 'great grace' that 'Our Lord' had bestowed on him.[56] At first sight he may just seem to be concealing the true course of events behind a façade of piety and humility. But for one who was convinced that the world was a mirror in which God's intentions were reflected, events never happened just 'by chance'. William Frederick was convinced that the causes of his good or bad fortune had to be sought in God's providence, even when he himself took a hand in it. Thus, his diary was not just intended to keep record of events and experiences, but helped him to articulate his special bond with God.[57]

William Frederick's belief in God's guidance was intimately connected with his conviction that the Lord had reserved a special role for his family. To confirm this belief, William Frederick often tried to explain incidents in his life by placing them in the context of his family history. He wrote, for example, that he did not owe the stadholdership of Friesland to God's help alone, but that it had been conferred on him 'through the love' of the Friesians 'for my late uncle count William, my late father and my late brother'.[58] He identified himself strongly with these predecessors, in whose 'footsteps' he firmly believed he must tread. In his autobiographical writings he therefore regularly looked for historical parallels between his own experiences and those of his ancestors. A case in point is his depiction of his own role as a servant of the prince of Orange as a mere variation on the relationship which his uncle William Louis of Nassau (1560–1620) had pursued with prince Maurice of Orange-Nassau (1567–1625).

However much his patronage roles may have evolved in reality, as they were shaped by his own choices and ambitions, William Frederick always spoke of them in the language of tradition and predestination. The result was that his writings suggest much continuity, and his own achievements are generally depicted as the natural outgrowth of family traditions. William Frederick thus gave a historical explanation and a religious meaning to his own experiences and his confessional and aristocratic frames of reference continually directed his writing of records and letters.[59]

Finally, it is noticeable that this religious frame of reference appears to have undergone some change in the course of William Frederick's career. As indicated, his notes in the later 1650s and 1660s clearly took on a more confessional and reflective tone. Possibly, as pietism came to dominate his religious experience, he felt a more urgent need to justify himself to God than he had had in the 1640s. This development has certain specific implications for this study. The count's distaste for certain types of social behaviour in court circles and among his clients became more marked as he grew older, giving the impression that customs and habits among his clienteles changed in the 1650s and 1660s. Yet it is not always clear if these practices and relationships themselves altered, or if this process is only suggested by the changing tone in which William Frederick wrote about them. This tension between the reality of clientage and the language in which people thought and spoke about it will be further investigated in this book.

Notes

1 This citation and other versions in *Gloria Parendi*, 738, 752, 757, 760.

2 Kettering, *Patrons, Brokers and Clients*, 3. For a survey of her publications on patronage see also Kettering, *Patronage in Sixteenth- and Seventeenth-century France*.

3 Blok, 'Variations in Patronage', 365; Landé, 'The Dyadic Basis of Clientelism', xiii–xxvii; Wolf, 'Kinship, Friendship and Patron-Client Relations', 174–5. This description is also in Kettering, *Patrons, Brokers and Clients*, 6 ff.

4 Because of the asymmetrical nature of the relationship, anthropologists sometimes describe patronage as unequal friendship. Cf. Boissevain, 'Patrons as Brokers', 379–80; Ellemers, 'Patronage in sociologisch perspectief', 432–6; cf. Boissevain, *Friends of Friends*, Schmidt, *Friends, Followers and Factions*.

5 Blok, *The Mafia*, xvii–xx, 516 and 178–80; idem, 'Variations in Patronage', 365–6; Flap, *Patronage. An Institution*', 225–6; Gellner and Waterbury, *Patrons and Clients*, 1–6; Wolf, 'Kinship, Friendship and Patron-Client Relations', 174–5.

6 In art history patronage has a much wider meaning, and art commissions in general are usually described as patronage. Lytle and Orgel, *Patronage in the Renaissance*; Hitters, *Patronen van patronage*, 57–62. For patronage in the republic of letters see Stegeman, *Patronage and Services*.

7 Blockmans, 'Patronage, Brokerage', 117–26; Boissevain, 'Patrons as Brokers', 379–86; idem, *Friends of Friends*, 148–54; Dumolyn, 'Investeren in sociaal kapitaal', 417–38; Kettering, *Patrons, Brokers and Clients*, 3–11; Reinhard, 'Oligarchische Verflechtung', 47–62. In recent years, scholars have started to identify different forms of early modern agency. See Dayton, 'Rethinking Agency', 827–43; Keblusek, 'Profiling the Agent'.

8 Blok, *Wittgenstein en Elias*, 8–9 and 12–16; idem, *The Mafia*; Kettering, 'The Historical Development', 419–26; Piattoni, *Clientelism*; Schmidt et al., *Friends, Followers and Factions*.

9 Cf. Blockmans, 'Patronage, Brokerage'; Eisenstadt and Roniger, *Patrons, Clients and Friends*; Kettering, 'The Historical Development' , 419–26; Van Nierop, 'Willem van Oranje', 654–5.

10 Blockmans, 'Patronage, Brokerage', 117–26; Kettering, 'The Historical Development', 419–26; Marcus, *The Politics of Power*, 37–74. A survey is offered in Reinhardt, *Power Elites and State Building* and Mączak, *Klientelsysteme im Europa*.

11 Surveys in Asch and Birke, *Princes, Patronage and the Nobility*; Béguin, *Les Princes de Condé*; Droste, 'Patronage in der frühen Neuzeit'; Greengrass, 'Functions and Limits'; Harding, *Anatomy*; Kettering, *Patrons, Brokers and Clients*; Koenigsberger, 'Patronage and Bribery'; Peck, *Court Patronage*; Mączak, *Klientelsysteme im Europa*; idem, *Ungleiche Freundschaft*; Neuschel, *Word of Honor*; MacHardy, *War, Religion and Court Patronage*; Reinhard, *Power Elites and State Building*; Swann, *Provincial Power*.

12 Durand, 'Clienteles et fidélités', 3–24; Mousnier, *Etat et société sous François Ier*; cf. Greengrass, 'Noble Affinities', 275–312; Kettering, 'Patronage in Early Modern France', 839–62; Mączak, *Ungleiche Freundschaft*, 56–69; Swann, *Provincial Power*, 9–12, 15. Quotations taken from Pollmann, 'Dienst en wederdienst', 231–2; Haddad, 'Noble Clienteles', 75–109.

13 Aymard, 'Friends and Neighbours', 449–70; Kettering, 'Friendship and Clientage', 139–58; Kooijmans, *Vriendschap*, 14–18 and 132–48; Lytle, 'Friendship and Patronage', 47–61; Stone, *The Family, Sex and Marriage*, 97ff.; Tadmor, *Family and Friends*, 1–17.

14 Asch, 'Introduction', 18.

15 Cf. Asch, 'Introduction', 1–40; Greengrass, 'Noble Affinities', 275–312; Mączak, 'From Aristocratic Household', 315–28, and *Ungleiche Freundschaft*; Kettering, 'Patronage in Early Modern France', 841.

16 De Bruin, 'Het politieke bestel', 16–38; Duindam, 'Versailles als dwaallicht', 185–7; Price, *Holland and the Dutch Republic*, 141; Randeraad and Wolffram, 'Constraints on Clientelism', 101–4.

17 Cf. Huizinga, *Dutch Civilization*; Busken Huet, *Het land van Rembrandt*; Japikse, 'Cornelis Musch',

498–523. Compare Schama, *The Embarrassment of Riches* and Roorda, *Partij en factie*, 20–32.

18 De Bruin, *Geheimhouding en verraad*, 13–18; idem, 'Het politieke bestel', 16–38; Price, *Holland and the Dutch Republic*, 134–48; Rowen, 'Neither Fish nor Fowl', 30–4; Schilling 'The Orange Court', 451–2; Groenveld, 'C'est le pere'; Van Nierop, 'Willem van Oranje'; Spanninga, 'Patronage in Friesland'.

19 In recent years much attention has been paid to the cultural history of the court of the stadholders, especially in the form of exhibitions: cf. Keblusek and Zijlmans, *Vorstelijk vertoon*; Van der Ploeg and Vermeeren, *Vorstelijk verzameld*; Schacht and Meiner, *Onder den Oranje boom*; Zandvliet, *Maurits*; Groenveld, Huizinga and Kuiper, *Nassau uit de schaduw van Oranje*. More politically oriented studies are Bruggeman, *Nassau en de macht van Oranje*; Gabriels, *De heren als dienaren*; Mörke, 'Stadtholder' oder 'Staetholder'; Rowen, *The Princes of Orange*; Prak, 'Republiek en vorst', 28–52; Schilling, 'The Orange Court', 442–53.

20 Price, *Holland and the Dutch Republic*, 141.

21 A few examples of patronage research can be found in Van Nierop, 'Willem van Oranje'; Israel, 'Frederick Henry'; Groenveld, 'Willem II en de Stuarts'; Roorda, 'Le Secret du prince'; Spanninga, 'Patronage in Friesland', 11–26. The only comprehensive study of networks of this kind has been made for the eighteenth-century court of William V of Orange-Nassau; see Gabriels, *De heren als dienaren*, and for a recent regional study Franken, *Dienaar van Oranje*.

22 Cf. Groenveld, *Evidente factiën*; Mörke, 'Stadtholder' oder 'Staetholder'; Price, *Holland and the Dutch Republic*; Rowen, *The Princes of Orange*; General studies of the individual stadholders are: Swart, *William of Orange*; Van Deursen, *Maurits*; Israel, 'Frederick Henry'; Groenveld, 'Frederik Hendrik'; Poelhekke, *Frederik Hendrik*; Kernkamp, *Prins Willem II*; Groenveld, 'Willem II en de Stuarts'; Troost, *William III*; Roorda, 'Le Secret du prince'; Gabriëls, *De heren als dienaren*.

23 Cf. Asch and Birke, *Princes, Patronage and the Nobility*; Gabriëls, *De heren als dienaren*; Harding, *Anatomy*; Mączak, *Klientelsysteme*; MacHardy, *War, Religion and Court Patronage*.

24 Kettering, 'Friendship and Clientage', 139–58; idem, 'Patronage and Kinship', 408–35.

25 Duindam, 'Versailles als dwaallicht', 187–8; Lind, 'Great Friends', 124–5; Mączak, 'From Aristocratic Household', 316–21; Mörke, 'Sovereignty and Authority', 458–64.

26 Cf. Greengrass, 'Noble Affinities', 278.

27 *Gloria Parendi*, 727.

28 William Frederick's secretary Vegelin, for example, mentioned in an account of his travels 'the old duke Augustus of Wolfenbüttel, who was my great patron' (Tresoar, Eysinga, 485). The secretary of a Gelderland regent also wrote of being 'at the house of my patron' in 1650 (Tresoar SA, 37–4–I). The Groningen regent Osebrand Jan Rengers told William Frederick in that year of a flock of 'clients' who would be at his disposal in the Ommelanden (GA, Farmsum, 620). For this and other terminology see Greengrass, 'Noble Affinities', 275–300; Kettering, *Patrons, Brokers and Clients*, 12–18; Neuschel, *Word of Honor*, 1–37.

29 Neuschel, *Word of Honor*, 23. Cf. Droste, 'Patronage der frühen Neuzeit', 555–90.

30 'Did these verbal formulas mean the same at all times in all patronage relationships', Kettering asked rhetorically, 'or did their meaning change according to where, when and how they were used?' Kettering, 'Patronage in Early Modern France', 852–9. See also idem, *Patrons, Brokers and Clients*, 12–18, and more recently Mączak, *Ungleiche Freundschaft*, 18–28; Swann, *Provincial Power*, 9–15.

31 The literature is by now voluminous. Some recent surveys in Dekker, *Egodocuments*; Burke and Porter, *The Social History*; Dewald, *Aristocratic Experience*; Heller et al., *Reconstructing Individualism*; Mascuch, *Origins*; Porter, *Rewriting the Self*; and specifically for the early modern Netherlands: Blaak, *Geletterde levens*; Frijhoff, *Wegen van Evert Willemsz*, 47–64; Pollmann, *Religious Choice*, 12–24.

32 The published portion of the diary is referred to as *Gloria Parendi*.

33 The various autobiographical notes are found in KHA, WF, VIII–2, 3. Several detached notes are also found in Leeuwarden (Tresoar, SA) and Oranienbaum (LAD, Oranienbaum, A7b). For the diary see also De Moel, 'Moet mij voortaen' and the excellent treatment in Kooijmans, *Liefde in opdracht*.

34 Salman, 'Troebelen en tijdsordening', 8; Kooijmans, *Liefde in opdracht*, 41–2.

35 *Gloria Parendi*, 748. Years later William Frederick wrote the word 'bedrog' (deceit) alongside certain entries on Johan de Witt, KHA, WF, VIII, 3–I (notes for 21 September – 1 October 1655). Part of the diary for 1650 has been destroyed, but it is not clear if William Frederick himself or one of his descendants did this.

36 For example in KHA, WF, VIII, 3–I, II and III.

37 Compare the literature in preceding notes. As well as Blaak, 'Autobiographical Reading', 63–4; Van Gelder, *Naporra's omweg*, 461–6; Pollmann, *Religious Choice*, 16–24.

38 William Frederick advised his eldest son to follow his example by 'writing down everything that happened day by day'. KHA, WF, VIII, 3–II. Cf. also Baggerman, 'Autobiography and Family Memory', 161–73; Gietman, 'Het adellijk bewustzijn'.

39 *Gloria Parendi*, 113.

40 *Gloria Parendi*, 750.

41 *Gloria Parendi*, 339.

42 Kooijmans, *Vriendschap*, 136–9, and *Liefde in opdracht*, 41–2. See also Blaak, 'Autobiographical Reading', 78–9; Salman, 'Troebelen en tijdsordening', 8–10.

43 NA, ND, 893. William Frederick was in touch with several leaders of this tendency, such as Maximilian Teellinck, from whom he received several works, KHA, WF, VII, C–146 (correspondence of Johan Goethals and William Frederick, 1652–64); Tresoar, SA, 37–1652 (Johan Goethals to William Frederick, 7 August 1652, from Delft).

44 Above all in the notes in KHA, WF, VIII, 30–I, William Frederick presented his own experiences as *exempla* of divine providence. The selection of events described differs from that in the diaries in KHA, WF, VIII, 2. Cf. Pollmann, *Religious Choice*, 15–16.

45 Cf. *Gloria Parendi*, xxiv; Spanninga, 'Ick laet niet met mij gecken', 85; see also Breuker, 'Over de Nadere Reformatie', 26–31; Bergsma, *Tussen Gideonsbende en publieke kerk*, 309–34; Frijhoff, *Wegen van Evert Willemsz*, 354–61; Van Lieburg, *Levens van vromen*.

46 A list of William Frederick's library is kept in: NA, ND, 893.

47 Burke, 'Representations of the Self', 17–28; Blaak, 'Autobiographical Reading', 61–87; Frijhoff, *Wegen van Evert Willemsz*, 590–61; Ginzburg, *The Cheese and the Worms*, 21 ff.; Pollmann, *Religious Choice*, 16–24.

48 KHA, WF, VII, C–153 (Anthony van Haersolte to William Frederick, 1 December 1650, n.p.); *Gloria Parendi*, 521. Cf. Kluiver, 'Brieven', 41.

49 BL, Additional MS 21527 (William Frederick to an unknown person, 17–27 December 1653, from The Hague); KHA, WF, VI, 14 (letters from William Frederick to unknown persons, 1655); VII, C–153 (Anthony van Haersolte to William Frederick, 1 December 1650, n.p.); Tresoar, SA, 37–F (William Frederick to unknown person, c. 1650), 367–X (Dirck van Ruijven to William Frederick, 6 January 1651, from The Hague).

50 Dewald, *Aristocratic Experience*, 174–204; Greengrass, 'Noble Affinities', 275–300; also Bergsma, 'Een geleerde en zijn tuin', 103–6; Stegeman, *Patronage and Services*.

51 Cf. Kooijmans, *Vriendschap*, 14–18, 54–5 and 144–5.

52 Kettering, 'Patronage in Early Modern France', 839–62.

53 BL, Additional MS 21527, fols 60r–61r (William Frederick to the States of Zeeland, 17–27 December 1650, from Leeuwarden); NA, Aitzema, 20 (William Frederick to Lieuwe van Aitzema, 3–13 December 1650, from Leeuwarden); KHA, WF, VII, B–I/2a (William Frederick to Johan de Knuyt, 15–25 December 1650, from Leeuwarden).

54 *Gloria Parendi*, 738, Cf. KHA, WF, VIII, 3–I (note 1–11 December 1650).

55 Tresoar, Eysinga, 485 (notes of Vegelin, 1650).

56 Frijhoff, *Wegen van Evert Willemsz*, 60–1; Mascuch, *Origins*, 2–20.

57 Adamson, 'The Aristocracy', 184–7; Egmond, 'De aansprakelijkheid van God', 11–15; Frijhoff, 'Identiteit en identiteitsbesef', 614–34; Pollmann, *Religious Choice*, 16–24.

58 KHA, WF, VIII, 3–I (note 10–20 September 1640).

59 Frijhoff, *Wegen van Evert Willemsz*, 59–62; Mascuch, *Origins*, 15–26; Woolf, *The Social Circulation*, 73–98.

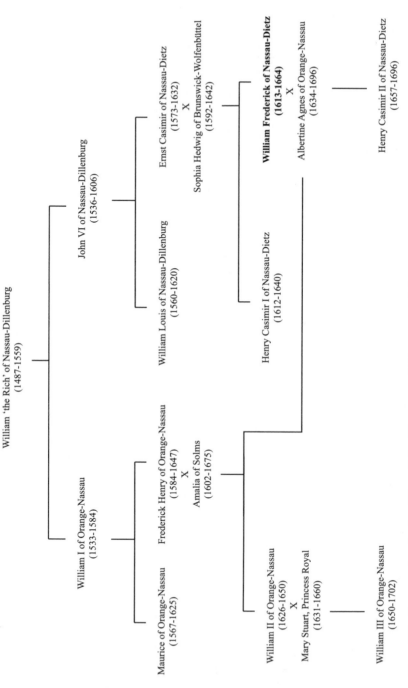

Simplified genealogical table of the Houses of Nassau and Orange

Part I

Patron in Friesland, 1640–1650

1

Loyalty on trial

It had all turned out 'very wonderfully', wrote William Frederick years later, looking back on the dramatic events of 1640. The death of his brother Henry, his nomination as stadholder of Friesland, and the ensuing quarrel with prince Frederick Henry of Orange, had made 1640 a year of extremes. William Frederick admitted that he had been 'perplexed' by the whole episode. It did not take much imagination to see the hand of providence in his ultimate appointment as stadholder and his restored relationship with the prince of Orange.[1]

It is in the summer of 1640 that William Frederick of Nassau-Dietz first makes his mark in archive sources and chronicles. He was then already 27 years old, but had led a rather inconspicuous life as an officer in the army of the Dutch Republic. Born at Arnhem in 1613, William Frederick was the second son of Ernst Casimir of Nassau-Dietz and Sophia Hedwig of Brunswick-Wolfenbüttel[2] (see table, page 18). As such he belonged to the 'Friesian' branch of the House of Nassau, so called because both his father and uncle had held the stadholdership of the province of Friesland, in the north of the Republic. They usually combined it with the same office in Groningen and Drenthe. As a second son William Frederick did not at first appear eligible for any of those positions, and it was entirely according to plan that his elder brother Henry Casimir became head of the family and also stadholder of the three northern provinces in 1632, when Ernst Casimir was killed on the battlefield at Roermond.

That long-planned arrangement, however, was abruptly ended eight years later. The Dutch Republic's war against Spain, which had already lasted nearly seventy years, took its toll once more in 1640 when Henry was seriously wounded in a skirmish near the Flemish town of Hulst. William Frederick was by his brother's side when Henry died of his wounds at the age of 28 on 12 July, unmarried and childless. The summer of 1640 therefore brought a radical change in the life of Ernst Casimir's second and sole surviving son and heir: William Frederick had to take up an unforeseen new family role and to begin an unexpected political career. As his own recollections of that turbulent year suggest, the 27-year-old was completely unprepared for this task.

The years before 1640

Years later William Frederick blamed the troubles of 1640 above all on his own inexperience and unfamiliarity with the provinces where his brother had been stadholder. Looking back, he felt that he had been 'very young', and could not recall having been in Friesland 'in ten years'. The most important result of this, he concluded, was that he had not had 'any backing, knowledge or credit in the province'.[3] This down-to-earth self-analysis is also the first indication of the function of patronage in William Frederick's career. In fact the count himself gives the impression that before 1640 he had nothing like a clientele or circle of close confidants. It appears that his recollection was of beginning his career as stadholder of Friesland under a patronage handicap.

The picture sketched by William Frederick should be treated with some caution, not only because his notes were written years after the event, but chiefly because they were intended above all to help him understand important moments in his life as manifestations of God's providence. From that point of view it was not so important for William Frederick, when looking back, to list all the friends and acquaintances whose support he may have counted on. Indeed, by minimising their contribution, he made the miraculous element in the events appear even more telling. If we ask what role clientage really played in William Frederick's early career, his pious self-examination will not supply the whole answer. Unfortunately William Frederick's other archives are equally uninformative about the people who belonged to his circle before his accession, and where these contacts originated. The count recorded in his autobiographical writings only that in the first twenty-five years of his life he had 'always lived in Germany with my lady mother or stayed with my company'.[4] By this he meant his ancestral castle of Dietz, where he had gone to live with his mother Sophia after the death of his father. In the summer months he had regularly exchanged Dietz for the camps of the Dutch army, as the second part of his remark suggests. The House of Nassau owed its prestige a great deal to its military successes in the Dutch war against Spain, and so it was hardly surprising that William Frederick should have expected to make a career in the first place in the Dutch 'States' army. Since 1631 he had held the rank of troop captain.[5]

A study of the nature and extent of William Frederick's patronage must therefore necessarily begin in the year in which Henry died and William Frederick succeeded him as the new head of the family. To whom did the count try to put out feelers in that year, and how much had these attempts to do with the network his brother had previously built up? The question of the origins of William Frederick's clienteles is thus intrinsically linked to that of the durability of existing patronage connections. Among scholars there is no agreement about the extent to which early modern clientage networks were generally passed on or continued after the death of the patron.[6] Discussion of the matter is complicated by the failure of many patronage studies to make it clear if clientage as such was taken over, or if the relations that continued merely had some of their apparent characteristics. In other words, we have to distinguish between the possible takeover of Henry's contacts and the form William Frederick later gave to them. For this a short introduction on Henry's management of his relations is necessary.

The inheritance of patronage

The scanty literature about the Friesian stadholders does not tell us if Henry Casimir ever formed contacts that we can describe as 'clientelistic', still less what the precise extent and composition of this network was.[7] At most, there are signs that appear to suggest the existence of it. It is clear, to begin with, that Henry in his capacity as count of Nassau-Dietz maintained a household of his own. As head of that court and lord of several domains he supported a small group of about thirty employees. We could regard this network as a private clientele, dependent on the House of Nassau and Henry's position as count. These courtiers and retainers were not attached to the office of stadholder or to any of the institutions of the Republic.

In his capacity as stadholder Henry had other opportunities to build up a network of followers. Unlike his hereditary title of count, the stadholderships were purely administrative offices, to which he was appointed by the States of the respective provinces. For this reason the political importance of the stadholdership varied from province to province. Henry enjoyed the fullest authority in Friesland, where the stadholder had the right to appoint to various administrative and military posts. It seems likely that such a formal authority favoured habits of clientage. Yet there are very few hard facts about the nature and extent of such a stadholderly or 'public' clientele in Henry's case. Scant evidence from other stadholders in the Dutch Republic suggests that their clientele was not so much a clearly defined network as a collection of all kinds of contacts and lesser networks assembled over the years, of varying degrees of intensity and loyalty.[8]

What is certain is that Henry's death had different consequences in the 'private' and 'public' circuits, since he had recruited his household clients and his political clients in different ways. The courtiers on the count's household staff were most immediately affected by the death of their employer, for their financial and social incomes depended entirely on his resources, and their employment formally ended on his death. This was not the case in the administrative colleges in Friesland and Groningen. Although several office-holders and magistrates (collectively known as 'regents') too owed their positions to the stadholder's nomination, his death did not necessarily end their careers. Because Henry had played two different roles in these institutional spheres, we would expect those involved to react differently to the death of their patron.

This impression is confirmed by the crisis that flared up in the northern provinces only a few days after Henry's death. To the surprise of many, William Frederick was not the only candidate who claimed the vacant stadholderships in Friesland, Groningen and Drenthe. His father's cousin, prince Frederick Henry of Orange-Nassau, started a competing campaign to secure the appointments in the north for himself. As stadholder of the other five provinces of the Republic the prince had long dreamed of combining all the provincial stadholderships in his own person. The death of his relative Henry Casimir, however regrettable it might be, offered a suitable opportunity to realise this dream.[9] In the summer of 1640, therefore, a struggle arose within the House of Nassau over the succession to Henry Casimir's offices. The result was that, unlike the count's household staff, the political elite of Friesland and Groningen were faced with a choice between two successors and two possible patrons. That choice was to have important consequences for the line that William Frederick was to follow as Henry's successor, and the roles he was able to carve out for himself as patron.

Court clientele

William Frederick must have been aware that his brother's clienteles were recruited from different backgrounds, yet he left no explicit written statement of the consequences he drew from this fact. Did he have a clearly defined idea of how he ought to approach Henry's former contacts, take them over or simply ignore them? At any rate he had never been prepared for a possible succession as head of the family and stadholder. Because William Frederick's diaries do not begin until 1643, and the archive sources for the events of 1640 are sparse, it is not easy to determine what ideas and strategies he may have worked out to deal with these problems.

On paper William Frederick's position in the summer of 1640 was clearest in the domestic court sphere. As sole heir and new head of the family, his right to take over Henry's duties and responsibilities was undisputed. And because their employment had ceased on the death of his brother, in principle he could have replaced all the old courtiers with his own favourites. We know, however, that it was not unusual to renew such employment either explicitly or tacitly after the death of the lord. The House of Nassau was no exception to this rule. It is known, for example, that William of Orange (1533–1584), Maurice (1567–1625) and Frederick Henry (1584–1647) simply continued to employ many of the court personnel on their accession.[10] William Frederick seemed to wish to follow that family tradition. In later years he would regularly stress that as head of the dynasty he intended to tread 'in the footsteps of my forebears, to maintain what they obtained'.[11] William Frederick saw himself as a link in a long chain of generations. His task now was to hold what his ancestors had won and, he hoped, to pass it on to following generations. Continuity of personnel in his household could serve to reinforce William Frederick's self-image as a link in that chain.

The seventeenth-century chronicler Lieuwe van Aitzema, in his account of the events of 1640, indeed reports that Henry's secretary Johan Sohn 'was taken on again' by William Frederick as early as July.[12] On the very day that Henry died Sohn left for Friesland on William Frederick's orders, to protect his interests there. The secretary was not the only one who immediately gained the count's confidence. The steward Barthold van Oostheim was another who could expect to be continued in office, and in the same month he openly declared himself a representative of the count in Friesland, where he and Sohn coordinated the campaign to secure the stadholdership.[13] At the seat of the central government of the Republic in The Hague, meanwhile, a third confidant from Henry's entourage spontaneously came out in favour of William Frederick. This man, Reinier Casembroot, had been the late count's financial adviser. He used his letter of condolence to the new count as an open job application, expressing the hope that William Frederick would make use of his services, so that he could 'continue his affection and inclination' for the family of Nassau-Dietz.[14] William Frederick must have been happy to accept Casembroot's direct offer, for later that year the new administrator presented several letters on his behalf at the *Binnenhof* at The Hague, the home of the central administrative organs of the Republic.

It was not just the top men in the household who were prompt to continue their service almost seamlessly after Henry's death. No noticeable changes of personnel can be detected at the lower levels of the domains in 1640 either.[15] Presumably many courtiers expected no less than a continuation of their service. As we shall see, their relationship with the family often went back over several generations of service, so that their connection to the Nassau court was less an expression of a professional affiliation with the household than of years of loyalty to the House of Nassau in general. That background created mutual obligations, which William Frederick was unable and probably unwilling to evade.

His declared wish for dynastic continuity, however, can only have been one of the motives that decided William Frederick's conduct. In the circumstances there were also practical advantages in continuing the existing relationships. He had probably made few contacts of his own yet, while as a candidate for the stadholderships he needed to find well-informed men whom he could trust to help him. Because some members of the court had served his family for generations, he might assume that he could simply appeal to their discretion and loyalty. William Frederick's lack of political experience and his urgent need not to put a foot wrong in Friesland combined to rule out any thought of looking for new men to place in the top positions in his court. Perhaps we should regard Henry's household personnel as an intangible asset, which William Frederick inherited from his predecessor as naturally as his title of count and his domain lands. That background may explain the origin of his household network, but it does not sufficiently define the nature of the new relationships. At this early stage, therefore, to describe the courtly entourage that William Frederick continued in his service as a 'clientele' might be premature, for the roles that he and its members were to play would take time to be clearly defined.

Regent clientele

For the members of Henry's stadholderly networks, a transfer of loyalty to his brother was probably less self-evident, for these officeholders were not his employees. Within the complex political system of the United Provinces, the stadholderships had developed into administrative offices and the decision whether or not to appoint William Frederick to the vacant stadholderships was a matter for the States of Friesland and Groningen. While the continuity of Henry's contacts in the household sphere was more or less guaranteed, his relations in the republican sphere needed to be confirmed by the potential clients themselves. In other words, during the election procedure the roles of patron and client were in fact reversed. This became particularly clear when the Friesian and Groningen elites were offered a very tempting alternative after Henry's death. The powerful and experienced prince Frederick Henry of Orange might have more to offer them as a patron, in the long term, than the young and rather inexperienced count of Nassau-Dietz. William Frederick's position as his brother's successor in Friesland was further weakened by the conflict that had embroiled count Henry with the Friesian establishment a few years before his death.[16]

One of the core issues in this so-called 'Friesian revolution' was the stadholder's right to political appointments. It had been finally settled in Henry's favour in 1637, when it was decided that the magistrates in nine of the eleven Friesian towns would in future be chosen by the stadholder from a list of two names for every office.[17] This arrangement allowed Henry to exert great influence on the political complexion of the town magistracies, but three years later it was clear that the stadholder had won a Pyrrhic victory. In many of the towns the settlement was still a sore point, and the stadholder's influence on local government an irritant. Henry's former opponents, whom the stadholder had consistently kept out of office after 1637, still hoped for a new revolution that would restore them to power. The power base of the sitting regents was therefore weak. Now that the stadholder was dead, the 'malcontents' of 1637 naturally sniffed their chance, and hoped to use the succession to bring about a change of power in the towns and to curb the stadholder's authority. The prince of Orange may have been willing to agree to such a new settlement at the price of the stadholdership, and this made him a possible ally for Henry Casimir's former opponents.[18]

It was certainly no easy task for William Frederick to present himself to this divided Friesian elite as an attractive candidate for the stadholdership. Given his inexperience, he found it advisable not to draw too much attention to his own limited capacities, but to stress his intention to follow in 'the praiseworthy footsteps of our forefathers'. In a typically seventeenth-century manner, he reasoned that if he placed himself in the family tradition of the stadholdership, the prestige of his predecessors would make him appear a qualified and credible successor.[19] The count therefore presented his candidacy for the stadholdership, not as inaugurating a new period in the Friesian administration, but as the continuation of the existing order. To make the idea of continuity concrete, he gave the sitting regents a guarantee that he would leave their positions of power in the Friesian towns intact. Meanwhile Sohn and Oostheim did their best to cast doubt on the integrity of the count's adversary, the prince of Orange. The secretary dropped hints that Frederick Henry might 'seek to introduce the papist religion' in Friesland, and that the prince himself was 'not pure in the matter of religion'.[20] If the rival candidate could be put in a bad light and depicted as a threat to Friesian independence, William Frederick might well appear a more attractive alternative.

For such an inexperienced administrator as William Frederick, it was a puzzle to determine just which members of the Friesian elite he should favour with promises, and which local regents he could trust. In the summer and autumn of 1640, therefore, the count familiarised himself in detail with the antecedents of these magistrates. His brother's archives probably helped him, for his correspondence in 1640 contains many notes that must have come from Henry and Ernst Casimir's papers. It can be deduced from these documents that William Frederick's predecessors had employed several selection criteria to test the suitability of local brokers and confidants. Persons of a suspect religious background ('papists, Mennonites, Arminians') or inadequate financial resources ('peat carriers, hauliers, wood carriers, labourers') were evidently regarded as unfit for this role.[21] It appears that William Frederick used his predecessors' files to read himself into the job of stadholder. In the summer of 1640 they helped him decide whom to lobby in Friesland, and which of Henry's connections he could continue to trust.[22]

The impression is confirmed by William Frederick's own letters, for the regents singled out for positive mention in the notes appear to be the same men with whom the count opened a correspondence. One such man, Frederik van Inthiema ('sound in religion and way of life, of a sober and capable life, with good means'), advised William Frederick on the election of magistrates in the town of Workum later that year. He would also assist the count as an army officer during the disturbances in the Friesian port town of Harlingen. The Dokkum apothecary Tjeerd Gauma ('a member of the Church, a politic person') and the local secretary Petrus Veltdriel ('capable of government') also acted as advisers to the stadholder in 1640.[23] Both men had been among Henry's protégés in Dokkum for years. Because the malcontents in the town were growing restive and raising the issue of the magisterial elections, Gauma and Veltdriel had a great interest in getting Henry's brother nominated as stadholder, and thereby securing their own positions. The same applied to the burgomasters Adriaan van Velsen of the town of Bolsward and Epeus Oosterzee of the smaller town of Sloten, who presented themselves to William Frederick as belonging to 'the good party' in Friesland. In 1640 this select group of intimates would support the count's candidacy as stadholder in the States of Friesland, where the Friesian towns and countryside jointly deliberated on the administration of the province and the nomination of a new stadholder.[24]

The strategy William Frederick applied to bring the hard core of Henry's network under his control is finally illustrated by his letter to the regent of Bolsward Willem Lamminga of August 1640. The count acknowledged that 'in the time of our late brother count Henry of Nassau' Lamminga had always sided with 'the good corresponding party'. His attitude then gave William Frederick confidence that 'Your Honour will continue in such a good will and intention from henceforth, and in particular in these times'. The count asked Lamminga to 'enter into a good correspondence with the burgomaster Velsen and the other friends, and to lend a hand'.[25]

While William Frederick approached Henry's former confidants in the towns himself, his campaign in the Friesian countryside largely escapes our view. It is doubtful that there was any question of an existing stadholder's clientele there, since the *grietmannen*, who represented the administration in the rural areas, could generally afford to take a much more independent line toward the stadholder.[26] Henry had not had powers to appoint the *grietmannen* himself. Yet William Frederick's strategy to win support for his candidacy in the countryside cannot have been very different from the line he followed in the towns, however different the conditions themselves may have been. This is illustrated by the letter of the *grietman* Johan van Aylva to Sophia Hedwig, written as early as 16 July; Aylva – one of the key figures in the Friesian elite – announced that he had had talks with several like-minded *grietmannen* 'to prepare the work somewhat'. More specifically, he added that he would recommend William Frederick's candidacy to his friends and family in Friesland and Groningen.[27] It can be inferred from this that William Frederick enjoyed the preference of at least some of the sitting officials in the Friesian countryside as well.

Frederick Henry

In the meantime, however, the count's opponent was not idle. Thanks to his princely rank, his military leadership in the war against Spain, and the concentration of numerous functions in his own person, Frederick Henry, on paper, was a much stronger candidate than William Frederick. Jonathan Israel, who studied the way in which Frederick Henry built up his power base in the Republic, believed that his widely ramified clientele probably reached its greatest extent in the years around 1640.[28] The prince's followers clearly had an interest of their own in seeing all seven provinces united under the prince of Orange, for they could then hope to profit from the greater number of offices in his gift.

Orange's lobbying in the summer and autumn of 1640 gives the impression that it was coordinated on two levels: officially by the chief clerk of the States-General in The Hague, Cornelis Musch, and privately by the prince's secretary, Constantijn Huygens. Musch had risen in the highest organ of government in The Hague under Frederick Henry's protection, and as the prince's 'creature' he also had a widespread network of his own, which was allegedly maintained by bribes, among other means.[29] At the end of July the clerk discussed with Huygens the tactics that they could employ for a successful campaign. They considered the possibility of prevailing on the States-General to send a deputation to the north, to give Frederick Henry's candidacy an official character. A few days later, in fact, Musch managed to persuade the States-General to take this unusual step.[30]

The deputies Gerard van Arnhem and Johan van Reede van Renswoude set off for Friesland and Groningen on behalf of the States-General on 1 August. Officially their task was to convince the provincial States of the importance of bringing all the Dutch provinces under a single stadholder. Informally, Musch gave them more precise instructions, advising them to exploit the political discord that existed in Friesland and Groningen. Musch knew that in Friesland in particular opinion was divided over the vacancy, because many notables wished to curtail the stadholder's influence on the appointment of magistrates. This unstable political situation created an opening for an outsider such as Frederick Henry to put himself forward as stadholder. Musch hoped to win over the malcontents, above all, by tempting them with the prospect of free elections to the magistracies.[31]

Arnhem and Renswoude probably knew that Constantijn Huygens was at the same time doing his best to mobilise local support for Frederick Henry. The prince's private secretary was in fact a kind of super-broker in Frederick Henry's network, who had his informants in several towns and provinces.[32] Huygens shared Musch's belief that it made good sense to exploit William Frederick's inexperience and the existing political instability as far as possible. To develop more concrete plans to achieve this, he lost no time after Henry's death in approaching some kindred spirits who were familiar with Friesian politics or had family ties with notables in the province.[33] A leading role was reserved for Sweder van Haersolte, who had been Frederick Henry's adviser in the province of Overijssel for some time. From the town of Zwolle he kept Huygens informed that summer and advised him on the tactics to be used in the campaign. Haersolte was on good terms with the *drost* (sheriff) of the province of Drenthe, Roelof van Echten, who had also promised his support for Frederick Henry's candidacy. It was suggested that Haersolte should travel to Friesland, as if by chance, to direct the informal lobby there.[34]

While Haersolte sent his reports to Huygens from Overijssel, the secretary received further advice from his brother-in-law David de Wilhem, who considered himself an expert on Friesian politics, because he had spent a few years as a student at the Friesian University of Franeker. De Wilhem compiled for Huygens lists of names of influential regents in Sneek, Dokkum, Harlingen and elsewhere, and backed Musch's strategy of cultivating those factions who had been kept down by Henry Casimir in the last few years. To gain their confidence, it was best to approach them on the spot. De Wilhem wrote that Haersolte could take on this job, but that it might be more effective to send Johan de Knuyt to Friesland. As Frederick Henry's representative in the province of Zeeland and a member of the Nassau Domain Council, De Knuyt was a skilled operator in situations of this sort.[35] De Wilhem optimistically argued that Huygens did not need to spend much time on the Friesian deputies in The Hague, for they had little influence in the province.[36]

It is a striking fact that Frederick Henry himself does not appear in the archive sources for the election of 1640. To be sure, he must have had discussions with his confidants Musch and Huygens, who managed his campaign at the different levels, but his patronage network was so hierarchically structured that there was no question of the candidate himself approaching the local regents in Friesland directly. That also delayed communications between the top and the base of his clientele. It was Huygens, for example, who used Haersolte to recruit the *drost* of Drenthe, after which Van Echten gave instructions to his local followers.[37] Because of the extent and stratification of the network, and the distance between The Hague and Leeuwarden, the prince's brokers, Huygens and Musch, could potentially exert great influence, but were less able to anticipate developments in Friesland itself.

William Frederick exploited this weakness. Although his newly formed following may have been regional and immature, it was less stratified. The count and his courtiers were in direct personal contact with the Friesian notables, while Frederick Henry remained a potential patron whom most Friesians had actually never seen. For this reason the sitting regents in Friesland in particular assumed that their personal interests would best be served by continuing to support the 'local' House of Nassau. The provincial States were also irritated by the attempt of the States-General in The Hague to interfere in the election. William Frederick's followers turned this irritation to their advantage by forcing the resolution to nominate him through the States of Friesland on 2 August. The historian Lieuwe van Aitzema acutely remarked that Arnhem and Renswoude only arrived in the Friesian capital Leeuwarden a few days later, 'to find the deal done in Friesland'.[38] William Frederick was thus spared an open confrontation with Frederick Henry in Friesland.

Conflict

When the news of William Frederick's appointment reached the Orange court in The Hague, the prince and his supporters reacted with indignation. 'A contemptible manner of behaving', wrote David de Wilhem, while Huygens refused to accept the decision of 'these rude peoples' ('ces rudes peuples') in Friesland, and Cornelis Musch proposed that, if necessary, William Frederick should be compelled to resign. Sweder van Haersolte interestingly interpreted the 'impertinence and thoughtlessness of this young gentleman' as a sign of shameless disloyalty, adding that William Frederick 'had behaved as no one from that great House had ever done before, by setting himself up against the head, on whom they ought all to depend'. Haersolte, in short, saw the count's presumption in standing against the prince as a breach of the proper relationship between a patron and his client.[39]

There are indications that William Frederick himself would not have denied his role as a subordinate of the prince of Orange. Although there are no surviving documents from 1640 in which he defined his attitude toward Frederick Henry in those terms, the development of the relationships within the House of Nassau in the previous decades clearly reflected a process of growing hierarchy and dependency.[40] Although both branches of the Nassau family descended from count William the Rich (1487–1559), since then the family of his eldest son William of Orange-Nassau (1533–1584), had become a dynasty of European standing and prestige (see table, page 18). In the following decades the combination of their princely title, their many possessions in the Low Countries, and their military leadership of the Dutch Revolt against Spain raised the Oranges to the rank of first family in the nascent Republic.

The descendants of William the Rich's second son, John of Nassau (1535–1606), in these circumstances, found themselves in a prominent but secondary position. For example, while the counts of Nassau-Dietz generally came to hold the stadholderships of Friesland and Groningen, the Oranges held this post in the other five provinces, including the most powerful of all, Holland. This growing difference in status between the two families of stadholder's rank had already caused friction more than once in the years before William Frederick appeared on the scene. Indeed, these family quarrels made it all the more painfully obvious that the counts of Nassau-Dietz in practice were too dependent on Orange to permit themselves to stand up to their princely cousins. Characteristically, William Frederick in his later diaries would consistently refer to Frederick Henry as 'the Boss' and to himself as his 'servant'. It will become clear that these titles also reflected the complicated relationships within the family in the summer of 1640.

William Frederick must have been aware of his family's strong dependence on the Oranges, but in the summer of 1640 he had to weigh its importance against his need to uphold the dignity of his own branch of the family as stadholders in Friesland. The count found it a troublesome task to reconcile these conflicting interests, and had to wrestle with the consequences of his dual roles for years afterward. In the summer of 1640 he appears to have taken the advice of his mother Sophia Hedwig, who made it very clear to him that he must not let slip his claims to the positions held by his late brother.[41] Sophia Hedwig herself asked the prince of Orange in early August to grant his 'very faithful servant' William Frederick the 'place' that had previously been held by his father and brother.[42] She represented the succession of her only surviving son as a continuation of the bonds of service between the two branches of the family.

But 'the Boss' himself did not see it in that light. For Frederick Henry the election in Friesland meant a public loss of face; it also threatened to wreck the negotiations in progress with the English royal family for a marriage between Mary Stuart and his son William.[43] Moreover the prince felt that, as illustrious head of the House of Nassau, he had been slighted in his self-evident role as patron. To restore some of his damaged prestige, he decided not to recognise the stadholdership of his great-nephew, but to force the count either to make a humiliating public submission or to 'oblige him to resign'. If William Frederick was not prepared to submit, then, according to the Gelderland nobleman Alexander van der Capellen, the prince would 'seek to ruin' the count.[44]

Before he began his punitive campaign, Frederick Henry made sure that matters were taken in hand in Groningen and Drenthe, where the succession had not yet been arranged. There too he employed unorthodox means of pressure. The deputation of Arnhem and Renswoude had left for Groningen immediately after their disgrace in Friesland. To bring the Groningen regents round to the prince's way of thinking they treated them lavishly to 'brandy and Spanish wines to obtain their votes for His Highness'. According to initiates these alcoholic gifts were supplemented by more substantial forms of corruption and bribery. William Frederick's later secretary, Philip Ernst Vegelin, wrote that it was obvious that 'the gentlemen of Groningen had allowed themselves to be bought for money'. Reinier Casembroot heard stories in The Hague later that year of the 'indirect and wholly unfair procedures' by which Orange's frustrated following had tried to secure the stadholdership.[45]

William Frederick had no choice but to repeat his successful Friesian strategy in Groningen. In the city he sought out the regents who, according to his information, had enjoyed his brother's confidence.[46] As in Friesland, family ties helped him make a claim on loyalties in Groningen. Lieuwe van Aitzema remarked that the burgomaster of the city of Groningen, Pieter Eyssinga, was 'zealous for count William, being closely allied with the secretary Sohnius'.[47] At the same time Reinier Casembroot made attempts in The Hague to win the Groningen deputies in the States-General for the good cause. One of them, Wigbold Aldringa, was asked by William Frederick to unobtrusively eavesdrop on Cornelis Musch's conversations in the corridors of power in The Hague. Could Aldringa perhaps inform him about the strategy the Orange camp would use in Groningen? The deputy was also instructed to 'penetrate' the rival party 'in secret'.[48]

William Frederick's ingenuity was in vain. Eyssinga and his followers in the city were in fact fighting a rearguard action in Groningen, where the States, which had to decide on the vacancy, consisted of representatives from two centres of power: the city itself and the Ommelanden, the rural areas surrounding it. The elite in the Ommelanden had long felt that they could expect to gain by choosing the prince as their stadholder, while the votes of the most influential regents in the city were said to have been bought. At the decisive moment Frederick Henry also managed to play the city and the Ommelanden against each other. Because of their rivalry, each was eager 'to stand better than the other in The Hague'.[49] Nor did the prince leave anything to chance in the third province where there was a vacancy, the *Landschap* of Drenthe. Here he had an influential protégé, the *drost* Roelof van Echten. The prince had helped Van Echten to win this office in 1639, and a year later he claimed his reward for this gesture. Van Echten, who was said by insiders to have 'the most direction' in Drenthe, joined forces with the Overijssel clan of Sweder van Haersolte to put pressure on the States of Drenthe, and having achieved a successful result, waited on Frederick Henry in person to offer him the stadholdership.[50]

Disorder in Friesland

Frederick Henry was not mollified by the consolation prizes of Groningen and Drenthe. In Friesland William Frederick was to find that flouting the prince's authority in the House of Nassau would earn him public humiliation and exclusion from the family. The prince found his opportunity ready to hand in the discontent that was still felt in the towns over the magisterial nominations, and the rancour that still lingered since Henry's intervention in 1637. Lieuwe van Aitzema relates that several 'domestics and creatures' of the prince were secretly sent to Friesland in late 1640 to support the 'malcontents' in the province. Members of these opposition movements were encouraged to come to The Hague, if necessary, to discuss their strategy at court. This was more or less officially approved by the States-General, which also sent some deputies to Leeuwarden 'to fan the flames there'.[51]

Aitzema reports that these Orange sympathisers tried to sabotage the new stadholder's unstable power base by openly challenging his right to nominate in the Friesian towns. Backed by the prince of Orange, several dissatisfied Friesian notables saw their opportunity, and boldly declared that they would not recognise William Frederick's choice of magistrates. How effective this opposition to the young stadholder would really be did not become clear until December, when new magistracies had to be chosen in the towns of Friesland. William Frederick's first nominations would be seen as a test of his authority in the turbulent province. In the months prior to the elections, Sohn and the young stadholder therefore selected a trustworthy man in each city who could enlighten and advise them on the local state of affairs, as a rule the burgomaster or secretary who had enjoyed Henry's confidence.[52]

Even so, the elections of 1640–41 in Friesland were chaotic, and local disorders broke out with the 'underhand incitement' of Frederick Henry. In Sneek things got out of hand on 27 December, during the election from the duplicate list, when eleven 'sworn members of the community', including Matthias Vierssen, left the town hall in a bad temper, 'notwithstanding being admonished and begged to remain'. In Dokkum too the 'men of ill-will' had absented themselves, because they believed that the elections were a matter for the Court of Friesland. In Harlingen, William Frederick's worst fear was realised: 'to the great contentment and acclamation of the whole community', two burgomasters were chosen without his knowledge, a flagrant snub to his authority.[53]

The States of Friesland, who feared that if the stadholder's nominations were questioned, their own power base would be undermined as well, understood that it was time to intervene.[54] With their backing William Frederick dared to send in troops to restore order. In Sneek some of the ringleaders were arrested and imprisoned in January. Soldiers were also sent to Harlingen, where, led by Frederik van Inthiema, they occupied the town hall and church. The self-styled burgomasters were held captive and replaced by William Frederick's preferred candidates. A few of the opposition leaders were arrested. Meanwhile, the magistrates of Bolsward were surprised by a troop of soldiers, which took up strategic positions in the town. Finally, in Dokkum the local garrison used 'force and violence' to prevent the opposition from entering the town hall.[55]

William Frederick's action made little impression on the puppeteer in The Hague who had staged the Friesian unrest, or his puppets in the States-General. Frederick Henry even invited the harassed Friesian opposition to come to The Hague to make their complaint. In November William Frederick indeed heard that several notables from Harlingen, Dokkum and Sneek wished to go to The Hague to bring the magistrates' appointments before His Highness.[56] This band of dissidents also had the covert support of some of the Friesian nobles who, hoping to be better off under Frederick Henry as stadholder, had gone to The Hague to pay their court to him. Among them was Sjuck van Burmania, whose involvement did not surprise William Frederick, since he 'had always been against my brother and father'.[57]

To put more pressure on William Frederick, further difficulties were put in his way. Frederick Henry ensured that Henry's regiment in the Republic's army, which had also been under the command of Ernst Casimir, was awarded to the count of Solms. William Frederick must have found this appointment extraordinarily insulting, because as stadholder of Friesland he now only bore the rank of a 'simple *ritmeester*'.[58] The prince took further steps to banish the companies commanded by William Frederick's courtiers Barthold van Oostheim and Johan Snabel to unattractive places, and both men were the butt of insults from the Orange following in The Hague.[59] When Oostheim visited the city in November that year, he was warned by the captain of the guard not to come to court or into the prince's sight.[60] Johan Sohn was summoned before the States-General to explain the 'wicked remarks' he was alleged to have made 'to the detriment of His Highness' in Friesland.[61] In the meantime, when William Frederick himself visited The Hague in January 1641, he found that he 'was looked at coldly at court and by everyone who wanted to be in favour at court'. Lieuwe van Aitzema says that William Frederick felt so vulnerable that he dared not take his seat in the Council of State, to which he was entitled as stadholder.[62]

Relationships restored

This continued sabotage and public humiliation must have made a deep impression on the young Friesian stadholder. 'Count William took the matter very much to heart', wrote Aitzema in his chronicle, 'for he fell into a grave illness, which kept him down for a long time'.[63] The problems in which William Frederick was now entangled were complex indeed. The count felt that he could not possibly shirk his duty to defend the stadholderly dignities acquired by his ancestors, but at the same time he associated his identity as count very strongly with the House of Nassau as a whole. To become *persona non grata* at the court of the head of the family, the 'Boss', went against all the principles that William Frederick felt bound to uphold as a nobleman. Several sources suggest that William Frederick fell into a great despair that winter, allegedly as a result of the sustained emotional strain caused by his competing roles as patron in Friesland and client in The Hague. William Frederick himself never did mention the physical or mental consequences of the prince's campaign of harassment. Yet it is noticeable that in later years in his diary William Frederick would often refer to the tensions of 1641 as 'that troubled time'.[64] The memory continued to haunt him, and it clearly served as an ominous example of the precarious balance he had to keep between his two contradictory patronage positions.

With that result, Frederick Henry's plan might appear successful. William Frederick was urged from several sides to give in to the prince's demands. In a letter of 12 October 1640, Reinier Casembroot had already warned his new master of the impossible position in which he was likely to put himself, and advised him to seek earnestly for 'means to repair' such a breach. The quarrel between the prince and the count, indeed, was damaging to the family but it was also a threat to William Frederick's own followers. 'Time may heal it, but in my opinion rather more is required', Casembroot wrote, in a cautious attempt to induce his master to make concessions.[65]

William Frederick was sensitive to these arguments, and in February 1641 he saw no way out of the impasse except to make a public submission to Frederick Henry. But because the prince had by now come to realise that to force his great-nephew out of office would 'cause too much scandal' he was content to secure the reversion of the office to his son William. That meant that on William Frederick's death his stadholdership would pass automatically to Frederick Henry's son prince William, placing all seven provinces at last in the hands of a prince of Orange.[66] That was not all that Frederick Henry demanded; he also required a purge of William Frederick's household to normalise the troubled relationship. The steward and secretary had lost so much credit at the Orange court that their positions had become untenable. William Frederick also saw the necessity of their departure, and in spring he let both men leave his service. Oostheim and Sohn thus paid for their loyalty to the count's family with their dismissal.

Interestingly, however, their departure did not put an end to their contacts with William Frederick as such. The formal tie of employment was dissolved, but informally Oostheim and Sohn were still able to invoke their patron's aid. The steward was found a new post in the army, and in later years he was a

regular guest at the count's court.[67] William Frederick also continued to corre-
spond frequently with Johan Sohn, who owed his appointment as president
of the council of war (*Krijgsgerecht*) in Groningen to the count's intervention.
And ten years later, when William Frederick made a new attempt to secure the
stadholdership of Groningen, Sohn was once more an active campaigner on his
behalf.[68] Thus the turmoil of 1640–41 did not end the patron-client relationship
as such, but merely altered the form it took. As we shall see, the court sphere in
which these relationships had originated was responsible for this continuity.

To underline his renewed dependence on Orange, William Frederick also
began 'spontaneously' asking the prince's advice in 1641 on filling military vacancies that were in his gift as stadholder of Friesland. In a sense he was putting
his own patronage resources at his patron's disposal, allowing Frederick Henry
in future to help his own favourites to army posts that were officially on the
Friesian payroll. William Frederick wrote to the Delegated States of Friesland, in
a rather apologetic tone, that he expected them 'not to be unwilling to consider
his aforesaid Highness's disposition agreeable'.[69] Frederick Henry, for his part,
was ready to do something in return for William Frederick. He immediately
abandoned the Friesian opposition and even lent a helping hand to William
Frederick to restore his authority as stadholder. The Friesian nobles and regents
who had come to The Hague watched with dismay as the prince's 'creatures and
domestics' lost interest in their cause. In these changed conditions it was now
in Frederick Henry's interest to strengthen the power base of his great-nephew
in Friesland. And since the succession of his son was in prospect, the prince also
wanted to be sure that William would inherit undiminished privileges when he
became stadholder of Friesland.

William Frederick also tried to come to a new understanding with Frederick
Henry's courtiers, sending Huygens, for example, some plants for the garden of
his newly built country house at Hofwijk.[70] The secretary had already broken the
ice by recommending a successor to Sohn: Philip Ernst Vegelin, who was on good
terms with Huygens. In the winter of 1641 Vegelin took over Sohn's duties, and
apparently made himself agreeable to William Frederick, who thanked Huygens
cordially a few months later for sending him 'such a capable man'. Thanks to
his close relations with Huygens, Vegelin acted as a bridge between the two
stadholders' clienteles, which had previously been at odds. It was Vegelin, for
example, who first sounded Huygens out about the possibility of the reversion
of the stadholdership of Friesland for Orange's son William.[71]

Yet William Frederick's submission to Orange was no guarantee that the
rest of his career in Friesland would run smoothly. In the years after 1640 it
became clear that taking over Henry's old contacts had been useful, but that
the trust that was necessary to build up a stable patronage network could only
grow over time. It was only after 1641 that William Frederick could really begin

to shape his clientele. While his inexperience had forced him to lean heavily on the advice of Henry's former contacts, in the following years he sought to establish a more independent position both as stadholder and as count. His efforts to develop a role for himself as patron in both circuits ran in parallel with a transformation of his standing as a client at the Orange court. In fact, these two themes dominated the years 1640–50, when Leeuwarden and The Hague competed for William Frederick's attention and devotion.

Notes

1 KHA, WF, VIII, 3-1 (note of 10–20 September 1640 et seq; 18–28 May 1642); VI, 5 (William Frederick to Wigbold Aldringa, 22 August – 1 September? 1640, n.p.).

2 For William Frederick's biography and his youth see Kooijmans, *Liefde in opdracht*, 9–21; Kleijn, *De stadhouders*, 90–112; Spanninga, 'Ick laet niet met mij gecken'.

3 KHA, WF, VIII, 3-1 (note of 10–20 September 1640); *Gloria Parendi*, 600. William Frederick's remark is contradicted by Christian von Dohna, who had certainly met the count in Leeuwarden before 1640, Borkowski, *Les mémoires*, xi.

4 KHA, WF, VIII, 3-1 (note of 10–20 September 1640).

5 Kooijmans, *Liefde in opdracht*, 10–16.

6 Kettering, *Patrons, Brokers and Clients*, 13ff; Greengrass, 'Noble Affinities', 275–300. See also Blok, *The Mafia*, 178; Wolf, 'Kinship, Friendship and Patron-Client Relations', 168 and 174–6. For the Dutch Republic see Gabriëls, *De heren als dienaren*, 147–9; Mörke, 'De hofcultuur', 76.

7 Groenveld, 'Nassau contra Oranje'; Kooijmans, *Liefde in opdracht*, 10–16; Kleijn, *De stadhouders*, 79–89.

8 Price, *Holland and the Dutch Republic*, 134–48; Israel, *The Dutch Republic*, 300–6 and 489–99. Cf. also the studies of Groenveld, *Evidente factiën*, and Rowen, *The Princes of Orange*. For the Friesian stadholders in particular Cf. Bergsma, 'Willem Lodewijk', 191–228; Kooijmans, *Liefde in opdracht*, 27–30; Kleijn, *De stadhouders*, 81–9.

9 Groenveld, 'Gemengde gevoelens', 30–41. Frederick Henry was also said to have made an attempt in this direction in 1632: Rowen, *The Princes of Orange*, 70–1.

10 For the personnel taken over by William of Orange see Delen, *Het hof*, 93–4; for Maurice, Van Deursen, *Maurits van Nassau*, 26; Scherft, *Het sterfhuis van Willem van Oranje*, 33–4 and 60–1; Zandvliet, 'Maurits' Haagse hovelingen', 439–45; for Frederick Henry, Tiethoff-Spliethoff, 'De hofhouding van Frederik Hendrik', 41–62; for William II, Groenveld, 'Een out ende getrouw dienaer', 17–19.

11 KHA, WF, VIII, 3-1 (note of William Frederick 15–25 August, 10–20 September 1640); *Gloria Parendi*, 413 and 600. A similar justification is also found in his correspondence for 1640: KHA, WF, VI, 5 (William Frederick to Wigbold Aldringa, 12–22 August 1640, n.p.; Reinier Casembroot to William Frederick, 2–12 October 1640, from The Hague).

12 Aitzema, *Saken van Staet en oorlogh*, II, 707.

13 Ibid., II, 707–9; Sohnius 'Brieven betreffende', 128–32.

14 KHA, WF, VI, 5 (Reinier Casembroot to William Frederick, 29 July – 8 August and 2–12 October 1640, from The Hague); KHA, WF, VII, A-XII (Reiner Casembroot to William Frederick, 5–15 July 1640, from The Hague). Cf. also Groen, *Archives*, III, 283. On Casembroot see Van der Aa, *Biographisch woordenboek*, III, 218–19; *NNBW*, VIII, 264–5, in which Casembroot's activities for the Friesian stadholder are not mentioned.

15 So far as the archives offer any details of this, see KHA, WF, V; Tresoar, Eysinga, 537, 476 and 544. See also Van Nienes and Bruggeman, *Archieven van de Friese stadhouders*, 622–7, which shows that Gosewijn Wiedenfelt, Achatius van Hohenfelt and other personnel had already been in service in Ernst Casimir's time. William Frederick did not formally inherit the barony of Liesveld until the death of Sophia Hedwig.

16 For the troubles of 1640 in general see Groenveld, 'Nassau contra Oranje', 27–8; Kooijmans,

'Hoe Willem Frederik', 205–17, and idem *Liefde in opdracht*, 22–35; Spanninga, 'Ick laet niet met mij gecken', 57–9 and 69–71.

17 Breuker, *It wurk van Gysbert Japix*, II-1, 204–10; Kuiper, 'Profijt, eer en reputatie', 179–82; Spanninga, 'Ick laet niet met mij gecken', 70.

18 Boomsma, 'Een werck van factie en staetsucht', 12–14; Breuker, *It wurk van Gysbert Japix*, II-1, 204–10; Kooijmans, *Liefde in opdracht*, 30; Guibal, *Democratie en oligarchie*, 29, 112.

19 Cf. KHA, WF, VI, 5 (Henry Casimir to the States of Friesland, 30 June – 10 July 1640, from the army camp at Reeck).

20 Aitzema, *Saken van Staet en oorlogh*, II, 707–9; Sohnius, 'Brieven betreffende', 128–32.

21 KHA, WF, VI, 5. These may be partly copies. Wiebe Bergsma found identical documents in the stadholder's archives in Leeuwarden: Bergsma, *Tussen Gideonsbende en publieke kerk*, 333–4. For a detailed discussion of these and other criteria see chapter 2.

22 Tresoar, SA, 276 (documents on the appointment of magistrates); 267 (recommendations on the appointments of magistrates); 305 (notes on Groningen).

23 Tresoar, SA 267 and 272 (documents on the appointment of magistrates); 285 (documents on Dokkum); 290 (documents on Workum); KHA. WF, VI, 5 (correspondence with Veltdriel, Gauma, Inthiema and others, 1640). For the long career of Inthiema see Lindler, *Raad van State, Repertorium*, 131 (n. 225).

24 This list of names is probably incomplete. It is quite possible that correspondence with other confidants has been lost. KHA, WF, VI, 5 and 6; Tresoar, SA, 267, 272, 285, 290.

25 KHA, WF, VI, 5 (William Frederick to Willem Lamminga, 3–13 August 1640, n.p.). Other letters of 1640 also refer to the continuance of Henry's patronage by William Frederick. The Dokkum *vroedschap* member Gerrit Harmens applied to Johan Sohn, remarking that he had been on the *vroedschap* under Henry and would be glad to continue his 'services' under the new stadholder (KHA, WF, VI, 6, Gerrit Harmens to Johan Sohn, 15–25 December 1640, from Dokkum). In 1642, Johannes Veltdriel recommended someone to William Frederick, because 'I know well that Your Honour has always been a true friend to His Excellency Count Ernst Casimir and His Excellency Count Henry Casimir of noble memory, and always kept an eye to the service of Your Excellency'; UBL, Coll. Hanschr. HUG 37 (Johannes Veltdriel to William Frederick, 22 September – 2 October 1642, from The Hague.)

26 Kuiper, 'Profijt, eer en reputatie', 179–98; Price, 'The Dutch Nobility', 82–113; Spanninga, 'Ick laet niet met mij gecken', 77–86. For more detail on the position of the Friesian nobility see chapter 2.

27 KHA, Ernst Casimir, IX, 46a (Johan van Aylva to Sophia Hedwig, 6–16 July 1640, from The Hague).

28 Israel, 'The Holland Towns' and 'Frederick Henry'. Cf. Groenveld, 'Frederik Hendrik', 21–6.

29 Well analysed by Knevel, *Het Haagse bureau*, 123–44; see also Japikse, 'Cornelis Musch'; Poelhekke, *Frederik Hendrik*, 425–7.

30 NA, SG, res. 75 (19–29 July and 22 July – 1 August 1640); Aitzema, *Saken van Staet en oorlogh*, II, 707; Van der Capellen, *Gedenkschriften*, I, 49; Worp, *Briefwisseling*, III, 81.

31 KHA, WF, VI, 5 (William Frederick to Wigbold Aldringa, 12–22 August 1640, n.p.); *Gloria Parendi*, 600; Worp, *Briefwisseling*, III, 81.

32 For Huygens's position as broker see Groenveld, 'Een out ende getrouw dienaer'.

33 Among the notables whom Huygens sought to contact was the courtier Cornelis van Aerssen van Sommelsdijk, who was related to the Friesian regent Peter van Walta. *Gloria Parendi*, 600; Groen, *Archives*, III, 264–7, 284–8; Worp, *Briefwisseling*, III, 83–4.

34 Worp, *Briefwisseling*, III, 68, 74–5; Poelhekke, *Frederik Hendrik*, 511–15.

35 Groen, *Archives*, III, 264–7 and 284–8; Worp, *Briefwisseling*, III, 83–4.

36 Groen, *Archives*, III, 260–2; Worp, *Briefwisseling*, III, 69–72.

37 Although the *drost* later paid a personal call on Frederick Henry: Heringa, *Geschiedenis van Drenthe*, 390–1 (note 139); Israel, *The Dutch Republic*, 538; Poelhekke, *Frederik Hendrik*, 514.

38 Aitzema, *Saken van Staet en oorlogh*, II, 707. Cf. Kettering, *Patrons, Brokers and Clients*, 65ff.

39 *Gloria Parendi*, 600; Groen, *Archives*, III, 284 and 288; Worp, *Briefwisseling*, III, 81 and 86. Cf.

Kooijmans, 'Hoe Willem Frederik', 213–14, and *Liefde in opdracht*, 32–3 and 281.

40 For this process see Groenveld, 'Nassau contra Oranje'.

41 Kooijmans, *Liefde in opdracht*, 27–35.

42 BL, Additional MS 21527 (Sophia Hedwig to Frederick Henry, 30 July – 9 August 1640, from Willing).

43 Groenveld, *Verlopend getij*, 93–6; Rowen, *The Princes of Orange*, 70–3.

44 Van der Capellen, *Gedenkschriften*, II, 50.

45 KHA, WF, VI, 5 (unknown person to Johan Sohn, 15–25 July 1640, from Groningen). Philip Ernst Vegelin referred to the bribes two years later: Tresoar, Eysinga, 485 (1642). Casembroot's report is in KHA, WF, VI, 5 (Reinier Casembroot to William Frederick, 2–12 October 1640, from The Hague). Some Groningen regents were rewarded by Frederick Henry after the election with 'a silver ewer and basin of five hundred guilders'. Aitzema, *Saken van Staet en oorlogh*, II, 708. For these gifts see also chapter 7.

46 KHA, WF, VI, 5 (correspondence of William Frederick with various Groningen regents, 1640). The States of Friesland also sent a deputation to Groningen: Tresoar, SvF, 47 (resolution of 25 July – 4 August 1640).

47 Aitzema, *Saken van Staet en oorlogh*, II, 708; Waterbolk, 'Staatkundige geschiedenis', 242.

48 KHA, WF, VI, 5 (William Frederick to Wigbold Aldringa, 22 August – 1 September? 1640, n.p.; Reinier Casembroot to William Frederick, 29 July – 8 August 1640, from The Hague). At that time Aldringa was a deputy for Groningen in the States-General. Lindler, *Raad van State. Repertorium*, 135 (n. 259).

49 The city had initially leaned toward William Frederick, but the regents feared that if the Ommelanden turned to Orange, 'the Ommelanden would thereby gain a great advantage in The Hague'. Aitzema, *Saken van Staet en oorlogh*, II, 707–8; Waterbolk, 'Staatkundige geschiedenis', 242.

50 KHA, WF, VIII, 3-I (note of 1–11 December 1650); Heringa, *Geschiedenis van Drenthe*, 390–1; Israel, *The Dutch Republic*, 538; Poelhekke, *Frederik Hendrik*, 514.

51 Aitzema, *Saken van Staet en oorlogh*, II, 747–8. See also Spanninga, 'Ick laet niet met mij gecken', 59, 70–1.

52 Cf. KHA, WF, VI, 6 (recommendations from Bolsward, Harlingen, Dokkum and Sneek); and Tresoar, SA, 282 (Sneek); 285 (Dokkum), 286 (Harlingen).

53 KHA, WF, VIII, 3-I (notes of 18–28 May 1642); Tresoar, SA, 282 (declaration of the magistrates of Sneek, 17–27 December 1640); 285 (Tjeerd Gauma and Petrus Veltdriel to William Frederick, 26 December 1640 – 5 January 1641, from Dokkum); 286 (Paulus Jansen Innema to the States-General, n.d. 1641; Frederik van Inthiema to William Frederick, 15–25 January 1641, from Harlingen).

54 KHA, WF, VI, 65; NA, SG, Bijlagen, 12548.20 (documents on the disorders in the towns of Friesland, 1641).

55 NA, SG, Bijlagen, 12548.20 (documents on the disorders in Harlingen, Dokkum, Sneek and Bolsward); Tresoar, SA, 282 (States-General to William Frederick, 23 January – 2 February 1641, from The Hague); 286 (Paulus Jansen Innema to the States-General n.d., 1641; Frederik van Inthiema to William Frederick, 15–25 January 1641, from Harlingen).

56 NA, SG, Bijlagen 12548.240 (Remonstrances to the States-General by, among others, P. Jansen Innema [Harlingen], M. Vierssen [Sneek], R. Tijmens [Workum], F. Hansa [Bolsward], Joh. Claes [Dokkum], A. Popma [IJlst], unknown [Sloten]). William Frederick was kept well informed about these: KHA, WF, VI, 6 (Renaerd Gedses (?) to Joh. Sohn, 29 October – 8 November 1640, from Harlingen); Tresoar, SA, 282 (magistrates of Sneek to William Frederick, 18–28 January 1641, from Sneek; States-General to William Frederick, 23 January – 2 February 1641, from The Hague); 285 (Tjeerd Gauma and Petrus Veltdriel to William Frederick, 28 December – 7 January 1641, from Dokkum; idem to Johan Sohn, 9–19 January 1641, from Dokkum).

57 NA, SG, Bijlagen, 12548.240 (Remonstrance of Sjuck Burmania and Regnerus Bruinsma to the States-General, n.d.); Tresoar, SA, 286 (magistrates of Harlingen to William Frederick, 29 January – 8 February 1641); *Gloria Parendi*, 205; Aitzema, *Saken van Staet en oorlogh*, II, 747.

58 Aitzema, *Saken van Staet en oorlogh*, II, 747.

59 Aitzema, *Saken van Staet en oorlogh*, II, 709. For Snabel, KHA, WF, VI, 6; Worp, *Briefwisseling*, III, 68.

60 Aitzema, *Saken van Staet en oorlogh*, II, 709.

61 Sohnius, 'Brieven betreffende', 129–31.

62 Aitzema, *Saken van Staet en oorlogh*, II, 709 and 747.

63 Aitzema, *Saken van Staet en oorlogh*, II, 708.

64 Ibid., II, 708; Kooijmans, *Liefde in opdracht*, 34; *Gloria Parendi*, 318, 332.

65 KHA, WF, VI, 5 (Reinier Casembroot to William Frederick, 2–12 October 1640, from The Hague).

66 Aitzema, *Saken van Staet en oorlogh*, II, 748. The States of Friesland ultimately agreed to the arrangement: Tresoar, SvF, 48 (resolution 19–29 March 1641).

67 *Gloria Parendi*, inter alia 55 and 457 ('Oostheim was with me, spoke to me for a long time'; 'Oostheim spoke to me and ate with me this evening'). Oostheim pursued his career in the States' Army and died as a captain in 1654.

68 Reinier Casembroot warned William Frederick in April 1642 that his continued contacts with Johan Sohn were provokig criticism in The Hague: KHA, WF, VII, C-115 (Reinier Casembroot to William Frederick, 4–14 April 1642 from The Hague). The correspondence with Sohn: KHA, WF, VII, B-I, 18a (Johan Sohn to Vegelin, 9–19 May, from Groningen); B-I, 33 (Johan Sohn to William Frederick, 24 January – 3 February 1658, from Groningen); B-I, 46 (Johan Sohn to William Frederick, 10–20 December 1658, from Groningen); Tresoar, SA, 37, 1-L (William Frederick to Johan Sohn, 1–11 December 1650, n.p.); 340 (various letters of William Frederick and Sohn as president of the council of war). See also *Gloria Parendi*, 199 and 588.

69 Tresoar, SA, 30, 1st bundle (William Frederick to the Delegated States, 22 July – 1 August 1642, from the army camp). Other examples: Tresoar, SA, 30, 3rd bundle (William Frederick to Delegated States, 6–16 October 1644); KHA, WF, VII, A-II, 1–15 (Frederick Henry to William Frederick, 1641–45); UBL, Coll. Handschr. HUG 37 (William Frederick to Johannes Veltdriel, 25 September – 5 October 1642, from the army). Amalia van Solms 'spoke in such a way' to William Frederick that she persuaded him to promise her brother Johan Albrecht the commandership of the Teutonic Order if William Frederick should die without children. Tresoar, Eysinga, 485 (1642); *Gloria Parendi*, 42.

70 Worp, *Briefwisseling*, III, 280.

71 UBL, Coll. Handschr., HUG 37 (Correspondence of Huygens and Vegelin, 1642); Worp, *Briefwisseling*, III, 261, 264, 267 and 269. The ex-steward Oostheim was succeeded in 1641 by Gozewijn Wiedenfelt, who had been in Ernst Casimir's service as chamberlain. Van Nienens, *Archieven van de Friese stadhouders*, 624.

2

The stadholder becomes a patron

In 1656 Johan de Witt, the pensionary of Holland, wrote to William Frederick, describing him as the 'chief director' of affairs in Friesland. The description was undoubtedly intended to flatter the recipient, but there was probably more to De Witt's choice of words than mere courtesy. Other political insiders around 1650 also remarked on the significant political power wielded by the Friesian stadholder. One of them, the burgomaster of Leeuwarden Alle van Burum, had heard in 1651 that rumours were current in The Hague, that the Friesian deputies in the States-General 'dared do no more than what suited the stadholder'. Two years earlier his colleague Pieter Walta had to admit that William Frederick had 'had so much credit' in Friesland for some time, whereas his predecessors 'had never had such credit'.[1]

Much must have changed in ten years. While in 1640 William Frederick's authority as stadholder had been openly challenged, by 1650 he had apparently become the central figure in Friesian politics for friend and foe alike. He himself was well aware of this political transformation. By his own admission he had consciously been working on a sophisticated network of local brokers in Friesland – 'one in each town' – over the last few years. William Frederick recognised that this network had only been assembled fairly recently; 'I could not do it' [earlier], he wrote, 'because it was in the beginning and in that troubled time.'[2] William Frederick thus depicted the formation of his provincial patronage network as a gradual development, which he himself had initiated cautiously but deliberately after the crisis of 1640.[3]

However revealing William Frederick's remarks may be, they do not really explain how broad the alleged power base of the Friesian stadholder was, and still less how exactly it had been formed over the years. The same can be said about other seventeenth-century stadholders, as historians have not yet been able to reconstruct the ways in which processes of patronage took shape in the highly decentralised, and often puzzling republican state system.[4] In order to make more sense of the position of the stadholders in the Dutch Republic and to understand the transformation of William Frederick's role in Friesian politics, we must first analyse the formal instruction that he was given at his installation in 1640.

Instructions

Formally William Frederick became a civil servant of the States of Friesland when he took office as stadholder. The States represented the highest authority in the province, and thus determined the powers and duties of their highest official. The States of Friesland were made up of the three rural quarters, Oostergo, Westergo and Zevenwouden, and the city quarter. These four bodies were represented in the assembly by *volmachten* (literally, proxies or holders of powers), some of whom sat in the *Mindergetal*, a preparatory committee of the States. Because the full States assembly met only once a year as a *Landdag* or Diet, there was also a standing committee, the *Gedeputeerde Staten* or Delegated States, which ran the day-to-day administration of the province. Important matters such as the definition of a new stadholder's duties were reserved for the States themselves, however, and William Frederick's appointment was no exception.[5] His functions were described in the twelve articles of his 'instruction' formulated by the States of Friesland on 2 August 1640, when they appointed him.[6]

Such an instruction was not indispensable, however. William Frederick's uncle, William Louis, had served as stadholder from 1585 to 1620 without one. In the province of Holland too, the stadholders traditionally had only a letter of commission, in which their duties were described in the most general terms.[7] In a sense that arrangement was more attractive to a stadholder, for instructions were usually intended to limit his influence. Yet William Frederick appears to have found his instruction an acceptable guideline, since from 1644 he began virtually every year by transcribing it into his diary, setting down in writing what his official duties would be in the coming year. His version of the text shows us that they fell broadly into two categories: political (as stadholder) and military (as captain-general). In practice this division partly coincided with the geographical distinction between William Frederick's networks in the Friesian towns and in the countryside. That means that the stadholder's political rights were exercised mainly in the towns, while his military powers were more useful to him in the country. Before analysing these powers, first of all a more precise description of his rights and duties is required.

William Frederick's first duty was 'to pay due honour and respect' to his formal employer: the States of Friesland and their Deputies. Next, the stadholder was instructed to uphold the Reformed religion, whose doctrines had been laid down in the decisions of the Synod of Dordt in 1619. William Frederick was expected to defend them 'without being able to make any alteration therein, or to suffer it to be made by others'.[8] Some other rules were formulated in similarly negative terms: the stadholder might not buy any land in Friesland, because the ownership of land in the province conferred the right to vote, and a policy of purchases by the count might have political consequences. He was also forbidden to solicit a reversion or succession of his office.[9]

Besides his duties, William Frederick was assigned some closely defined rights, although the privileges of the stadholder were not always clearly distinguished from those of the captain-general. The fifth and sixth articles stipulated that virtually all army commissions were to be awarded by William Frederick, acting in conjunction with the Delegated States. The stadholder sat in this college, and also in the *Mindergetal*. Thanks to this structure, he was able to exert direct influence on the government of the province and to share in the nomination of the *grietmannen*, who headed the administration and the judicial system in the *grietenijen*, into which the three rural quarters were subdivided.[10]

At first sight this may seem to exhaust the stadholder's duties in Friesland. Yet in fact William Frederick's privileges were much wider, as the stadholder's instructions left some remarkable gaps. For instance, the instruction of 1640 did not mention his additional right to choose the magistrates from a duplicate list of names submitted to him in nine of the eleven Friesian towns, Leeuwarden and Franeker excepted. From the early 1640s, moreover, it became customary for William Frederick to appoint to the so-called 'ambulatory' offices of the city quarter.[11] These were temporary but lucrative posts, such as representatives to the Delegated States, the States-General, the Council of State or an Admiralty college.[12] Finally William Frederick enjoyed several powers that were awarded to him ad hoc or for part of his term of office. In 1652, for instance, the representatives of the rural quarter of Westergo decided to leave the appointment to their offices for the coming year to the stadholder. Their colleagues in Zevenwouden did something similar the following year, when they asked William Frederick to appoint to 'the first councillor's place in Zevenwouden'.[13] In 1653 William Frederick added the dignity of *curator magnificentissimus* of the University of Franeker, in which capacity he could influence academic appointments.[14] All of these incidental duties enhanced the stadholder's standing in Friesland as an informal dispenser of favours and potential patron.

The discrepancy between the stadholder's written instructions and his privileges in practice make it clear that for a study of patronage customs a fixation on the stadholder's formal authority is short-sighted. This becomes all the more relevant, since stadholder's instructions in the seventeenth-century Republic did not only leave significant gaps, they were often vaguely worded as well.[15] As we shall see, William Frederick made a shrewd use of the possibility of interpreting to his own advantage such unclear rules for appointment to certain offices. His patronage resources thus became far more extensive than the nominal system of government in Friesland would suggest. William Frederick was certainly no exception in this; in the other provinces too, the personality of the stadholder strongly influenced the real extent of his powers. In the republican system, a patronage network could therefore be built up by the exercise of formal rights of appointment, but it could also grow through the informal intervention of a stadholder, whose preferences were not to be lightly ignored.

The election of magistrates

The written and unwritten privileges of the Friesian stadholder suggest that William Frederick's patronage process will be most clearly visible in the towns, and his diaries bear out this assumption. In December and January, the months when the magistrates were elected and preparations were begun for the annual *Landdag*, the stadholder's agenda was dominated by writing letters of recommendation, receiving visits and organising dinners with the town regents. William Frederick prized his right to appoint the town magistrates, and never failed to exercise it during his twenty-four years in office as stadholder. The privilege was so jealously guarded because it had only been regained recently, in 1637, when Henry Casimir had definitively secured it. Moreover, the appointment of the magistrates was *the* means of acquiring political influence in the province. For William Frederick, therefore, the elections were an annually recurring test case. The tensions that preceded them and the relief that he felt afterward are recorded in his diary. 'December went off well and happily, by God's blessing', he sighed in 1649, 'the council appointment passed off peacefully and quietly, at Leeuwarden too it is quiet.' Two years earlier the election 'God be praised, was completed quietly without trouble or opposition'.[16]

The appointment of magistrates was not officially included in the stadholder's instruction, but it was bound up with rules that were defined elsewhere and with customs that had grown up over the years. In each town William Frederick was presented with a list of names, two for every vacancy. The candidates were nominated from within the *vroedschap*, although each town had its own customs. In most of them the nomination was left to 'five *vroedschap* persons chosen by lot, who may not vote for themselves'. These five were 'to have regard to qualified persons, without ambition or favour'. Their discussions took place in 'a chamber apart', and they were not permitted to leave or to communicate with anybody. In Dokkum and Harlingen they were not even allowed food or drink, to prevent interminable meetings and possible drunkenness.[17]

The day on which all this took place also differed from town to town. Bolsward, Sneek, Staveren, Workum, IJlst, Sloten and Hindeloopen nominated fourteen days before New Year's Day, Dokkum and Harlingen 'the day before Christmas Day'. The number of vacancies varied from one burgomaster a year in IJlst to two burgomasters and two councillors in Harlingen, but the criteria for eligibility were the same in most of the towns. Only men of Friesian birth could be nominated, while they had to be members of the Reformed, 'public' Church 'or at least well-affectioned, attending services and properly baptised'.[18] Once the nominations had been made according to these rules, the duplicate lists then had to be sent to the stadholder in a 'sealed missive'. He was not given much time to ponder his choice, for his messengers and halberdiers had to deliver the result to the towns not later than New Year's Eve. To help himself despatch the business efficiently, every year from 1643 William Frederick drew up a table, in which he listed the towns, the vacancies and the names of the nominees. This gave him a good conspectus of the candidates, and he could insert the name of his preferences in the scheme. Mostly those chosen were marked with a cross on the official letter of nomination.[19]

William Frederick's archives clearly demonstrate how such an appointment procedure favoured the local habits of clientage. Anyone in Friesland who wished to be considered for a post in the civic magistracy had to make himself known and agreeable to the stadholder. Friesian regents who were named in the lists of nominees therefore did their best to meet William Frederick personally at least once in December. It was also shrewd policy to persuade their friends and relatives to do the same, or at least to prevail on them to write a letter of recommendation. 'I spoke to many people who wanted to be burgomasters', the stadholder characteristically noted on 21 December 1649. As usual, over the following days regents known and unknown waited on the stadholder to recommend themselves while the postal system came under pressure 'because of the election, since letters arrive every day'. Occasionally William Frederick was so busy that he forgot whom he had met: 'four *vroedschappen* from Dokkum recommended to me their man for burgomaster', he jotted down on 26 December. 'Don't forget that Haubois recommended those from Sneek to me', he added elsewhere. By William Frederick's own admission, it was not just a poor memory but a shortage of offices that let him down: 'almost all the gentlemen from the towns have been to see me. Everyone wants an office, and there are only three'. To satisfy everyone was simply impossible: 'one cannot help all those people at the same time'.[20]

William Frederick's reports further indicate that the candidates used their visits and letters not only to emphasise their qualities, but also to assure the stadholder of their 'service, correspondence and friendship', if they should be chosen for office. That suggests that they saw appointment to a public office as a kind of service, which assumed a service in return. In 1649 a newly appointed burgomaster hastened to assure William Frederick that he 'would always be my friend and grateful to me'. On 19 February 1646 we read that 'burgomaster Klinckebijl thanked me for making him burgomaster'. Dealing with regents who sought office therefore became, for William Frederick, a way of managing his relations. By honouring someone with a post, he gained 'credit', to use his own word, on which he could draw at any moment.[21]

Indeed, the Bolsward regent Adriaan van Velsen praised himself in 1649, when he assured the stadholder that he would 'always remain serviceable, thankful and true as best I can'. Another colleague was recommended because he was accustomed to carry out the 'designs' of William Frederick. Evert Evertsz was said to be exceptionally suitable as burgomaster of IJlst in 1640, because he allowed himself to be 'used'.[22] The stadholder from his side deliberately tried to reinforce and to capitalise these expressions of dependence. To enhance the effect of his right of appointment, William Frederick reminded himself, when dealing with applications and recommendations, 'to act as if I were unwilling, so that afterward, when I do it, I have all the more thanks for it'.[23]

Selection criteria

William Frederick's comments show that his choices were rarely random. The many notes and tables in his archives illustrate that the stadholder thoroughly investigated the candidates' talents and backgrounds before he made his final choice. William Frederick had adopted this habit immediately after he arrived in Friesland, using his predecessors' notes. Over the years he was to make a systematic practice of this preliminary vetting, and to formulate more precise demands on the available candidates. What were the selection criteria by which William Frederick informally tested the urban elites? In other words, what did his potential clients in Friesland look like?

Officially, the appointed burgomasters and other office-holders must, of course, serve only the civic community. But as his earlier remarks showed, William Frederick felt justified in demanding from the regents a certain responsibility to himself. In a sense the stadholder was requiring a double loyalty from the magistrates. However, the ambiguity was not so obvious to the count himself, who believed that the segmented structure of the Friesian administration, and indeed of the Republic as a whole, was best served if he played a unifying or even a directing role. Like many of his contemporaries, William Frederick found it hard to imagine how such a decentralised state system could function without a compensating, centralising force. Moreover, according to William Frederick, the very roots of the Dutch Republic were inseparably intertwined with the history of the House of Nassau. 'Where would freedom, ... religion and the Union be,' he once asked rhetorically, 'if my forefathers had not been there?' The blood they had sacrificed for the good cause was for William Frederick the proof that 'their descendants succeeding to their offices ...' would maintain 'their zeal and inclination to serve this country'.[24] In short, the stadholder did not believe that by making further demands on the regents, he was seeking to aggrandise his own power; rather, it was part of his task to guarantee 'unity' in the public administration, as his forefathers had done before him. In this way the count appealed to historical parallels to legitimise the role that he evidently hoped to develop as patron.

Being so preoccupied with the construction of a clientage network, William Frederick regularly wrestled with the question of whom to trust and reward. In 1649 he resolved 'to choose the best and wealthiest and most honourable'.[25] Later he filled in the details of this rather broad set of requirements. According to William Frederick, the ideal client must be of unimpeachable conduct, that is of 'good name and fame'. Other recommendations included a 'sound understanding', 'knowledge of government' and some education. The stadholder could appreciate a man who was 'pleasant in his dealings with everyone', and in his tables of candidates he also noted those regents he thought 'of little understanding'. William Frederick believed that limited intellectual powers often went hand in hand with excessive drinking – a very frequent observation in his diaries. Folpert Hansma of Bolsward was eager to point out in 1647 that Joost Schenckel 'would be very serviceable, since he is a person who has an aversion for strong drink'. Haring Fongers was another who was said to be 'not inclined to drunkenness' and 'completely sober'. The Harlingen regent Gerrit Keth wrote enthusiastically in 1644 that his colleague Frederik Krol was not only averse from drink, but 'from tobacco and long conversations in taverns'.[26]

Yet a respectable *curriculum vitae* was no guarantee of success. In general it was not a man's personal qualities but his social background that qualified him for public office in the seventeenth century. Religion, money and family connections were the yardsticks.[27] William Frederick's resolve suggests that he too was convinced of the rightness of these criteria. He made careful notes on the candidates' occupations and whether they earned enough money. The information was relevant, because a good income would guarantee financial independence, making a regent less open to blackmail or bribery, and thus capable of running the public administration.[28] Frederik van Inthiema advised William Frederick to appoint two of his friends in Workum, 'as the said persons are very wealthy people'. His colleague Johan Veltdriel praised an acquaintance who was very rich and therefore 'incorruptible in all things'.[29]

Often the wealthy also came from the right milieu, for ideally financial and social capital went hand in hand. The stadholder therefore kept an eye on family backgrounds, and placed more trust in testimonials from relatives than in paper qualifications. Conversely, many Friesian notables also regarded their public offices as family perquisites. Douwe van Hottinga boasted of being 'a burgher's son from father to son, whose father, grandfather and great-grandfather had always been in the government here as burgomasters, with good reputation'. Haring Fongers of Bolsward was recommended by being a cousin of the town secretary. His other family connections were indisputable as well. His colleague Anne Heerkes was not sure if it had been Haring's grandfather or great-grandfather, but in any case one of them had 'gone into exile for religion's sake' in the 1560s and had been actively involved with the Revolt against Spain. Several local sources could even confirm that a forebear of Haring's had been at the famous capture of Den Briel by the count of Lumey in 1572, the celebrated start of the Revolt in Holland.[30]

Confessional segregation

Strictly speaking there was only one indispensable formal requirement which the stadholder was bound to verify when judging candidates for office: their religious background. Persons who were not members of or regular attenders to the Reformed, Calvinist Church were by definition ineligible to hold any public office. Unsurprisingly, candidate burgomasters often proclaimed that they were members or 'sympathisers' of the so-called 'public' Church.[31] Yet not all the notables of Friesland were attenders, let alone members of the Reformed Church of the Republic. This was the result of the way in which the Reformed community had developed over the previous decades, and the place in society which the authorities were willing to acknowledge to it.

The Reformed Church had enjoyed a privileged status since the Dutch Revolt, in Friesland since 1580. That meant that it had the exclusive use of church buildings in the Republic, and that the stipends of its ministers were paid by the secular authorities. At the Synod of Dordt in 1619 its exclusive status as the sole recognised public Church was further confirmed, while the tenets of its Calvinist doctrine were defined more precisely. Yet for all its privileged status the Reformed Church was not a state Church, nor was it the home of all believers in the Republic. Since the Union of Utrecht of 1579 guaranteed a rather vaguely defined 'freedom of conscience', joining the public Church remained a voluntary choice. Even attendance at its services was not obligatory for anyone, and adherence to another faith was permitted – although the 'private' freedom of conscience did not generally imply freedom of 'public' worship. By making public Church membership a matter of choice, the Reformed were at any rate unable to impose their confessional agenda on all believers in the Republic. At the same time, it gave them ample opportunity to present their Calvinist Church as an exclusive congregation: a community of the elect.[32]

Wiebe Bergsma, who has made a thorough study of the implications of this policy in Friesland, has shown that although the membership of the Reformed community in Friesland increased in the early seventeenth century, it certainly had not won the formal allegiance of more than half of the population by 1650. It is not easy to give precise figures in this connection, but circumstantial evidence suggests that a large part of the regular churchgoers did never become formal members. Locally, these so-called 'sympathisers' with the Reformed Church could be up to 30 per cent of the entire population. What's more, Catholics, Mennonites and other more or less tolerated groups could count on the adherence of a further sizeable proportion of local communities in the province.[33] The religious 'market' in Friesland, and in the Dutch Republic in general, was therefore highly fragmented, and all denominations, privileged or not, were in that sense minority Churches.

A great deal has been published on the practical consequences of this religious pluralism, and on the way in which religious divisions guided contacts in daily life.[34] Simon Groenveld has argued that the coexistence of confessional minorities in the Republic around 1650 in fact led to a situation in which each denomination lived a largely separate life.[35] If this assumption is correct, clientage networks will probably have reflected and reinforced this practice of 'confessional segregation'. In that case William Frederick's nascent clientele in Friesland must have had an overtly Calvinist character.[36]

Yet the hypothesis of separate, parallel confessional communities in early modern Dutch society has been challenged in recent years, whereas the possible connections between clientage networks and religious allegiances have never been fully examined. As Judith Pollmann has pointed out, it remains difficult to see how such separate confessional networks functioned in practice, if a substantial proportion of the population was not formally connected to any Church at all. It's clear that the ideal of confessionalised society and strict separation was propagated by the Church elites, but how far it was in fact adopted by (unattached) churchgoers remains an open question.[37] Recent publications that take this approach 'from below' indeed suggest a practice of mutual cooperation in everyday daily life, rather than a form of self-imposed segregation. It may also be that this practice of 'tolerance' applied to certain social areas only, and that the habits of separateness and confessionalisation prevailed in other social spheres.[38] This obviously raises the question of how far forms of patronage upheld or challenged such customs and unwritten codes.

We find a good test case of these questions in William Frederick's patronage practices in the towns of Friesland. To be sure, the count himself was a professing member of the Reformed community, although his active involvement in the public Church and his interest in Reformed pietism did not prevent him from occasionally attending the services of the Amsterdam Lutheran congregation, among others.[39] Moreover William Frederick's notes reveal that he was well aware of the social risks implied by the coexistence of so many confessions. He knew, for instance, that Catholic landowners in Friesland could still exert political influence. William Frederick heard that the *grietman* Ulbe van Aylva 'always used the priests to get the papists' votes' and that 'the Catholics had such great power here through their votes'.[40]

These rumours alarmed William Frederick, because in his mind Catholicism and public administration formed a dangerous combination. Like his forefathers, the count went into battle against the Spanish Catholic armies every year, and the reality of that permanent war also made him alert to the internal dangers that threatened the Republic. For William Frederick, Catholic sympathies were close to treason.[41] 'All the Catholics are against me, ... seek our ruin and downfall, to make their views and the king [of Spain] master again', he wrote in 1651, three years after the Peace of Münster.[42] The existence of Anabaptist or Mennonite communities appeared less threatening, since on principle they refused to bear arms or take part in the government.[43] Their attitude to the hereditary enemy Spain was also less ambivalent, but even so, any hint of political ambitions on the part of the Catholic and Mennonite elite in Friesland appeared undesirable to William Frederick.

The stadholder therefore kept a very sharp eye on how Van Aylva and his followers voted, and noted the names of those *grietmannen* who were said to receive secret support from papist landowners.[44] It is no surprise that William Frederick also kept himself informed of the confessional preferences of the town regents, and adhered strictly to the rules in his appointments in the towns. Regular attendance at the Reformed Church was the minimum requirement for an administrative career, but full members always enjoyed William Frederick's preference. His urban clientele thus bore an explicitly Calvinist character. Conversely, many Catholics had cause to feel excluded by William Frederick and his followers. When one Catholic was asked for the loan of his coach during the stadholder's wedding festivities in 1652, he replied; 'why should I lend count William my coach? He gives us Catholics one affront after the other'.[45]

The Reformed tone of William Frederick's republican clientele may appear predictable and self-evident, yet on closer inspection it was less uniform – and William Frederick's policy more ambiguous – than the examples cited suggest. For instance, it is striking that the Reformed William Frederick also recorded in his diary dinners at his court with Catholic nobles, from whom he also regularly received gifts. Moreover, the count went hunting with the Mennonite merchant Hobbe Jans Baerdt, while goods for the court were ordered from Catholic and Jewish merchants.[46] Catholics were even prominent in William Frederick's immediate entourage. His servant Gilles Marez, with whom the count often dined, was a Catholic. Their confidential relationship is also evident from the numerous missions on which he was employed by William Frederick. Marez clearly was one of the count's inner circle, and in 1646 he was rewarded with the rank of reserve officer in the stadholder's guard.[47]

Gilles Marez's case was not exceptional; there were other courtiers with a Catholic background. The captain of the guard Doecke van Hemmema, for instance, was William Frederick's closest military advisor. He accompanied his master in 1650 in the assault on Amsterdam, and twelve years later carried out his orders for military intervention in Groningen. Hemmema and his colleague Johan van Herema were both known 'papists', but for William Frederick this deviant confessional background apparently formed no obstacle to their service at court and friendly relations. On Easter Monday 1648, for example, he dined with Herema and discussed 'religion and the holy communion'; and about a week later the count's diary recorded: 'dined with Hemmema, we were very merry. We went to Hemmema's brother's house and saw the altar'. Interestingly, this visit to the private Catholic altar in the house of Hemmema's brother did not prompt any expression of distaste in the count's diary.[48] Just as noteworthy was the little verse with which William Frederick ended the year 1647:

> the zeal of a papist
> the good life of a Mennonite
> the doctrine of a Calvinist
> together make a good Christian.[49]

How is the confessionally diverse clientele in the private sphere of William Frederick' court to be reconciled with his strictly Reformed patronage in the Friesian towns? It may be that political expediency led the count to practise such selective tolerance. In other words, William Frederick may have chosen to include influential Catholics in his court clientele in order to attach them to himself in a way that was not open to him in the public sphere as stadholder. Yet if this is true, it is still remarkable that he never said anything about this possible strategy in his diaries. Therefore, it might be more sensible to look for another explanation of this noticeable discrepancy between William Frederick's republican (public) and domestic (private) patronage spheres. It was suggested above that the structure of the government in the Dutch Republic to some extent enabled William Frederick to develop different patronage roles in these two distinct institutional circuits. As stadholder, he dispensed patronage as part of his official duties; this made clientelism possible, but also influenced the way in which it was practised. As count of Nassau, William Frederick had opportunities in his household and domains to attach people to him by appointing them to offices and granting other favours. This private patronage, however, was not restricted by any official regulations; William Frederick was therefore free to exploit different possibilities for patronage in both circles or social spheres.

The remarkable differences in the religious aspects of his patronage policy thus appear to be the result of the different roles that he found appropriate as patron in public and domestic settings. In his capacity as stadholder William Frederick probably felt that an efficient public administration required unity of government, as the motto on the Republic's coat of arms – 'unity makes strength' – proclaimed.[50] That political unity had to be reinforced by confessional uniformity, so that religious passions could not divide the public administration. A uniform allegiance to the Reformed Church was therefore desirable in his public network of republican office-holders.

Yet evidently William Frederick did not consider such exclusiveness indispensable in every social role. Catholic individuals whom he explicitly had excluded from the public office-holding could still enjoy his confidence and patronage in the private sphere of his court. Clearly, the role that the count had to perform in a given context was decisive for the importance he attached to a man's confessional preference. There was a place for tolerance and a place for intolerance.[51] As a result, William Frederick's patronage policy sometimes deliberately contributed to confessional segregation, while at the same time he was forging links between those of different faiths in another social sphere.

William Frederick's differential patronage norms in religion were not exceptional. Willem Frijhoff, Benjamin Kaplan and Judith Pollmann have identified similar public and private circles and distinctions in the Republic, within which confessional allegiances were judged by different criteria. In these studies, however, the importance and relevance of distinctive social spheres for seventeenth-century people were associated exclusively with religion.[52] The case of William Frederick makes this connection problematic, because it raises the question of whether 'confession' was in fact the reason for, or no more than one of the characteristic results of, the distinction between public and private spheres of patronage. In other words, we need to know how far William Frederick's public and private clienteles contrasted in other, non-religious respects as well. To answer this question the next chapter reconstructs his court network more systematically, and determines how far William Frederick adjusted his other selection criteria to the social sphere in which he developed a role as a patron.

The role of the patron

The selection and nomination procedure in the Friesian towns was only the beginning of William Frederick's intended project. It reveals the social background that the patron demanded of his potential clients, but not how they behaved as clients. How far did the regents actually keep their earlier promises to serve their patron, and how far could William Frederick invoke them in practice? Similar questions have been asked for other stadholders and the matter remains generally in doubt in the literature. Some authors have suggested that the several stages of the appointment process prevented stadholders from effectively gaining the magistrates' allegiance. A choice restricted to a duplicate list of names made their preferences only partly relevant.[53] From that point of view, William Frederick's choice of office-holders could have only a limited effect.

To test this hypothesis, and to examine the precise meanings to be attributed to the language used by patrons and clients, it is important to assess the different means available to William Frederick to strengthen his informal position as patron; for the choice of magistrates was not the only authority vested in the stadholder. William Frederick's tactics in appointing to the ambulatory offices, and in acting as go-between on other occasions, can reveal how he gradually manoeuvred himself into a key position during the 1640s.

The case of Alle van Burum can serve as a specific example. It is characteristic that this burgomaster from the 'free' city of Leeuwarden soon proved – or was forced to become – willing to harmonise his political agenda with the stadholder's. In March 1645 William Frederick wrote that Van Burum had paid him a visit to assure him 'of his service and friendship at all times'. Specifically, the burgomaster promised to consult the stadholder informally about the offices that were in his gift as a magistrate. Indeed, that same year the stadholder recorded that Van Burum had promised him 'not to do anything in the matter of the sheriff's place without my knowledge'. Thanks to his connection with the stadholder, Van Burum for his part hoped to gain influence on the ambulatory offices, to which William Frederick made the appointments. The stadholder was perfectly aware of this. In 1647 he mentioned that he had 'discussed the offices' with Van Burum, and he regularly repaid his credit by appointing Van Burum's protégés and friends from Leeuwarden to office.[54]

Van Burum's case illustrates the growing social credit that William Frederick managed to accumulate in Friesland in the 1640s, as the central dispenser of favours in the province. William Frederick himself also deliberately sought to exploit his opportunities to the full, using his official rights to appoint where he could, and making unsolicited recommendations where he could not. Abraham Roorda advised the stadholder on 26 January 1645 to appoint Wibrant Wibrandi to the *vroedschap* of Workum, even though on paper the office was not William Frederick's to bestow.[55] Undeterred by these limits on his authority, William Frederick decided to write 'immediately to the town of Workum and Inthiema, in the man's favour'. This Frederik van Inthiema was the burgomaster of Workum who, with his followers, had been kept in office every year since 1640 by William Frederick. Van Inthiema was now instructed to arrange the appointment of Wibrandi to the *vroedschap*. Even though he had initially promised the post to a friend, Van Inthiema felt that he could not refuse William Frederick's candidate.

He assured the stadholder that 'His Excellency's recommendation will not be unfruitful', and decided that, if the *vroedschap* should try to thwart him, he would if necessary resign his own place to Wibrandi, so that the latter 'might come to enjoy the effect of his recommendation'.[56]

Wibrandi's example was not isolated, for there was a surprisingly large number of vacancies to which William Frederick had no right to appoint, but for which he nonetheless spontaneously put forward a candidate in a recommendation, 'of which we have no doubt that the same shall be agreeable to Your Honours'. Burgomasters and *vroedschappen* were mostly very wary of refusing someone who enjoyed William Frederick's preference, since a decision to snub the stadholder could have serious consequences for their own careers. In the 1640s the custom developed in Friesland for local clerkships, pensionaries' or secretaries' offices to be filled by men whom the stadholder preferred. Even candidates for the ministry beat a path to William Frederick's court.[57] The stadholder's increasing readiness to issue recommendations in the 1640s confirms Pieter Walta's earlier observation that William Frederick was systematically building up his role as patron from 1640. His success in this also appears to have made him more socially confident, so that in 1645, for example, he felt able to refuse a solicitation from a local regent in these words: 'I had thought that you would have moderated your desire somewhat, and been satisfied that your son has been in the Chamber of Accounts for two years'. In future, clients in the towns must know their place.[58]

This firmer grip on the process of network building was explained by William Frederick's ability to exert consistent pressure on appointments to offices. Once the stadholder had acquired 'credit' with a magisterial appointee, he could draw on it later by making a recommendation. Clientage was therefore not a static phenomenon or a status that could be achieved at a given moment. William Frederick's patronage in the Friesian administration was much more a work in progress; its characteristics and consequences only became evident over the years, and could therefore also change gradually. At first, the implications of William Frederick's tactics were most manifest in his spontaneous advice and informal recommendations to those who were appointed by him.[59] In so doing he himself claimed to have succeeded in 'bringing peace to Friesland again, which is a great good fortune for me, and will be a great honour to me'.[60] The selection criteria he used, however, reveal that the attempt 'to bring the country out of unrest and back to quietness' was closely related in William Frederick's mind with a broader ideal of confessional unity and social discipline. In the public sphere of his stadholdership, patronage also had to help him keep an eye on church attendance and suppress deviant or undesirable behaviour among the regents.

On 29 December 1648, for instance, William Frederick recorded his irritation that Johan van Aylva had been drunk that afternoon, because he had 'been boozing with Swartzenburg'.[61] William Frederick considered it one of his duties as patron to reprove and restrain such unseemly conduct. In 1659 a regent from Sneek received a final warning, 'since we have again been grieved to learn that Your Honour still will not refrain from drunkenness'.[62] His motives for such reprimands probably were not purely altruistic, since socially unacceptable behaviour by his 'creatures' reflected badly on his own reputation as a patron. For the same reason, in 1648 the magistrates of Hindelopen cautiously suggested that it would not be wise to comply with William Frederick's recommendation of the local debauchee Lambert Camp, since if they did so, 'we should be the laughing stock of the whole community and be held up to ridicule'.[63] Such examples also make us realise that the effects of William Frederick's disciplinary offensive should not be exaggerated, certainly in the early stages.

Not everyone in Friesland was willing to adjust to the new order. 'This is a wonderful country', sighed William Frederick in 1647, 'one cannot rely on anyone in the world. Those who were your greatest and most trusted friends one day, in a short time become your greatest and bitterest enemies.' Mutual liking was therefore not an indispensable feature of William Frederick's patronage in this context. The terms 'friendship' and 'friend', which recur so often in his correspondence, rather refer to a social obligation of mutual service, and not necessarily to an emotional bond or affection.[64] William Frederick had few illusions about the opportunist motives of the regents' conduct: 'when they have to deal with me, they give me good words; otherwise they pay me no heed'.[65] These remarks indicate that the stadholder viewed Friesian politics from above as a patron, but at the same time he kept a sharp eye on the strategies of his clients.

Brokers

William Frederick gave an acute social analysis when he wrote that his action as patron was regularly hindered by his limited knowledge of local politics and the great distance between Leeuwarden and The Hague: 'when I am absent, they can do everything as they please and see fit'. Effective patronage demanded permanent supervision. Particularly in the early years of his stadholdership, William Frederick's recommendations could be ignored if he was not there to enforce them quickly and effectively. In 1642 the Friesian Admiralty college announced that it could not comply with his recommendation, because the office in question had already been given to another.[66] Such an open rejection of his own candidate was a painful experience for a patron-in-the-making, since every unsuccessful recommendation weakened his credibility and influenced his perceived social credit. William Frederick tried to solve these logistical problems by adopting a stratified system of patronage in Friesland, which allowed him to farm out the recruitment and control of his clients.

Local intermediaries or brokers had to meet this need for intensified super-vision. Often they were local regents, such as Frederick van Inthiema or Alle van Burum, who already had a clientele of their own in their home town and were thus both patrons and clients. Their task as brokers was twofold: in the first place they had to keep the stadholder regularly informed of the political situation in the localities; and secondly they had to advise him during the annual election of magistrates. William Frederick was not altogether enthusiastic about using brokers as a means of control, since he knew from experience that ultimately only personal contact was a sufficient guarantee of trust and loyalty. William Frederick's ideal of an effective patron was one who would 'caress his clients, ... at least receive them as his guests, treat them and live familiarly with them, let himself be frequently seen by them'.[67] Brokers made it possible to acquire more influence locally, but at the same time they were an obstacle to direct contact between the patron and his local clientele.

It is not easy to determine how original William Frederick's idea of brokerage was. The crisis over his appointment in 1640 suggested that Frederick Henry must already have had men he could trust at the centre of affairs in his provinces, but little research has been done on the emergence of such stratified clienteles in the Republic.[68] To be sure, Jos Gabriëls has made a thorough study of the eight-eenth-century brokers' networks of William V (1751–95), but he was unable to say exactly when they originated. According to the pensionary Simon van Slinge-landt, brokers had been employed by William III (1672–1702) 'to overcome the obstacles that arose from the constitution of the government, which he now and then encountered in the management of affairs, by bringing the government and the regents into a sort of dependence'.[69] Gabriëls assumed that the practice in many provinces, including Friesland, was of relatively recent origin. He consid-ered it 'by no means certain' that the use of local brokers or 'premiers' had been current as early as the first half of the seventeenth century.[70]

William Frederick's correspondence partly confirms Gabriëls's impression. At any rate, there was no sign of any network of brokers in Friesland in 1640. Only eight years later, however, William Frederick himself unmistakably referred to such a system in the towns of Friesland, when he discussed patronage tactics with his second cousin William II: '[William] thinks of getting one man in every town [in Holland], like me in Friesland, whom he can rely on', wrote the count in his diary.[71] In itself this remark does not prove that a network of brokers was already in existence in Friesland, but it does indicate that William Frederick must have intended to create one.

From the stadholder's archives we can identify two different types of broker during William Frederick's years in office: Alle van Burum exemplifies the first. The account given above suggested that it was probably the burgomaster himself who had taken the initiative, to make up for William Frederick's limited opportunities to bring a favourite to the top through his own nominations in Leeuwarden. Because Van Burum had offered himself as a broker, and William Frederick needed him to acquire a clientele in Leeuwarden, Van Burum had a strong negotiating hand to play. The relationship between patron and broker was consequently less asymmetrical than in other Friesian towns. This is the form of brokerage that we also find in most of the studies of patronage for neighbouring countries. On the basis of the French situation Sharon Kettering emphasised that most provincial brokers already ran a local clientele. This type of 'independent' broker offered his local network to a more highly placed patron, in the hope of strengthening his position.[72]

Yet in William Frederick's case Van Burum was not typical. In the nine 'unfree' towns in Friesland the different form of government created another type of broker, exemplified by Cornelis Haubois of Sneek. Like Van Burum in Leeuwarden, Haubois was already burgomaster before William Frederick appeared on the scene, but since the magistrates of Sneek were appointed by the stadholder, his position was much more precarious than Van Burum's. 'If I wish, he cannot become a *volmacht*, and so I am rid of him', said the stadholder confidently in 1648. Yet the many reports of conversations between Haubois and William Frederick show that the stadholder was consistently willing to retain him in office. '[Haubois] hoped I should help him next year', he wrote in 1646, 'which I shall do if it is possible for me'. The table on the following page shows that the Sneek regent indeed held one office or another virtually without a break during the 24 years of William Frederick's stadholdership.

In this period Haubois also came up for nomination in Sneek three times, in 1646, 1651 and 1656, and in all three cases William Frederick chose him.[73] In short, Haubois owed his whole political career to the stadholder's favour. But there was a price to be paid: William Frederick expected regular information from him, and did not shrink from telling him how to operate as burgomaster, member of the Chamber of Accounts or of the States-General; and Haubois was also expected to insert William Frederick's preferred candidates in the list of nominees for office in Sneek. The election from the duplicate list was thus an effectively orchestrated performance, in which the broker often recommended the magistrates to be chosen. 'Haubois was with me, recommended those in Sneek to me', the stadholder noted after a discussion in December 1646; a week later he added; 'Haubois was fairly satisfied with my election at Sneek, and gave me good words.'[74] Johan de Witt once crushingly dismissed the Sneek broker and his colleagues as 'the aforementioned Mr Haulbois and other creatures of count William'.[75]

De Witt's characterisation was correct up to a point, for unlike Van Burum, Haubois was not in an independent position. Of course from the patron's point of view a broker of Haubois's type was the most attractive intermediary, yet

Table: Ambulatory offices held by Cornelis Haubois, 1640–64

1640			CA		1653		MG	
1641	DS				1654		MG	
1642	DS				1655	DS		
1643	DS				1656	DS		
1644					1657	DS		
1645			CA		1658			SG
1646		MG	CA		1659		MG	
1647				SG	1660			
1648				SG	1661	DS		
1649	DS			SG	1662	DS		
1650	DS				1663	DS		
1651	DS				1664			
1652				SG				

DS member of the Delegated States
MG member of the *Mindergetal*
CA member of the Chamber of Accounts (of Friesland)
SG member of the States-General

Based on data from Tresoar, SA, 242 (name indexes), 276 (magisterial nominations) and 278 (regulations for the election of magistrates), supplemented by Engels, Naamlijst. See also the notes of J. Visser (Tresoar).

William Frederick realised that the use of such 'creatures' had its disadvantages. Brokers like Haubois could easily become potentates in their own towns. In Sneek there were many who complained that Haubois thought of himself as 'stadholder of Sneek'. This led William Frederick to use him with caution, occasionally rejecting his advice, to remind him of his dependence. In 1645 for example Haubois believed himself to be so certain of a new career as a member of the Delegated States that he congratulated himself in public even before the *Landdag*, letting slip the words 'I fear that people will be jealous of my good fortune and favour'. It was this overconfidence that William Frederick was so keen to curb; the very same day he put Haubois in his place by offering the post to a regent from Franeker. He was not really forgotten, for a day later he waited on the stadholder to thank him for the office of treasurer, which had been given him as a consolation prize. In this way, William Frederick intended to demonstrate that he 'would not allow himself to be governed'.[76]

Because the stadholder's network of brokers was still being assembled in the 1640s, every Friesian town in this decade presented a different picture. In Bolsward and Harlingen, for example, both politically unstable, there were rival factions, which frustrated the implementation of an effective broker system. In the smaller towns such as Workum, Dokkum and Hindelopen the situation was more clear, and there too brokers of the Haubois type emerged in the early 1640s. Frederik van Inthiema of Workum had been one of Henry Casimir's confidants whom the new stadholder simply took over in 1640. At the end of Van Inthiema's career, the Workum broker typically recommended his nephew Frederik junior as his successor. After his prompt appointment to the *vroedschap*, the young man did indeed act as William Frederick's new favourite in Workum from 1649.[77]

Patron in the countryside

At first sight William Frederick's patronage appears to have been a largely urban affair, since his instructions gave him scarcely any powers in the country. The studies of Luuc Kooijmans and Hotso Spanninga have already drawn attention to the stadholder's lack of opportunities to build up clienteles outside the towns. Yme Kuiper agreed, claiming that 'instrumental friendship seems to be the best term for his relationship with the most powerful nobles in the province'.[78]

This negative conclusion should not be accepted without reservations. It became obvious from the description of the Friesian towns that William Frederick did not always feel constrained by a lack of formal powers; and that limited privileges did not always exclude clientelistic habits. It seems rather that William Frederick's patronage took a different form in the countryside, because the institutional framework and the social background of his potential clients differed from those in the towns. To analyse his distinctive strategies in these surroundings, it is useful to distinguish between the stadholder's political and military authority.

The extent of his political powers was best illustrated by his influence on the appointment of the *grietmannen*. These officials were the heads of the thirty *grietenijen* into which the three rural quarters were divided. They were responsible for administration and parts of the system of justice in their districts, and thus comparable to some extent with the burgomasters in the towns. Their social background, however, was very different. Often, but not always, the *grietmannen* were drawn from an elite of noble families, whose ownership of land gave them a more independent power base than the urban patriciate.[79]

The procedure for appointment of the *grietmannen* also differed from that for burgomasters. When a vacancy occurred, three candidates were first chosen by the electors in the *grietenij*. The right to vote was attached to the ownership of land, but over the seventeenth century several Friesian families succeeded in monopolising these voting rights, so that with whole villages at their command they could choose the list of three as they saw fit. The names of the three candidates were then submitted to the Delegated States, who had the right to appoint. It was in this final phase that the stadholder became involved; he sat in the college of Delegated States, probably with a full vote, and in practice he could also count on the votes of the towns, whose deputies he himself had selected.[80]

William Frederick's room for manoeuvre was therefore limited, but he was not completely without opportunities. In 1646 the post of *grietman* of Ooststellingwerf fell vacant, and Jacob Runia was one of those nominated. Interestingly, he began his lobbying for office by going to the stadholder, who noted that 'Runia was with me, and recommended himself to me for the *grietenij*'. Runia's rivals, led by Johannes Crack, also put their case to the stadholder: '[Crack] said, "I would rather give ten thousand guilders than that Runia should get the *grietenij*". Crack apparently believed that the nomination depended on William Frederick's preference: 'it is up to you alone, for Ulbe van Aylva will look to you alone'. These comments shed light on the lobbying in the Friesian corridors of power, and on the real power relationships in the province. Evidently William Frederick had more influence in the Delegated States than his two guaranteed votes. As Crack surmised, Ulbe van Aylva was also willing to vote the way the stadholder wanted. This was made clear a few months later, in April 1647, when William Frederick recorded that 'Ulbe van Aylva was with me, and thanked me for helping him into the *grietenij* of Wonseradeel, and assured me of his friendship; he told me he would like to change the secretary of Wonseradeel, and asked if I had anyone to recommend; he would be glad to take him'.[81]

Ulbe van Aylva was not a unique case. The Friesian nobles knew that the stadholder's support could be decisive at election time, and that it therefore made good sense to cooperate with him. In particular, the informal influence of the highest official in the province increased when the decision-making process was paralysed by internal squabbles within the administration, and such conflicts were almost continual. The critical Pieter Walta, for example, 'abused their lordships the Deputies, cursed and raged like a man out of his senses' after a vacancy had eluded him. His colleague Tjalling van Eysinga was so 'passionate' in 1647 that 'tears of rage came to his eyes'. The regents even came to blows regularly: Hans van Lijcklama and Saco Fockens 'had struck each other and threatened each other with knives'; Abraham Roorda did not shrink from attacking his colleagues 'with rapier and poniard'. When a summer evening dinner in 1649 at the house of Johannes Crack turned into a brawl, William Frederick feared for the consequences, 'since there were many daggers and knives there'.[82]

The stadholder exploited this permanent strife adroitly, by stepping in to mediate when passions ran too high. This and the votes he controlled in the Delegated States made him indispensable. In his own words, his mediating role in the countryside gave him 'credit' with those involved, on which he could draw when he needed it in other matters. On several occasions he reminded Ulbe van Aylva of how he had helped him in a case in 1647. In short, it was as a mediator that William Frederick tried to exact loyalty. Hans van Wijckel, when applying for a post as *grietman* in 1652, threw himself 'at the feet of Your Excellency', because a favourable letter from him to the Delegated States would probably be enough to ensure his 'advancement to the vacant *grietenij*'.[83]

Sometimes, however, William Frederick found it too risky to support a given candidate, and on such occasions he avoided loss of face by 'keeping quiet and neutral in the matter' or satisfying the candidates with other posts. On 1 January 1654 Philips van Boshuysen, accompanied by the deputy Tjalling van Eysinga, came to thank the stadholder for making him a *grietman*. But the disappointed runner-up, Anchises van Andla, also let it be known that he would 'always conduct himself and behave as may suit his Excellency', because William Frederick had appointed him provincial physician. The third candidate, Assuerus van Vierssen, was satisfied with the appointment of his cousin Abraham Mellinga as president of the military court, 'which he ascribed to me alone, and then presented me his service', as William Frederick wrote.[84]

Implicitly the rural elite themselves also gave proof of their growing dependence on William Frederick. In 1652 the representatives of Westergo decided to leave the distribution of their offices for that year to the stadholder. A year later the *grietmannen* of Zevenwouden waited on William Frederick to offer him 'the first councillor's place in Zevenwouden'.[85] In 1647 the stadholder was even able to report that a *grietman's* place would be filled with his 'approval and communication'. These incidental favours not only strengthened William Frederick's influence on the political complexion of the rural areas, but also illustrated the growing willingness of the nobles to let the stadholder act as mediator.[86]

Yet the difference between the urban and rural environments certainly had an influence on the nature of clientage. William Frederick's position as patron in the country depended far more on the extent to which the *grietmannen* were ready to let him play that role. He had almost no formal privileges to invoke, while the noble origin of many *grietmannen* could sometimes complicate his dealings with them. Creating dependants therefore demanded more time and different methods. 'I began to do my best to make a jealousy between Tjalling Eysinga and the Aylvas', the stadholder wrote in 1646, describing his tactics, 'for as long as the nobles are divided, nothing can be done against me.' Outsiders also gained the impression that William Frederick was much more cautious in dispensing patronage in the countryside; in 1649 he heard a rumour that 'I made it so, that all the nobles must eat out of my hand, and I had the towns and the Zevenwouden quarter all under my thumb, the rest had to follow'.[87]

A military trump card

William Frederick's transformation from a formal outsider to an informal patron in the country also owed something to the military regulations. As his instruction declared, the stadholdership was coupled with the captain-generalship. In the latter capacity William Frederick could appoint officers in the army, or at least influence their appointment, and it was the rural nobility that claimed most of these commissions. In practice, therefore, William Frederick used his military patronage as a means to bind the Friesian nobility more tightly to himself. Military and political clientage thus overlapped all the time, and although his powers were institutionally distinct, in practice there was no question of their being exercised separately, nor did the stadholder create a separate 'military' network in Friesland.[88]

The captain-generalship of the province was not a military rank but an administrative position. William Frederick was responsible for the portion of the Dutch or 'States' Army that the annual war budget scheme assigned to Friesland's responsibility for payment. In theory each province paid and maintained its own quota of the army, which did not mean only those troops who were quartered in its territory: provinces with a higher quota, such as Holland and Friesland, also paid for regiments that were based elsewhere. William Frederick's duties included supervising these 'Friesian' units, fortresses and garrisons. His privilege of appointing certain officers up to and including the rank of captain was summarily described: formally he had to act in conjunction with the Delegated States, while in the field the right of appointment was reserved to the captain-general alone; in all cases, the instruction prescribed that native Friesians must be preferred over 'foreigners'.[89] The captain-general had similar powers in the fleet, but William Frederick seems to have intervened scarcely at all in the appointment of naval officers, and to have concerned himself only with administrative posts in the Friesian Admiralty. Membership of the Admiralty was one of the ambulatory offices that were in the stadholder's gift in the city quarter, but his archives do not reveal any involvement in other maritime matters.[90]

All in all, very little came of the requirement for the stadholder and the States to act jointly in the appointment of army officers, since William Frederick simply managed to draw the whole process into his own hands. The letter which he sent to the Delegated States in 1642 in favour of Moritz Livingstone is typical of this: 'Kindly requesting your Noble Mightinesses to be pleased to provide him with the aforesaid vacant place of lieutenant, as we are very confident that he shall know how to perform such a charge as is fitting'.[91] The Delegated States must have accepted this informal way of appointment by their captain-general, for as far as we know they never made any protest.[92]

William Frederick made effective use of his right to name army officers, and repeatedly helped influential Friesian families, among them the Aylvas and the Grovestins, to secure commissions, either for themselves or for their acquaintances. The *grietman* Oene van Grovestins was honoured in 1661 with a company of horse for his son. 'I shall never forget this loyal good deed', the nobleman wrote, 'and my father in law and I, and all my friends ... will serve Your Princely Grace obediently in all submission.'[93] Hessel van Aylva could also congratulate himself on a military career for his heirs: his son Hans Willem became a captain in 1646, thanks to William Frederick, who admitted that it was not the young man's military talents which had earned him a recommendation. Hans Willem was only thirteen, so that perhaps 'his youth and inexperience may cause some reluctance', he wrote to the Delegated States.[94] Unsurprisingly, the same Hessel van Aylva, as commander of the garrison at Dokkum, kept William Frederick informed of local politics and the annual candidates for burgomasterships. Oene van Groevestins performed the same task for years at Bolsward.[95]

Group identity and ideology

The development of William Frederick's role in Friesland between 1640 and 1650 clearly altered his own vision of Friesian politics, but it may also have changed the self-image of those who became dependent on him. How far did his clients identify themselves as such, and how far did that identity create a fellow-feeling with other clients? A uniform answer to such questions can hardly be expected, as William Frederick's patron-client relationships varied so widely in intensity and mutual dependence. We have seen that the patron actively promoted confessional uniformity, exercised some social control over his clients and, up to a point, sought to direct their political course; but the degree to which he succeeded always depended on the conditions he had to work with when forming a relationship. In the towns of Leeuwarden and Franeker the patron could not make as many demands on clients as he could in the nine 'unfree' towns of Friesland, and even within the various circuits there were considerable differences. There was no typical client, and the language of loyalty and dependence that was common to all the regents could conceal very different interpretations of their roles.

Many Friesian regents, in their letters to William Frederick, explicitly cast themselves as 'servants' of their patron, and even suggested an emotional attachment to his House. Yet it is hard to say exactly what they meant by this self-proclaimed dependence, and how we are to read such an expression of identity. The sources occasionally tell us that a civic regent claimed to belong to the 'good party', apparently meaning William Frederick's clientele. But what the 'membership' of such a group implied remains rather unclear, nor can we determine how it originated. How far was this expression of group feeling explained by other – local, family or religious – ties? In other words, a specific, collective clientele identity among Friesian regents can hardly be deduced from the few scraps of evidence, and there is no proof whatever that such a group feeling emerged as a result of William Frederick's patronage policies. It is not so likely that clientage as such created a distinctive collective self-image in this political sphere. Patronage of this type did create 'vertical' dependence, but apparently no recognisable or lasting 'horizontal' solidarity, even though outsiders sometimes saw William Frederick's urban clientele as a clique of the 'creatures'.[96]

This conclusion has some relevance for an ongoing debate about the interpretation of early modern Dutch politics in terms of ideologically based parties.[97] Historians such as D.J. Roorda have argued that political factions in the Dutch Republic were almost invariably characterised by local family ties and based on short-term material self-interest.[98] More recently historians such as Jonathan Israel and J.L. Price have claimed that Roorda underplayed the importance of religious and political convictions and that 'ideology' did indeed help to determine political allegiances in the Republic.[99] More specifically, they point out that the pro-stadholder or 'Orangist' factions generally enjoyed the sympathy of the Reformed Church elite, and that patronage practices may have strengthened this connection. In the words of Israel: 'this linkage of factional and clientage characteristics with political ideology and theology was to prove one of the enduring, fundamental features not only of the Golden Age but [of] the entire history of the Republic'.[100] This general assumption has been difficult to prove so far, since local studies have revealed such a varied landscape of political factions, and ideological tensions and expressions only become clearly visible in moments of crisis.[101]

The case of William Frederick sheds a partial new light on these problems. Although there is nothing to suggest that his clientele acquired a unifying ideological basis, that does not mean that political thought and ideals played no part at all in patronage processes. To begin with, William Frederick certainly did use his selection criteria to recruit his clients from uniform confessional and social backgrounds. Over new men, he preferred families with which his predecessors had already had some connection. It was not surprising that a family such as the Van Inthiemas of Workum should appeal to a certain family tradition of service and attachment to the stadholder. And Haring Fongers was equally justified in boasting that his forebears had fought alongside the Nassaus in the Revolt. Fongers emphasised the bond that he believed to exist between the Reformed Church and the proponents of a strong stadholdership. The conviction that religious and political preferences went together was apparently shared by William Frederick himself, whose selection criteria can be regarded as an attempt to stamp his administrative clientele with a Reformed character.

But as we have seen, the effect of this policy must not be exaggerated. Some of William Frederick's chosen clientele did indeed share a common confessional and social profile, but for the patron this requirement was not so dominant that it became the distinctive feature of all his patronage. The examples of Gerrit Keth or Alle van Burum, who had openly attempted to frustrate his appointment in 1640, show that the stadholder himself could be flexible in the demands he made. Political ideology and religious preferences certainly mattered, but the importance attached to them could vary as local circumstances dictated. As we shall see, the crisis of 1650 and the 'stadholderless period' that followed it made political differences of opinion in the Republic more acute, with the result that clienteles came to be more ideologically defined. It was not the stadholder's patronage as such, but the circumstances in which it took shape, that decided the degree and the form of this ideological profiling.

Though William Frederick's patronage in Friesland failed to create a political group identity, it does seem possible that clientage had the negative effect of confirming group feeling among the rural nobility. William Frederick regularly received reports of complaints about his clientelistic practices: 'they said I wanted to make myself sovereign, and sought to draw all authority to myself'.[102] The self-image of the Friesian nobles certainly left no room for a possible role as clients of a count of Nassau, and many a nobleman reacted to William Frederick's increasing influence by harking back to the old ideal of 'Friesian liberty', in which there was no place for the institution of the stadholdership. Tjalling van Eysinga was one of these men, and argued that the political initiative ought to lie with the Friesian nobles, as it had done of old, 'for the nobles and the freeholders must rule the country, and not the stadholder'.[103] These comments show that there existed a tension between the reality of growing dependence and the self-image of unchanged autonomy cultivated by the nobles. Sjuck van Burmania felt that many Friesian families, his own among them, had a better historical claim to prestige in Friesland than that of William Frederick, and bragged that one day he would 'shave the beard' of that parvenu baldhead, the stadholder.[104] But these frustrations, and the tendency to accentuate local noble identities, in fact only confirmed that real power in Friesland was moving in the opposite direction, a process which these nobles saw as a threat. The vainglorious boasting of Van Eysinga or Burmania did not reflect a true growth of their influence, but was a response to the shift of political power in the stadholder's favour that had taken place since 1640.

Notes

1   Fruin, *Brieven van De Witt*, I, 350; *Gloria Parendi*, 637 and 744.
2   *Gloria Parendi*, 332 and 534.
3   Historians have not always recognised this process of patronage in Friesland. A recent handbook concludes that the stadholdership of Friesland 'around 1650 had a mainly symbolic function with little political authority'. Frijhoff and Spies, *Dutch Culture in European Context*, 79.

Also Fockema Andreae, *De Nederlandse staat*, 6; Rowen, *The Princes of Orange*, 71, 88–91 and 101. A more nuanced approach is offered by Kooijmans, *Liefde in opdracht*; Spanninga, 'Ick laet niet met mij gecken'.

4 See the references in the Introduction. Good overviews of the formal position of the stadholders within the republican system are given by Fruin and Colenbrander, *Staatsinstellingen*, 218–24, and Fockema Andreae, *De Nederlandse staat*, 6–11. More recent are Van Deursen, 'Staatsinstellingen', 354–61; Israel, *The Dutch Republic*, 300–6; Price, *Holland and the Dutch Republic*, 134–48; Rowen, *The Princes of Orange*. The Friesian stadholdership is discussed in Kleijn, *De stadhouders*. A thorough analysis of the eighteenth-century stadholdership is offered by Gabriëls, *De heren als dienaren*.

5 Fockema Andreae, *De Nederlandse Staat*, 58–61; Kalma et al., *Geschiedenis van Friesland*, 303–7.

6 KHA, WF, VI, 4 (copy of the instruction for William Frederick as stadholder of Friesland, 1651). This version agrees with Thoe Schwartzenberg en Hohenlansberg, *Groot Placcaat- en Charterboek*, V, 459–61.

7 Guibal, *Democratie en oligarchie*, 230–4. Fruin, *Staatsinstellingen*, 221–2. This Holland custom was, however, a topic of repeated discussion. Cf. *Gloria Parendi*, 542.

8 KHA, WF, VI, 4 (copy of the instruction of William Frederick as stadholder of Friesland, 1651). The instruction explicitly stated that the 'church order', or method of appointing ministers, should not follow the rules laid down at Dordt. Bergsma, *Tussen Gideonsbende en publieke kerk*, 94 and 191–5.

9 This rule remained a dead letter. As mentioned in chapter 1, in 1641 the States agreed to a reversion for William II. In 1659 William Frederick again managed to secure a deed of reversion, this time in favour of his son Henry Casimir II. See chapter 7.

10 Some sources claim that the stadholder had no more than an advisory voice in the Delegated States and the *Mindergetal*. Cf. Israel, *The Dutch Republic*, 305; Fockema Andreae, *De Nederlandse Staat*, 7; Gabriels, *De heren als dienaren*, 48; Kuiper, 'Profijt, eer en reputatie', 181; Van Nienes, 'Inleiding', 17–18 and 20; Spanninga, 'Ick laet niet met mij gecken', 70–4.

11 At any rate this was the custom from 1643. Tresoar, SA, 241 (letters about the ambulatory offices); KHA, WF, VIII, 3-I (note of William Frederick, 3–13 June 1658); *Gloria Parendi*, 337. Spanninga, 'Ick laet niet met mij gecken', 72–4. The States formally confirmed the appointment of the magistrates in 1642.

12 Guibal, *Democratie en oligarchie*, 23–4; Van Nienes, 'Inleiding', 17–20.

13 KHA, WF, VIII, 3-I (note of William Frederick, 10–20 February 1652); Tresoar, Eysinga, 485 (1653).

14 Guibal, *Democratie en oligarchie*, 24; Van Tuinen, 'Mars en Minerva', 57 and 66–9.

15 Remarkably, these unwritten customs are ignored in many studies. Cf. Gabriëls, *De heren als dienaren*; Groenveld, *Evidente factiën*; Van Nierop, 'Willem van Oranje'; Delen, *Het hof*, 89–128; Price, *Holland and the Dutch Republic*, 145.

16 *Gloria Parendi*, 323, 452, 470 and 736. It is not entirely clear if the Friesian stadholder only enjoyed the right to appoint magistrates when he was in the province, as was the case with the stadholder of Holland. For this see chapter 4.

17 Tresoar, SA, 279 (rules for the election of magistrates); in Sloten and Hindeloopen three *vroedschap* members nominated the candidates. See also Fockema Andreae and Bakker, *IJlst*, 37–42; Guibal, *Democratie en oligarchie*, 46–7; Obreen, *Harlingen*, 17–19. Different rules in Leeuwarden: Boomsma, 'Een werck van factie en staetsucht', 7–30; Spanninga, 'Om de vrije magistraats-bestelling', 128–58.

18 Tresoar, SA, 278 (rules for the election of magistrates). In certain towns there were also rules forbidding the combination of certain posts, for the awarding of civic offices, and on the age and financial resources of *vroedschap* members.

19 The results were mostly sent around 27 December. Tresoar, SA, 267 (documents on the choice of the magistrates). In the election season it was therefore necessary for William Frederick to remain in Leeuwarden, as he reminded Constantijn Huygens in November 1651: 'en decembre il fault que je suys de necessite icy a cause du changement de la magistrature, qui se faict

quatorse jours devant le nouvel annee', Worp, *Briefwisseling*, V, 123. See also William Frederick's remarks in *Gloria Parendi*, 470 and 536. His tables are in Tresoar, SA, 276.

20 The dates given here, exceptionally, are old style. Tresoar, SA, 267 (incoming and outgoing letters concerning the appointment of magistrates); *Gloria Parendi*, 107 and 732–4.

21 *Gloria Parendi*, 214, 479, 746.

22 KHA, WF, VI, 6 (Homme van Hittingha to William Frederick, 19–29 December 1640, from IJlst); Tresoar, SA, 267 (Adriaan van Velsen to William Frederick, 20–30 December 1649, from Bolsward; Folpert Hansma? to William Frederick, 22 December 1649 – 1 January 1650, from Bolsward).

23 *Gloria Parendi*, 738.

24 *Gloria Parendi*, 368.

25 *Gloria Parendi*, 734.

26 KHA, WF, VI, 5 (documents on the election of 1640); Tresoar, SA, 267 (Folpert Hansma? to William Frederick, 22 December 1649 – 1 January 1650, from Bolsward; Folpert Hansma to William Frederick, 20–30 December 1647, from Bolsward; Gerrit Keth to William Frederick, 24 December 1644 – 3 January 1645, from Harlingen); 276 (documents on the appointment of magistrates).

27 Cf. Van Deursen, *Een dorp in de polder*, 159.

28 Similar criteria in Roorda, *Partij en factie*, 40–4; Van Deursen, *Plain Lives*, 162–6, and *Een dorp in de polder*, 164ff.

29 Tresoar, SA, 276 (notes and schemes of William Frederick); 267 (Frederik van Inthiema to William Frederick, 19–29 December 1649, from Workum; Gerrit Keth to William Frederick, 25 December 1642 – 4 January 1643, from Harlingen). UBL, Coll. Handschr., HUG 37 (Johan Veltdriel to William Frederick, 22 September – 2 October 1642 from The Hague).

30 It is unknown if Haring's grandfather really did serve in Lumey's fleet. He is not named in De Meij, *De watergeuzen*. Tresoar, SA, 267 (Anne Heerkes and Folpert Hansma to William Frederick, 20–30 December 1649, from Bolsward; Folpert Hansma? to William Frederick, 22 December 1649 –1 January 1650, from Bolsward; Johannes Rodrigenius to William Frederick, 24 December 1649 – 3 January 1650, from Dokkum). Both Haring Fongers and Douwe van Hottinga were appointed by the stadholder that year.

31 Tresoar, SA, 267 (Jan van Marsum to William Frederick, 19–29 December 1645, from Bolsward). Numerous other examples in KHA, WF, VI, and Tresoar, SA, 267 and 272. See also Bergsma, 'Kerk en staat', 158–72.

32 On the position of the Reformed – public – Church see, among others, Hsia and Van Nierop, *Calvinism and Religious Toleration*; Berkvens-Stevelinck et al., *The Emergence of Tolerance*; Benedict, *Christ's Church Purely Reformed*.

33 Bergsma, *Tussen Gideonsbende en publieke kerk*, 96–150; idem, 'Godsdienstige verhoudingen', 93–103. See also Spaans, 'Violent Dreams', 158–9; Woltjer, 'De plaats van de calvinisten', 18. Another vision in Breuker, 'Over de Nadere Reformatie', 23–5, and idem, 'Nogmaals over de positie', 39–42.

34 Kaplan, 'Dutch Religious Tolerance', 21–5; Prak, 'The Politics of Intolerance'; Price, *Holland and the Dutch Republic*, 78–9 and 85–9; Spaans, *Haarlem na de reformatie*, inter alia 109–38, and 'Religious Policies', 77–86.

35 Groenveld, *Huisgenoten des geloofs*.

36 Connections between clientage networks and confessional allegiances have been the subject of debate. Compare Greengrass, 'Noble Affinities', 285–6; Harding, *Anatomy of a Power Elite*, 68–87; Kettering, 'Clientage during the French Wars of Religion', 221–39. See also Benedict, 'Introduction', 1–21; Neuschel, *Word of Honor*, 30–2; MacHardy, *War, Religion and Court Patronage*, 183–207 and 210–11; Reinhard, 'Oligarchische Verflechtung', 57–62.

37 Pollmann, *Religious Choice*, as well as idem, 'The Bond of Christian Piety', 53–4. Cf. Kaplan, 'Dutch Religious Tolerance', 25–6.

38 Frijhoff, 'Dimensions de la coexistence', 213–37. Cf. Dorren, *Eenheid en verscheidenheid*, 63–7; Israel, *The Dutch Republic*, 637–45; Kaplan, *Calvinists and Libertines*, 261–96; Prak, 'The Politics

of Intolerance'; Spaans, *Haarlem na de Reformatie*, 109–38 and 228–32.

39 *Gloria Parendi*, 228. William Frederick wrote that he preferred the Lutheran church in Amsterdam 'to remain incognito'.

40 LAD, Oranienbaum A7b, 103 (notes of William Frederick on the appointment of *grietmannen*, 1642–58); *Gloria Parendi*, 505 and 733; the last passage refers to the situation around 1635.

41 Bergsma, 'Kerk en staat', 165; *Gloria Parendi*, xvi–xviii; Price, *Holland and the Dutch Republic*, 262–3; Spaans, 'Violent Dreams', 152–5.

42 *Gloria Parendi*, 733 and 745. In 1649 William Frederick noted 'Makkum is full of papists, and they greatly annoy our co-religionists'. Other examples in Spanninga, 'Ick laet niet met mij gecken', 85.

43 Bergsma, *Tussen Gideonsbende en publieke kerk*, 142–6; Zijlstra, 'Anabaptism and Tolerance', 112–21. In practice anabaptists were active politically at a local level, as warnings against their political influence in Friesland from sitting magistrates indicate.

44 LAD, Oranienbaum, A7b, 103 (notes of William Frederick on the appointment of *grietmannen*, 1642–58).

45 KHA, WF, II, 19 (Allard Pieter Jongestal to William Frederick, 25 May-4 June 1652, from Leeuwarden). The stadholder's tables in Tresoar, SA, 276. Correspondence on the subject in SA, 267. For a similar habit of Ernst Casimir and William Louis, see Bergsma, *Tussen Gideonsbende en publieke kerk*, 333–4ff.

46 Dinners with Catholic nobles: *Gloria Parendi*, inter alia 323, 503 and 512. See also Bergsma, 'De godsdienstige verhoudingen', 83. Purchases from Jewish and Catholic traders: KHA, WF, V (documents on the court); Tresoar, SA, 289 (incoming and outgoing letters, 1660–62); 30 to 32 (incoming and outgoing letters, 1640–64).

47 *Gloria Parendi*, 314. Cf. Kooijmans, *Liefde in opdracht*, 305.

48 *Gloria Parendi*, 512 and 515. Hemmema was commandant of the stadholder's guard: Ten Raa and De Bas, *Het Staatsche leger*, IV, 236; Tonckens, 'Het proces Schulenborgh', 66–93. For the role of house altars such as that of Hemmema's brother see Kaplan, 'Fictions of Privacy', 1030–64.

49 *Gloria Parendi*, 477.

50 Cf. Frijhoff, 'Religious Toleration', 33–52; Price, *Holland and the Dutch Republic*, 270–1.

51 Frijhoff, 'Dimensions de la coexistence', 228–37; Kaplan, *Calvinists and Libertines*, 261–96; Pollmann, *Religious Choice*, 194–203.

52 Pollmann, *Religious Choice*, 201–3; Kaplan, 'Fictions of Privacy'; Frijhoff, 'Religious Toleration'.

53 Gabriëls, *De heren als dienaren*, 48 and 173–82; Groenveld, *Evidente factiën*, 33–5 and 40; Van Nierop, 'Willem van Oranje'; Price, *Holland and the Dutch Republic*, 140–1.

54 KHA, WF, VII, 3–I (note of 1–11 January 1662); Tresoar, SA, 278 (regulations for the ambulatory offices); *Gloria Parendi*, 113, 128, 202 and 336; Boomsma, ˋEen werck van factie en staetsucht', 7–37.

55 In some towns it was customary that when a *vroedschap* member died, the vacancy was offered to William Frederick to fill, possibly by presenting two names to choose from. That was also done if there was disagreement in the town itself. Tresoar, SA, 278 (regulations on the appointment of magistrates); Van Nienes, 'Inleiding', 18.

56 Finally William Frederick proposed to advise Wibrandi 'for the future, when a place in the *vroedschap* should become open ... that he should have the benefit of it before others': Tresoar, SA, 290 (Frederik van Inthiema to William Frederick, 31 January – 10 February and 9–19 February 1645, from Workum; the magistrates of Workum to William Frederick, 9–19 February 1645, from Workum; William Frederick to the magistrates of Workum, 13–23 February 1645, from Leeuwarden); *Gloria Parendi*, 101 and 102. Cf. also William Frederick's lobbying for Wibrandi in 1648: Tresoar, SA, 282 (William Frederick to the magistrates of Sneek, 13–23 May, from Leeuwarden).

57 For clerkships: KHA, WF, VII, B-III/2 (William Frederick to Johan van Aylva et al., 8–18 July 1652, n.p.); B-I/32 (Dirck van Ruijven to William Frederick, 17–27 August, from Leeuwarden); *Gloria Parendi*, 3. Pensionaries: Tresoar, SA, 31 (William Frederick to Frederik

van Inthiema, 12–22 October 1656, from Halle); *Gloria Parendi*, 225, 326–7. Secretaries: KHA, WF, VII, B-I/36 (A. van Hobbema to William Frederick, 28 April-8 May 1658, from Ijlst); *Gloria Parendi*, 225. Ministers: KHA, WF, VII, B-III/2 (William Frederick to Johan van Aylva et al., 2–12 May 1652, n.p.); Tresoar, SA, 31 (William Frederick to the Delegated States, 16–26 July 1655, n.p.; William Frederick to Oene or Sicke van Grovestins, 19–29 October 1655, n.p.; William Frederick to the Delegated States, 21–31 March 1659, n.p.). Cf. Bergsma, *Tussen Gideonsbende en publieke kerk*, 207–11. Professors: Tresoar, SA, 31 (William Frederick to the Delegated States, 24 March – 3 April 1659, n.p.); Worp, *Briefwisseling*, V, 196–7; Van Tuinen, 'Mars en Minerva', 57–70. On appointments to 'subaltern' offices in general: Vries, 'Geschapen tot een ieders nut', 329–32.

58 *Gloria Parendi*, 94, 103, 106–8, 121, 126 and 631.
59 For examples see chapters 6 and 7. The same remark is made by Israel, *The Dutch Republic*, 701–13; Geyl, *Orange and Stuart,* 72–3; Kooijmans, *Liefde in opdracht*, 188 and 218–28.
60 *Gloria Parendi*, 448.
61 Ibid., 613–14.
62 Tresoar, SA, 282 (William Frederick to an unknown correspondent in Sneek, 15–25 January 1659, from Leeuwarden).
63 Tresoar, SA, 292 (magistrates of Hindelopen to William Frederick, 19–29 February 1648, from Hindelopen).
64 Kooijmans, *Vriendschap*, 132–48.
65 *Gloria Parendi*, 312, 438 and 443; Kooijmans, *Liefde in opdracht*, 187.
66 Tresoar, SA, 30 (William Frederick to the Admiralty in Dokkum, 7–17 February 1642, from Leeuwarden, and vice versa, 12–22 February 1642, from Dokkum); *Gloria Parendi*, 121.
67 *Gloria Parendi*, 578.
68 Cf. Israel, 'Frederick Henry'; Groenveld, 'Frederik Hendrik' and *Evidente factiën*, 240–2. See also chapter 1.
69 Cited in Gabriëls, *De heren als dienaren*, 146.
70 Gabriëls, *De heren als dienaren*, 145–9 and 487 (note 88). Gabriëls uses the term 'premier', which was current in eighteenth-century Friesland. These were specifically urban brokers. Other types of broker can be found at the Orange court earlier in the seventeenth century. See for example Groenveld, 'C'est le pere', and idem, *Evidente factiën*, 34–8.
71 *Gloria Parendi*, 534.
72 Kettering, *Patrons, Brokers and Clients*, 40–60; Mączak, 'From Aristocratic Household', 315–27; Greengrass, 'Noble Affinities', 275–300; Lind, 'Great Friends', 124–46.
73 Tresoar, SA, 276. Meetings between William Frederick and Haubois: *Gloria Parendi*, 37, 103, 104–5, 109–10, 120, 204, 211, 317, 325, 334, 337, 470, 613 and 732. Cf. Kooijmans, 'Haagse dames', 262–3.
74 *Gloria Parendi*, 317 and 325. Haubois's first recommendation, in 1641, can be found in KHA, WF, VII, C-158 (Cornelis Haubois to William Frederick, 17–27 December 1641, from Sneek). Other recommendations in Tresoar, SA, 267 (letters on Sneek); 282 (appointment of magistrates in Sneek). William Frederick also borrowed money from the regent, as shown by the inventory of his debts in 1666, in which Haubois is named as his creditor for 7,000 guilders: KHA, WF, IV, 8 (inventory of debts and charges, 1666).
75 Fruin, *Brieven van De Witt*, I, 187.
76 *Gloria Parendi*, 105, 109, 112–13. The last passage refers to Gosewijn Wiedenfelt as well as to Haubois.
77 Tresoar, SA, 267 (correspondence of Frederik van Inthiema sr and jr with William Frederick); 290 (documents on Workum); *Gloria Parendi*, 330, 610 and 636. In Sloten Epeus Oosterzee appears to have acted as broker, but the data from this town are incomplete: Tresoar, SA, 288 (documents on Sloten).
78 Kuiper, 'Profijt, eer en reputatie', 197; Kooijmans, *Liefde in opdracht*, 193–8; Spanninga, 'Patronage in Friesland'; idem, 'Ick laet niet met mij gecken'.
79 The term 'nobility' is complicated for the seventeenth-century rural elite in Friesland.

Cf. Kuiper, 'Eer, profijt en reputatie'; Price, 'The Dutch Nobility', 87 and 100; Visser, 'Adel en "Adel", 430–57.

80 There was an exception in the Bildt, where the stadholder had a long-established right to appoint the *grietman*: Faber, 'De oligarchisering', 39–65; Gabriëls, *De heren als dienaren*, 64–5 and 223; Guibal, *Democratie en oligarchie*, 38–9; Spanninga, 'Kapitaal en fortuin', 19–26.

81 *Gloria Parendi*, 311–13 and 371.

82 In 1648 the military court heard a case about 'blows and pushing between troop-captain Ernst van Haren and captain Douwe van Sijthama, which took place at the court of His Excellency, over the drinking of a glass of wine': Tresoar, SA, 340 (documents on the military court, 1648); *Gloria Parendi*, 317, 496, 522 and 673. See also Kooijmans, *Liefde in opdracht*, 187.

83 KHA, WF, VII, C-266 (Hans van Wijckel to William Frederick, 24 April – 4 May, 26 April – 6 May 1652, from The Hague, and 27 November – 7 December 1653, from Leeuwarden).

84 Tresoar, SA 30, 3rd bundle (Assuerus van Vierssen to William Frederick, 30 June – 10 July 1644, from the Bildt; William Frederick to the Delegated States, 6–16 June, from the field and 25 October – 4 November 1644, n.p.; Anchises van Andla to William Frederick, 7–17 October 1644, n.p); *Gloria Parendi*, 56, 93, 110–11 and 116).

85 KHA, WF, VIII, 3-1 (note of William Frederick, 10–20 February 1652); Tresoar, Eysinga, 485 (1653).

86 According to William Frederick the opportunity to appoint to these offices 'had never fallen to any of my predecessors': KHA, WF, VIII, 3-1 (note of William Frederick, 10–20 February 1652); *Gloria Parendi*, 460.

87 Douwe van Hottinga was said to have spread the story. *Gloria Parendi*, 204 and 661; Kooijmans, *Liefde in opdracht*, 195. William Frederick also kept notes on the election of *grietmannen*: LAD Oranienbaum, A7b, 103 (notes of William Frederick, 1642–58).

88 Cf. Mörke, 'Stadtholder' oder 'Staetholder', 115–22; Price, 'The Dutch Nobility', 95; idem, *Holland and the Dutch Republic*, 146–8.

89 The instruction did not distinguish between the various ranks, but there were different rules for ranks above captain. The appointment of the senior officers, e.g. colonels and generals, was a matter for the States-General and not for the provincial governments. The States-General also laid down further rules for both senior and junior officers; KHA, WF, VI, 4 (copy of the instruction of William Frederick as stadholder of Friesland, 1651); Guibal, *Democratie en oligarchie*, 54–66. Cf. Ten Raa and De Bas, *Het Staatsche leger*, IV, 178–9; Zwitzer, 'De militie', 30–8.

90 Cf. Gaastra, 'Friesland en de VOC', 184–96; Roodhuyzen, *De Admiraliteit*; Guibal, *Democratie en oligarchie*, 54–7.

91 Tresoar, SA, 30, 1st bundle (William Frederick to the Delegated States, 1642, n.p.); Ten Raa and De Bas, *Het Staatsche leger*, IV, 405. Other examples of recommendations and appointments in Tresoar, SA, 30 to 32.

92 Tresoar, SA, 31, 2nd bundle (William Frederick to Augustinus? van Lycklama, 17–27 October 1655, n.p.). For a similar case in Frederick Henry's time: Poelhekke, *Frederik Hendrik*, 132.

93 KHA, WF, VII, C-149 (Oene van Grovestins to William Frederick, 24 July – 3 August 1661, n.p.).

94 Tresoar, SA, 30, 4th bundle (William Frederick to the Delegated States, 7–17 September 1646, n.p.); *NNBW*, I, 202–3.

95 Tresoar, SA, 267 (letters of Hessel van Aylva to William Frederick, including 26 December o.s. 1642, from Holvert; letters of Oene and Sicco van Grovestins, 1648–50); 368 (summaries of garrisons in Friesian towns, n.d.). J.A. Faber showed in 1973 that in his 24-year term of office William Frederick appointed almost exclusively Friesian noblemen to officers' commissions: Faber, *Drie eeuwen Friesland*, II, 512; Ten Raa and De Bas, *Het Staatsche leger*, IV, 235–7 and 475–7.

96 Fruin, *Brieven van De Witt*, I, 350; *Gloria Parendi*, 744; Thurloe, *A Collection*, II, 537.

97 There are good surveys of the discussion in Groenveld, *Evidente factiën*, 10–13, and Price, *Holland and the Dutch Republic*, 57–69. Cf. also Van der Bijl, *Idee en Interest*; Israel, *The Dutch Republic*, esp. 392, 700–3, 725–6 and 758–66; Geyl, 'Het stadhouderschap in de partij-litera-

tuur'; Van der Klashorst, 'Metten schijn van monarchie getempert'; Roorda, *Partij en factie*.

98 Roorda, *Partij en factie*, 1–8, 11–36, and 55–6; Roorda and Van Dijk, *Het patriciaat van Zierikzee*, 3–7. Cf. Groenveld, 'Adriaan Pauw', 432–9.

99 Israel, *The Dutch Republic*, esp. 758–66; Price, *Holland and the Dutch Republic*, 57–69 and 154–71. See also Van der Bijl, *Idee en Interest*, 166–95. A recent reassessment of the importance of political thought in the Dutch Republic is offered in Velema, 'That a Republic', 9–19.

100 Israel, *The Dutch Republic*, 392.

101 Cf. Groenveld, *Evidente factiën*; Price, *Holland and the Dutch Republic*, 57–69; Van der Plaat, 'Lieuwe van Aitzema's kijk', 341–72; Rietbergen, 'Beeld en zelfbeeld', 643–4.

102 *Gloria Parendi*, 194.

103 'Did we win freedom for this', Eysinga asked on another occasion, 'to stand under those of Nassau?', *Gloria Parendi*, 219 and 448. Cf. Kooijmans, *Liefde in opdracht*, 193; Woltjer, *Friesland in hervormingstijd*, 185–96.

104 *Gloria Parendi*, 38. Also in Kooijmans, *Liefde in opdracht*, 194.

3

The count as patron

Although the stadholder's court at Leeuwarden served as the main informal political centre in Friesland, the provincial regents were not the only users of the stadholder's residence. William Frederick's own personnel were constantly in attendance as well. This household was in a sense the count's private affair, and to that extent it is misleading to speak of it as the 'Friesian' or 'stadholder's' court, since those names would suggest that the court in the Republic was also a state or provincial institution. In fact William Frederick's princely household as such had little to do with his position as stadholder or with the Dutch state as a whole. Because sovereignty in the United Provinces was not vested in the House of Nassau, its court was, at least on paper, a separate institution, privately owned by the prince.[1]

This practice seems to have developed in contrast to arrangements at most foreign, monarchical courts where such a distinction between the public (state) and private (household) spheres was not always easy to draw. To be sure, in the monarchies too the government of the state and the household of the prince were formally distinct, but in practice their interrelationship developed along other lines. At many early modern courts noble families combined functions in the royal household with a high office in the state, so that there appears to have been little or no discrepancy between 'public' and 'private' patronage. And even at those royal courts where the combination was less usual, members of the household and the administration at least took part in the same court life.[2] The question remains as to whether or not that personal connection was equally self-evident in the Dutch Republic, and what practical significance was assigned to the distinction between public stadholdership and private household.[3]

The only explicit treatment of this key issue in the Dutch republican system is that of Olaf Mörke. He has suggested that the first connections between princely 'household' and 'public administration' in the Republic did not become visible until Frederick Henry's time, while the personal ties that bound them together were further tightened under William III (1650–1702).[4] In a sense, by appointing his courtiers to republican functions the prince brought public administration increasingly within his private, household sphere. Because the office of stadholder was also declared hereditary under William III, and the powers attached to it were expanded in nearly all the provinces, the stadholdership of the Dutch Republic gradually took on a quasi-monarchical status. Yet there are still few empirical data about this process, while the consequences of the striking distinction that the republican body politic drew between public and private spheres remain little studied.[5] One way to measure this gap and its practical relevance is to take William Frederick as a case study, and compare his patronage policy as count with his activity in the role of stadholder.

Houses and domains

The term 'Friesian court' is not just formally inaccurate as a name for William Frederick's household, but inappropriate for other reasons as well. The household was in fact seldom concentrated in Leeuwarden, while most of the count's courtiers did not come from Friesland at all. Only between December and March, the months when the magistrates were appointed and the *Landdag* (Diet) met, was William Frederick invariably to be found in Friesland. How far he felt it necessary to remain in the province for the rest of the year depended on the political situation, but for most of the time he did not. Until 1646 William Frederick usually spent his summers in the southern provinces of Brabant and Flanders, campaigning against the Republic's enemy Spain. He passed much of the rest of his time in The Hague, the seat of central government in the Republic, where his fellow-stadholders the princes of Orange also resided. In the years after the Peace of Münster (1648) The Hague remained his most important place of residence. William Frederick's house on the fashionable Lange Vijverberg was where his children Amelie (1650), Henry Casimir II (1657) and perhaps Sophia Wilhelmina (1664) were born. His household became even more closely identified with The Hague after his marriage in 1652, when it was joined by the retinue of his second cousin and now wife Albertine Agnes of Orange-Nassau. Finally, the count varied his regular journeys between Leeuwarden and The Hague by paying visits to the country houses of his relatives. The castle of Turnhout in Brabant, a domain of Amalia van Solms, was his usual summer destination from 1657.[6]

What's more, William Frederick did not own any lands or houses in Friesland, for all his family estates lay elsewhere in the Republic or in the Holy Roman Empire. This was partly because of his German (Nassau) descent, and partly because the Friesian States wanted it that way; their instruction for the stadholder forbade him to buy land in the province.[7] Financially, this was not unattractive for William Frederick, who enjoyed the free use of stadholder's residences in Leeuwarden and later also in Groningen, placed at his disposal by the States.[8]

From that point of view, it was only his administrative position that bound William Frederick to Friesland; as a great nobleman his attachments lay outside the northern provinces. As a count of Nassau-Dietz he owned substantial estates in the Holy Roman Empire, such as the castle and lordship of Beilstein and the county of Dietz, where he had lived with his mother for some years before 1640. A third group of German possessions consisted of the county of Spiegelberg, near Hanover, which William Frederick had acquired through his mother. Together these estates and castles represented a large capital, at least on paper, but in William Frederick's lifetime the situation on the ground was frankly wretched as a result of the Thirty Years War. Countless campaigns of pillage and plunder in the 1630s and 1640s had reduced many villages to ruins. When William Frederick's secretary Vegelin visited Spiegelberg in the 1650s, he noted that the farms and the population were still in a deplorable condition.[9] William Frederick did make some attempts to restore the infrastructure of his counties, but never revisited his German estates after 1638.[10]

Besides his possessions abroad, William Frederick owned a small Dutch estate, the barony of Liesveld, which consisted of a castle and several polder villages in the province of Holland. Yet also in this case, the count largely left the running of his estate to his local bailiff or his secretary.[11] The only properties of which he made intensive personal use were his town mansions in The Hague; at first he lived in his house on the 'Poten', and in 1645 he gained the possession of two more residences on the 'Lange Voorhout' and the 'Lange Vijverberg'. Because of its grandeur William Frederick decided to make the last one his permanent residence in The Hague in 1649, and after unsuccessful attempts to sell them the other two properties were let for the time being.[12]

The surviving inventories reveal that the furnishings of this collection of castles and houses grew gradually in size and value over William Frederick's life.[13] All in all the value of his movable property in 1651 must be estimated at 250,000 guilders. The count's other assets included his landed estates in Liesveld and in the Holy Roman Empire (together 500,000 guilders), and his houses in The Hague (100,000).[14] A fortune of 900,000 guilders in real and movable property was large, but not exceptional. By 1650, the first millionaires appeared among the merchant elite of Amsterdam, and a noble family such as that of the Van Aerssens was almost as wealthy as the count of Nassau-Dietz. Yet William Frederick's cousins, the Oranges, took the prize and could boast a fortune in the millions. Their annual income from their private assets alone was around half a million guilders.[15]

By comparison William Frederick's income was modest. On the eve of his marriage to Albertine the count drew up an account of his income and expenditure. Dietz, Spiegelberg, Beilstein and Liesveld were said to be good for respectively 20,000, 10,000, 8,000 and 7,500 guilders a year, an optimistic estimate, for the incomes from the devastated German estates often proved very disappointing. His leased houses brought in a further 1,500 guilders, but the greater part of William Frederick's income came from his official duties. From 1650 he combined the stadholdership of Friesland with those of Groningen and Drenthe. The Friesian post received a salary of 32,364 guilders a year, while Groningen paid 16,300 in 1650. Compared with this his salary of 2,250 guilders from Drenthe was not much more than a tip. The count's military functions provided him with additional income: his colonelcy earned him 11,000 guilders, and the command of the Teutonic Order another 18,000 guilders. All in all the count could look forward to an annual income of 126,814 guilders.[16]

This was not enough to cover his expenses. 'More paid out than received: 4,950 guilders', William Frederick noted in 1647; and the following years were not much better. In spite of rigorous attempts to economise and numerous instructions to his court personnel, the count's burden of debt grew remorselessly. 'If only I were once free of my debts', he sighed a year later. The list of creditors drawn up after William Frederick's death shows that his marriage was a financial disaster for him. Building activities and increasing orders to suppliers of luxury goods forced him to take out one loan after another from 1652, and the bills he received revealed both his own embarrassed financial situation and the ambition of William Frederick and Albertine to give their court a certain international allure by ordering luxuries from Amsterdam, Antwerp and Paris.[17]

William Frederick's marriage thus inaugurated a more elaborately 'courtly' way of life. In the years before his marriage his household had impressed visitors as rather sober and predominantly military in tone. This modest lifestyle was probably the result of William Frederick's limited financial resources rather than a principled rejection of frivolity and courtly ceremonial, for the Calvinist count took part in all manner of courtly amusements at the court of the Oranges.[18] After 1652 William Frederick appears to have caught up: the houses in Groningen and Leeuwarden were rebuilt in the 1650s and 1660s and equipped with galleries and gardens, while commissions to painters, tapestry weavers and silversmiths also grew more frequent in this period. Even the formalities at court appear to have been influenced by the arrival of Albertine. William Frederick's diaries for the 1640s often record dinners alone or with only his servant for company; but after his marriage these simple dining habits made way for ceremonial dinners, served during successive sittings and courses.[19]

William Frederick left no comments in writing about the reasons for this change in the court manners or the function it served, but he seems to have associated court culture chiefly with his noble identity and not with the office of stadholder. In spite of patriotic assumptions expressed in the older historiography, there is very little to suggest that William Frederick felt any personal attachment to Friesland. To be sure, in his letters to the States he wrote of his 'sincere love for Friesland in particular', but such courtesies were part of formal discourse. We find the same phrases in his correspondence with the States of Groningen and Drenthe, and in later letters soliciting favours from the States of Overijssel, Gelderland, Utrecht or Zeeland.[20] Moreover, there is nothing in William Frederick's extensive archives to suggest that he had any knowledge of the Friesian language. The count himself wrote mostly in Dutch, while his correspondence with family members was exclusively in French or German. The books he owned also testify to an international, noble taste. William Frederick's collection was typical of the kind of library a seventeenth-century *honnête homme* ought to possess, but Dutch literary authors such as Pieter Cornelisz Hooft, Jacob Cats or even Constantijn Huygens were absent from it.[21] As the grandson of a daughter of a king of Denmark the count identified himself in the first place with his peers in the international high nobility, and the paintings or books with which he surrounded himself were intended to emphasise that illustrious descent. This cultivated self-image of the House of Nassau was only partly related to the province of Friesland, where the count served as the highest official.

Courtiers

Little data exist on the actual size of the Nassau court. 'His household was limited, and formed with a view to modesty and dignity, rather than pride and vanity', Ubbo Emmius famously (1547–1625) wrote of the court of William Frederick's uncle William Louis.[22] Emmius' evaluative description, however, tells us little about numbers and functions. It is certain that the households of the counts of Nassau were formed on the Burgundian model, which divided the household into departments (the kitchen, the chamber, the stables), whose tasks were defined in a household ordinance. This method of organisation had been introduced in the Nassau families by William of Orange in the sixteenth century.[23]

From William Frederick's own household ordinance it can be concluded that three categories of courtiers could be distinguished: the permanent staff; the military officers who combined a commission in the States army with more or less permanent duties at court; and finally a group of young noblemen attached to the court as pages. William Frederick thus controlled three funds of patronage that he could use to build up a court clientele.

Estimates of the size of the first group, the personnel, varied from source to source. The number of personnel fluctuated from the 1640s to the 1660s, whereas some courtiers were employed permanently in one place, and others accompanied William Frederick on his travels. The court personnel was not a sharply defined body. Be that as it may, all this personnel came under the control of the steward, Gosewijn Wiedenfelt. He was responsible for William Frederick's servants and lackeys, and also supervised the various menservants, maids and linen-keepers. In addition, Wiedenfelt had to run the kitchen department, consisting of a kitchen master, kitchen clerk, butler, preserves cook, dispenser, several cooks and kitchen maids. In the stables the steward supervised two grooms, the coachmen, stable lads, outriders and running footmen. Concierges and several halberdiers completed the paid establishment. All in all these domestic staff in 1655 numbered about thirty.[24]

Yet this did not exhaust the number of personnel. Several higher functionaries at court were not formally subordinates of Wiedenfelt, the most prominent example being William Frederick's secretary Philip Ernst Vegelin.[25] The count's financial adviser, first Reinier Casembroot and later Anthony Pieterson, was not a member of the personnel either. Both of these men also combined their roles with other positions: Casembroot was commissioner of the finances of the States-General, while Pieterson was a *vroedschap* of The Hague, where he rose to become burgomaster.[26] At the count's court they cooperated closely with the officials of the domain lands, such as the bailiffs Georg Clenck and Jacob van Gramberringen at Liesveld, and Achatius von Hohenfelt at Dietz. Finally there were a few who were omitted from the steward's payroll lists because they received board and lodging only. This also applied to the army officers and the pages. An undated summary in William Frederick's archives lists a total of seventy-eight persons who enjoyed meals at court. It appears that this total was not reached every day, for during his wedding festivities William Frederick's retinue numbered only fifty-five people.[27] The explanation for the rise in the number of diners may be his alliance with Albertine Agnes. From 1652 William Frederick's court was enlarged by the princess's personnel, which formally remained a separate court. The precise size of Albertine's retinue is not known, however.[28]

If we assume that William Frederick kept at least thirty to forty permanent staff, his court was larger than those of his predecessors. William Louis is known to have had a household of about twenty.[29] Even so, William Frederick's court in 1650 was still small by international standards. At the courts of foreign princes the number of employees and courtiers could rise into the hundreds even in the sixteenth century; and in the seventeenth a royal court of more than a thousand was not uncommon. Nonetheless, William Frederick's household must have been one of the three largest in the United Provinces. The exiled Queen of Bohemia, Elizabeth Stuart (1596–1662), initially kept a court of around two hundred in The Hague, though it later shrank to fifty. The court of the Oranges also greatly outnumbered that of William Frederick: Maurice had had about two hundred household staff members, while under Frederick Henry their number rose to nearly two hundred and fifty.[30]

As indicated, William Frederick's court included more than his permanent staff alone; there was a second category, of those who combined a rank in the Dutch States army with a more or less permanent position at court. The presence of these army officers was a result of the ongoing war with Spain and of William Frederick's post as captain-general. They gave his court a strongly masculine and military atmosphere, all the more marked in the absence of a wife and her retinue until 1652. In addition, the States of Friesland had assigned their stadholder a lifeguard of sixteen halberdiers and a *garde de corps* of two hundred men. The captain of this stadholder's guard, Doecke van Hemmema, also acted as William Frederick's military adviser. Strictly speaking these officers were not part of the private court personnel, for their function at court was paid for out of 'public' funds.

Some overlap, however, existed between the military officers and the count's staff, for William Frederick used his authority as captain-general to bestow military posts on his top household members as a reward for services rendered. Gosewijn Wiedenfelt, for example, became a major in a Friesian regiment thanks to the stadholder's intervention, while his son-in-law Johan Snabel was honoured with a reserve commission in 1645. The count's manservant Gilles Marez held the same rank in the stadholder's guard, while his bailiff Jacob van Gramberringen, who was himself a captain, procured a reserve commission for his son Willem Lodewijk.[31] All this created ties between the Friesian officer corps and William Frederick's court, and strengthened the stadholder's influence on parts of the army. It was Hemmema and Wiedenfelt who accompanied their patron in the assault on Amsterdam in 1650.[32]

Finally, the pages attached to William Frederick's court were not part of the personnel either. The court of the count usually offered places for up to eight pages, mostly youngsters from noble families who spent some time in William Frederick's service as part of their education. A post as page at court must have carried some prestige among the Friesian and Groningen nobility, for William Frederick received regular requests to admit their sons to his court. Several examples show that the count made skilful use of these opportunities to maintain his ties with the provincial nobility.[33]

Public and private

Army commissions for courtiers and the admission of noble youths from Friesland or Groningen as pages show that there was some overlap between William Frederick's republican and domestic patronage spheres. This suggests that the boundary between the two circuits created by the Republic's state system was blurred in practice. Assumptions in the literature appear to confirm this impression. P. Breuker, for example, has described the count of Nassau's household as a markedly Friesian institution, and claimed that it formed a 'dominant unity' with the Reformed community in the province; indeed, that it even contributed to a 'Calvinisation' of Friesian culture.[34] Moreover, from Wiebe Bergsma's study of William Louis we may conclude that this predecessor of William Frederick did recruit several of his staff members from Reformed Friesian noblemen. In this case there appears to have been hardly any difference between 'public' and 'private' clienteles.[35]

Yet William Frederick's patronage policy and therefore the connection between private court and public administration was more complex than the example of William Louis would suggest. As the analysis in the previous chapter showed, the confessional profile of the two networks was rather different in William Frederick's case. As a stadholder he built up a clientele with a pronounced Reformed character. Yet in his role as count of Nassau, William Frederick had no objection to employing Catholics at his court, which even resembled a rendez-vous for several Mennonite and Catholic notables. Whereas the stadholder delib-erately encouraged confessional uniformity in the public administration of the Republic, the count did not see confessional diversity as a threat to his private household.[36]

William Frederick's different patronage norms in the public and private spheres were, however, visible in more than his religious selection criteria. The court personnel differed from the public clientele in their geographical origin as well. The top officials in the count's household were usually noblemen, but for the most part not of Friesian birth. Gosewijn Wiedenfelt and Philip Ernst Vegelin were both German nobles. The financial counsellors Reinier Casembroot and Anthony Pieterson both came from families of officials in The Hague. The ancestors of the Liesveld bailiffs Georg Clenck and Jacob van Gramberringen had been allied to the courts of William Frederick's relatives in Dillenburg and The Hague. In other words, the count did not recruit his senior personnel from the provinces of which he was stadholder. During William Frederick's stadholder-ship the princely court remained largely closed to the Friesian nobility as a place of employment. Only a few of them, such as Albertine's equerry Haring van Harinxma, made careers at court.[37]

The family background of the courtiers presented a third contrast with the clients from the stadholder's administrative network. The way in which William Frederick took over the court clientele of his predecessor in 1640 already showed that service to the Nassau family often went back several generations. The steward Wiedenfelt had been chamberlain under Ernst Casimir, while bailiff Georg Clenck and his son Coenraat (William Frederick's court purveyor and agent in Amsterdam) came from a Dillenburg family. The count's representa-tive in Dietz, Achatius von Hohenfelt, had previously served as Ernst Casimir's equerry and steward of Sophia Hedwig. Jacob van Gramberringen and Lamoraal van der Noot also had a family tradition of service to the family.[38] William Frederick's household clientele thus owed less to his own selection policy than to the consolidation of existing ties.

Against this backdrop, it becomes clear that confessional diversity at the court was only one of the characteristic results of the public and private patronage spheres in which William Frederick operated.[39] Moreover, there is nothing to suggest that he wished to change this policy or sought to integrate the two circuits. The distinct social spheres that the republican state system created continued to be relevant in William Frederick's practice, and determined how he defined and shaped his role as stadholder and as count.

The pronounced distinction between patronage roles appears at first sight to have little in common with the boundaries between public and private life in early modern Europe traced in the models suggested by scholars such as Georges Duby and Philippe Ariès. For example, an incipient awareness of intimacy or privacy does not appear to have been of vital importance to William Frederick. Spatial separation, which plays a role in many theoretical public/private paradigms, was equally irrelevant to the distinction between public and private spheres of patronage.[40] The members of the two networks continually rubbed shoulders and shared the same space in the court complex at Leeuwarden, which was itself formally 'public' property, being owned by the States. In fact, it was only a set of unwritten patronage codes that really demarcated the public sphere from the private, apart from the fact where relationships between patron and client were physically located. Therefore, the function and relevance of distinctive patronage *spheres* can only be derived from the different *roles* in which William Frederick and the others involved cast themselves. For a better understanding of the meaning of these social spheres and patronage codes, we must define more precisely the count's role as patron in his court.

The role of the court patron

It has often been remarked that the early modern court in a sense resembled a family in which the head of the house acted as *paterfamilias*.[41] That collective bond also imposed obligations on William Frederick, and these were not the same as those under which he lay in his role as stadholder. In his own words he often described the court indeed as 'our court family'. This was a sharp contrast with the public clientele, for the stadholder certainly never regarded the civic regents as members of his court entourage. As we shall see, the relationship between a lord and his courtiers displayed characteristic features of clientage as well, different from those found in the republican-administrative context.

As head of the family William Frederick's primary obligation was to offer his courtiers protection and an income. Yet the patron's responsibilities were not all written on paper. In 1640, for example, the count had felt obliged to take over his brother's court clientele. His willingness to reward such prominent confidants as Wiedenfelt, Marez or Gramberringen with military posts can also be read as a sign that he felt a duty to give them additional support. Even employees who had left his service for family reasons could look forward to continued patronage. We saw above how the secretary Johan Sohn and the steward Barthold Oostheim, after their enforced resignations, successfully appealed to the undiminished solidarity of their former employer.[42] There is more evidence which suggests that as count William Frederick followed certain habits in his patronage that differed from those he adopted as stadholder. For example, the patron was ready to support his courtiers in legal proceedings, while widows and orphans could also rely on his charity and protection. When the sheriff of Groot Ammers died, Jacob van Gramberringen thought it no more than natural that his family should receive assistance, 'out of compassion for the poor grieving widow and seven fatherless children'.[43]

But because such patronage norms were not enshrined in written agreements, William Frederick was also faced with clients who expected more solidarity from their employer than he was willing or able to offer. In 1657 it was Vegelin who felt that the count was neglecting his obligations to him. The secretary carefully listed the gifts and offices with which William Frederick had rewarded the services of other courtiers, and sourly remarked that he himself had never been favoured with such kindnesses.[44] Reinier Casembroot also felt that his services were not appreciated at their true value, when his son Gijsbert was overlooked for the position of bailiff in 1647. He even urged William Frederick several times to reconsider the appointment.[45]

The patron himself was particularly sensitive to such 'indiscretions' and regularly reproved his court clients for transgressing the unwritten codes of patronage. Gosewijn Wiedenfelt was rapped over the knuckles when he publicly announced his imminent promotion to major. Such behaviour disturbed William Frederick as he believed it undermined his prestige and authority in the outside world. When his concierge in The Hague, Johan Aleman, went bankrupt in 1664, William Frederick again believed that his own reputation was being tarnished, for financial mismanagement led to 'dishonour and ill-repute'. A client's bankruptcy equally damaged the social credit of his patron, and the discredited concierge was unceremoniously shown the door in the same year.[46]

William Frederick had equally definite views of just how far his courtiers could go in acting as brokers. While William Frederick as stadholder had deliberately built up a stratified clientele in the towns of Friesland, in his household it was Wiedenfelt and Vegelin who took the initiative to develop similar brokerages. Vegelin in particular, as the count's secretary, was in a key position. He dealt with all incoming and outgoing letters, which offered him a conspectus of William Frederick's clientele as well as of vacant posts. Vegelin was keen to steer his patron's thoughts in the direction that served his own friends and acquaintances, often with success. Wiedenfelt too had his own circle of clients, whom he served in the same way, but he was less subtle in his approach than Vegelin. William Frederick recorded that the steward was in the habit of 'going for a walk in the marketplace', where he was generous in offering to exploit his good relations with the count of Nassau. The patron himself was none too pleased with this behaviour, and several times put Wiedenfelt in his place by explicitly rejecting his recommendations.[47] William Frederick felt that the 'haughtiness, and good opinion of himself and presumption' that Wiedenfelt displayed as a broker were unbecoming. 'N.B., not to be forgotten', he typically recorded in 1647, 'that Wiedenfelt has not thanked me for giving an office to Ziercksma on his recommendation, and I believe this is because of his anger that I did not make Haubois a deputy [on his suggestion]'.[48]

The role of the court client

Because William Frederick strongly believed that the conduct of his courtiers touched his reputation and interests directly, he exercised a much tighter social control over them than over his clients in the public circuit. In a way William Frederick's clients were placed under a double obligation: their official duty and an unwritten one. The first was described in the court ordinance, which was more or less a job description for the courtiers. These guidelines were intended to guarantee 'good order and discipline' at court, and ideally also to 'set a good example for others'. The ordinance insisted that the reputation of the head of the family ought to be the chief care of his subordinates also. The 'court family' was to 'show loyalty to His Excellency, and in every way help to avert and ward off harm to us'. Specifically, 'if they should hear anything to our detriment, in the house or outside it, either in words or deeds, they shall inform our steward of such things'. Conversely they were forbidden to leak information outside the court; the chamber servants in particular were ordered 'not to divulge anything that they see or hear in our chamber of any secret matters, either in writing or orally, but to keep silent to the grave'.[49]

A second rule applied to all employees: they were to keep their costs down. The ordinance of 1647 was probably framed for this very purpose. In practice, the head of the kitchen was required to follow a policy that 'shall be most to the reputation of His Excellency but at the lowest possible cost'. The linen-keepers were carefully to count the washing that they collected from the bleachers, while penalties were imposed for wasting soap and peat. The concierge was also expected to strike the best possible bargain with suppliers.[50] Individual guidelines of this kind were issued for the top officers of the household, some of whom received a personal job description.[51]

The duties defined on paper were supplemented by several unwritten and ad hoc tasks. Although there was little connection between William Frederick's public and private clienteles, that did not prevent members of his domestic staff becoming involved in 'stadholder's' matters. The impression is given that William Frederick employed them when he did not find his public clients sufficiently trustworthy; and that he preferred court clients when dynastic interests, discreet information and confidentiality were at stake. Moreover, courtiers such as Reinier Casembroot, Anthony Pieterson and Coenraat Clenck were instructed to provide William Frederick with news from Amsterdam and The Hague on a permanent basis.[52]

William Frederick's strong interest in a reliable and regular private news service was clearly the result of his ambiguous position as stadholder.[53] As civil servants of the States the stadholders did not have automatic access to all the sources of information open to the republican institutions and authorities. As a result, most stadholders set up news networks of their own. Above all in times of political unrest and during William Frederick's lobbying for the offices of stadholder and field-marshal his senior courtiers were sent into the country to organise a reliable supply of news for him.[54] The regular reports that reached William Frederick from his courtiers supplemented those he received at the same time from his brokers in the Friesian towns, so that private and public clienteles contributed different types of information. Thanks to this sophisticated system, William Frederick as an official was often better, or at least sooner, informed than his political masters, the States of Friesland, themselves.

Besides, William Frederick kept a secret political informant who sent him information from The Hague. This man, Dirck van Ruijven, had been employed at the court of the Oranges in the 1640s, and in 1650 William Frederick invited him to work for him 'in dangerous things'.[55] In fact Van Ruijven became the stadholder's spy in 'republican' circles in Holland, and even infiltrated the office of the Holland pensionary Johan de Witt. Copies of De Witt's secret correspondence and state papers were thus delivered to William Frederick's desk.[56] Van Ruijven's motives seemed to have been of material as well as ideological nature. He clearly tried to induce William Frederick to bring about 'some advancement for himself and his children', but in 1655 he also told his judges that he had decided to undertake his dubious activities for William Frederick 'out of love for the prince of Orange'.[57]

It was more troublesome for William Frederick to build up similar news networks abroad. Because his patronage resources were largely confined to the

Dutch Republic, the count had little to offer as a patron to those who had no interest in the United Provinces. William Frederick therefore made use of regular, commercial news services from places such as London, Berlin, Brussels, Cologne or Hamburg. These handwritten letters were characterised by a standard layout, in which reports were arranged by topic or region.[58] They were often produced as a sideline by men who held official posts as local agents or diplomats. For example, the secretary of the embassy in London, Maarten Mazure, sent weekly reports to William Frederick in the later 1640s.[59] Matthias Römer did the same from Hamburg and Lübeck in the 1650s and 1660s.[60] Most of these correspondents served several subscribers at the same time. Although William Frederick's archives provide no concrete evidence of payment, the count probably paid for their services in cash. His informant in Cologne, Hendrik van Bilderbeek, sent identical newsletters to other, paying customers. He had supplied Henry Casimir with news before 1640, which gives the impression that William Frederick simply took over such commercial news services from his predecessor.[61]

The less mutually dependent the relationship between supplier and recipient of news, the less exclusive was the information. Moreover, the quality and reliability of the commercial news services left much to be desired. Mazure's news letters, for example, though frequent, were superficial in content. The Holland envoy Gerard Pietersz Schaep even warned Vegelin not to place too much credence in the so-called *nouvelles* that Maarten Mazure sent. Schaep felt that 'one should not make too much of them, as if he were very penetrating; *sed hec cursim*.' Schaep claimed to have been 'told this by an Englishman' who 'had remarked the same on opening his, Mazure's, intercepted letters'.[62] It was not surprising that William Frederick only used commercial and professional news services when his clients could not offer him a better – informal and exclusive – alternative.

Identity

In the towns of Friesland the extent and nature of the stadholder's patronage had grown and developed gradually. At William Frederick's court no such process was evident as clientage appears to have taken the form of consolidation of existing relationships. This had at least two important consequences. First, it meant that contact between patron and client was not necessarily the result of personal choices, but more often of long-term family circumstances. Secondly, it implied that many courtiers had no independent sources of power or income. Clients who were socially and financially so dependent on a single patron had to be ready to show a great deal of flexibility and loyalty. On the one hand they had far less room for manoeuvre than their 'public' counterparts, and yet on the other hand the courtiers could make larger and more frequent appeals to the service and protection of their patron. In that way court patronage created a family-like feeling, which apparently was rarely infringed by members of the 'court family'.

Even the names that clients gave their children could illustrate the 'sociability' in the court circuit. Coenraat Clenck typically named his eldest son 'William Frederick' after his former patron, and Albertine Agnes became the boy's godmother. Jacob van Gramberringen named his son 'William Louis'.[63] These clients were making a public statement of the attachment formed in their relationship with their patron. Clientage at William Frederick's court thus had an integrating effect, and created a degree of recognisable group identity, which the patron himself cultivated by distinguishing his 'court family' from his other clienteles. The outside world in turn acknowledged this exclusivity by making its criticisms heard when courtiers made use of the 'public' resources of the province of Friesland. Irritation was aroused, for example, by the appointment of Wiedenfelt and Marez to Friesian regiments.[64]

The exclusive and emotional bond among William Frederick's clients at court was not so exceptional. Numerous examples are known from the literature of early modern patron-client contacts reinforced by 'affinity' and affection. Some French historians have called this form of patronage *fidélité*, to distinguish it from *clientèle*, on the assumption that the latter rested on a purely material basis.[65] The use of these terms is not without problems, because seventeenth-century people themselves did not use a terminology that drew such a subtle distinction. For this reason the existence of this distinctive type of 'emotional patronage' has not been universally admitted.[66] Sceptics assume that clientage was essentially a material mechanism, which could not be sustained by friendship or affinity, but only by mutual reciprocity.[67]

Sharon Kettering has argued that emotional attachment certainly could play a part in early modern patronage contacts, but that unconditional *fidélité* was not common in practice.[68] She claimed that this kind of clientage was indeed presented as an ideal in letters, but that the practice was mostly more capricious and more varied. The case of William Frederick supports this reading. Affection or fidelity and a feeling of group identity indeed characterised his patronage only in exceptional cases, and it was precisely this exclusive form of clientage that ultimately proved enduring and capable of spanning generational and religious divides. Moreover, his example suggests that it was not the social distance between client and patron, but the social environment in which the relationship was situated, that was responsible for the durability of patronage and the creation of *fidélité*. Public or private spheres, rather than social distance, defined the characteristics of William Frederick's clientage roles and codes.

Notes

1 On the 'Friesian' court see Groenveld, Huizinga and Kuiper, *Nassau uit de schaduw van Oranje*; Bruggeman, *Nassau en de macht van Oranje*; Huizinga, *Van Leeuwarden naar Den Haag*; *It Beaken*, 60(3/4) (1998).

2 For an international perspective on the relationship between household and state administration cf. among others Asch, 'Introduction', 1–38; Adamson, 'The Making', 9–19; Duindam, *Vienna and Versailles*, esp. 3–13 and 90–128; MacHardy, *War, Religion and Court Patronage*, 1–12.

3 The issue has received little to no attention in the literature. Israel, 'The Courts', 119–21; Kuiper, 'Hofleven', 326–47; Mörke, 'Sovereignty and Authority', 455–64; Prak, 'Republiek en vorst', 28–52; Rowen, 'Neither Fish nor Fowl'; Schilling, 'The Orange Court', 441–53; Cf. also Kettering, 'Clientage during the French Wars of Religion', 222–5 and 238–9; Mączak, 'From Aristocratic Household', 315–27.

4 Mörke, *'Stadtholder' oder 'Staetholder'*. See also Roorda, 'Le Secret du prince'.

5 Cf. Schuurman and Spierenburg, *Private Domain, Public Inquiry*, and Wheelock, *The Public and Private*.

6 Cf. Kooijmans, *Liefde in opdracht*, 36–7. William Frederick also paid longer or shorter visits to Honselaarsdijk, Buren, Liesveld or Cleves. BL, Egerton MS 2538, fol. 95b; Tresoar, Eysinga, 476; *Gloria Parendi*, 435, 539–46 and 689; Morren, *Het huis Honselaarsdijk*, 46.

7 For this see chapter 2.

8 Guibal, *Democratie en oligarchie*, 230–4. In 1648 the States of Friesland made an exception and allowed William Frederick to lay out a garden behind the stadholder's residence, the present *Prinsentuin*. The rebuilding of the court in the 1650s and 1660s was also paid for by William Frederick himself. Mulder-Radetzky, 'Huizen van Albertine Agnes', 99–111.

9 Tresoar, Eysinga, 485 (several years); Kooijmans, *Liefde in opdracht*, 176–7.

10 William Frederick made plans to settle Friesian farmers on vacant farms on his German estates, to bring them back into cultivation. *Gloria Parendi*, 639.

11 The barony of Liesveld had come into the family relatively recently; Ernst Casimir had bought it, but the purchase was controversial. William Frederick occupied the barony in 1642, when his mother died. NA, ND, 5797ff.

12 *Gloria Parendi*, 720: ('Monday I saw the house on the Vijverberg, which suits me very well, and I wish to live there and sell the houses on the Poten'). Van Dam, 'Stadhouderlijke verblijven', 89–90; Van Diepen, 'Het hof van Friesland', 52–6; Drossaers and Lunsingh Scheurleer, *Inventarissen van de inboedels*, II, 76; Mensonides, 'De geschiedenis van de huizen', 228 ff.; Wijsenbeek, *Het Lange Voorhout*, 49 and 250. Until 1648 William Frederick also owned a house in his birthplace A r n h e m, which he sold to the States of Gelderland in that year. Van Nienes, 'Inleiding', 59.

13 Inventories of the estates: KHA, WF, IV, 7 (Vijverberg, 1657); Drossaers and Lunsingh Scheurleer, *Inventarissen van de inboedels*, II, 87–120; Mulder-Radetzky, 'Huizen van Albertine Agnes', 99–111. Paintings: Ekkart, 'Schilders aan het hof', 113–20; Janssen, 'De kunst van het kopiëren', 37–47. Books: NA, ND, 893 ('Catalogue ou register'). Diamonds: LAD, Oranienbaum, A7b, 134 (list of William Frederick's diamonds and jewels, 1647).

14 KHA, WF, II, 3 (survey of William Frederick's possessions, income and debts, 1651); Visser, 'Het huwelijk', 25.

15 Burke, *Venice and Amsterdam*, 62–8; Israel, *The Dutch Republic*, 347–8; Knevel, *Het Haagse Bureau*, 86; Van Nierop, *The Nobility of Holland*, 93–139; Veeze, *De raad van de prinsen*, 9–12.

16 KHA, WF, II, 3 (documents on the marriage, 1651–52); Tresoar, SA, 367, I (William Frederick to Dirck van Ruijven, 28 June – 8 July 1655, from Groningen).

17 KHA, WF, IV, 8 (statement of William Frederick's debts, 1666); *Gloria Parendi*, 332 and 485. Commissions to painters: Ekkart, 'Schilders aan het hof', 1130–20; Janssen, 'De kunst van het kopiëren', 37–47; RDO, 21 (Vegelin to Floris Borre van Amerongen, 6–16 February 1656, from Leeuwarden, and William Frederick to the same, 15 April 1656 from The Hague). Buildings: KHA, WF, B-1, 104 (Elias Jansen to William Frederick, 11–21 June 1662, from Groningen);

Tresoar, Eysinga, 477 (correspondence of William Frederick with Vegelin, 1647–64); Mulder-Radetzky, 'Huizen van Albertine Agnes', 99–111. Purchases of luxury goods and tapestries: Tresoar, SA, 38 (incoming letters and drafts, 1660–62); KHA, WF, VII, C-133 (Correspondence).

18 William Frederick was sometimes critical of the frivolities that the Oranges permitted themselves. See chapters 4 and 5. Vegelin for his part was irritated by the 'carnival' that the marriage to Albertine involved in 1652: Tresoar, Eysinga, 485 (1652).

19 It is not clear if the courtiers dined at the same time as William Frederick and Albertine, at separate tables, or if there were successive sittings for the various categories of courtier. KHA, WF, V, 2 (documents on the household). Cf. Kleijn, De stadhouders, 62–3; Waterbolk, 'Met Willem Lodewijk aan tafel', 296–315.

20 Cf. BL, Additional MS 21527; Tresoar, SA, 37; KHA, WF, VI, 5; VII, B-III/1a.

21 NA, ND, 893 ('Catalogue ou register').

22 Cited in Bergsma, 'Willem Lodewijk', 192.

23 Bruggeman, 'Het hof', 293–302; Delen, Het hof, 21–9; Vetter, Am Hofe, 14ff.; Zandvliet, 'Het hof', 37–63.

24 KHA, WF, V, 2 (list of salaries); Tresoar, Eysinga, 476 (lists of salaries).

25 In 1657 he succeeded the steward Goswijn Wiedenfelt. Tresoar, Eysinga, 469.

26 NNBW, VIII, 264–5; Smit, 'De ambtenaren', 384–8; Wijsenbeek, Het Lange Voorhout, 250.

27 KHA, WF, V, 2 (documents on the household). Several documents in this file date from 1692, so that the total of seventy-eight diners may refer to the court of Henry Casimir II. For the size of William Frederick's retinue during his wedding, Visser, 'Het huwelijk', 39.

28 Cf. KHA, WF, IX. According to the wedding arrangements, Albertine's household was to consist of twenty-two people. The retinue of William Frederick's son Henry Casimir II in 1660 comprised nine persons. RDO, 21 (William Frederick to Floris Borre van Amerongen, 5–15 June 1660, from The Hague).

29 Bergsma, 'Willem Lodewijk', 214–15. In the Habsburg period the stadholders of Friesland had about thirty persons in their service. In the eighteenth century, the household of the Friesian stadholder numbered about 120 members. Bruggeman, 'Het hof', 294–5; Van Nienes, 'Inleiding', 52–6; Mulder-Radetzky, 'Het hof', 68–9.

30 Mörke, 'Stadtholder' oder 'Staetholder', 96–104; Tiethoff-Spliethoff, 'De hofhouding van Frederik Hendrik', 41–62; Zandvliet, 'Het hof', 43. The retinue of the 'Winter' King and Queen of Bohemia probably numbered around 200 when they arrived, Groenveld. 'König ohne Staat', 174–82; Keblusek, 'Het Boheemse hof', 47–54.

31 KHA, WF, VII, C-205 (Gilles Marez to William Frederick, 17–27 August 1656, from Groningen); VII, V-III (appointment of Willem Lodewijk van Gramberringen, 1658); VII, VB-II/3 (list of army officers, 1653); Gloria Parendi, 123 and 484; Worp, Briefwisseling, II, 68; Kooijmans, 'Haagse dames', 262–3; Ten Raa and De Bas, Het Staatsche leger, IV, 236.

32 KHA, WF, VII, B-III (appointment of Doeke van Hemmema, 1645); Tresoar, SA, 367, E (statement of William II naming the officers involved in the assault, 19–29 July 1650).

33 Compare KHA, WF, VII, C-172 (C. van Iddekinge to William Frederick 5–15 November 1658, from Groningen); KHA, WF, VII, C-120 (correspondence of A. Clant with William Frederick, 1658–59); KHA, WF, VII, C-269 (Sweder? van Wijnbergen to William Frederick, 1–11 November 1662, n.p.); KHA, WF, VII, VB-I/97 (G. van Heerma to William Frederick, 20–30 October 1661, from Leeuwarden).

34 Breuker, 'Court Culture', 62. See also Breuker, 'Over de Nadere Reformatie, 25–9; Schutte, 'Nederland: een calvinistische natie', 698.

35 Bergsma, 'Willem Lodewijk', 221. Cf. Waterbolk, 'Met Willem Lodewijk aan tafel', 296–315.

36 His court ordinance at first sight suggests that his courtiers were drawn from an equally Reformed background, since the count encouraged regular worship, and even offered his personnel a financial incentive to attend morning and evening prayers. KHA, WF, V, 1.

37 Besides, the lower personnel were mostly recruited locally. For Wiedenfelt: Kooijmans, Liefde in opdracht, 305. For Vegelin: Worp, Briefwisseling, III, 261. For Pieterson: Wijsenbeek, Het Lange

Voorhout, 250. For Casembroot: *NNBW*, VII, 264–5. For Clenck: Elias, *De vroedschap*, II, 565. For Gramberringen: KHA, WF, VIII, 408; NA, ND, 5807.

38 Compare KHA, WF, VIII, C-216; Tresoar, Eysinga, 476. Kooijmans, *Liefde in opdracht*, 283; Van Nienes and Bruggeman, *Archieven van de Friese stadhouders*, 622–7.

39 Cf. the remarks on this in chapter 2. Pollmann, *Religious Choice*, esp. 201–3; Kaplan, 'Fictions of Privacy', 1030–64; Frijhoff, 'Dimensions de la coexistence', 213–37.

40 Cf. Ariès, *A History of Private Life*; Habermas, *The Structural Transformation*; Weintraub, 'The Theory'. For the Dutch Republic see Kaplan, 'Functions of Privacy', 1030–64; Schuurman and Spierenburg, *Private Domain, Public Inquiry*; Wheelock, *The Public and Private*.

41 Adamson, 'The Making', 11–15; Asch, 'Introduction', 7–11; Elias, *Die höfische Gesellschaft*.

42 See chapter 1.

43 NA, ND, 5807 (Jacob van Gramberringen to William Frederick, 11–21 October 1659, from Liesveld). For William Frederick's involvement in legal proceedings in the Court of Friesland, see chapter 7.

44 'And although I have travelled over a thousand miles in this work during ten years, I am still waiting for my recompense'. Tresoar, Eysinga, 485/1657.

45 NA, ND, 5807 (William Frederick to Jacob van Gramberringen, 28 May – 7 June 1653, from Leeuwarden); 5806 (correspondence of Reinier Casembroot with William Frederick); KHA, WF, VII, C-115 (Reinier Casembroot to William Frederick, 6–16 February 1647, from The Hague; vice versa, February 1647; 11–21 November 1652, from Leeuwarden).

46 KHA, WF, VII, C-50 (Johan Aleman to William Frederick, 3–13 April and 26 April – 6 May 1664, from The Hague). Cf. Janssen, 'De kunst van het kopiëren'.

47 Examples in *Gloria Parendi*, 112–13 and 339–41.

48 *Gloria Parendi*, 682.

49 KHA, WF, V, 1. Cf. similar terms in William Louis's time: Bergsma, 'Willem Lodewijk', 211–12.

50 KHA, WF, V, 1; VII, C-50 (Johan Aleman to William Frederick, 11–21 April 1661, from The Hague).

51 Steward: Tresoar, Eysinga, 469. Bailiff: NA, ND, 5903. Commissioners: *Gloria Parendi*, 244, 295, 310, 401, 405, 410, 532, 723. The bailiff of Liesveld, the steward and the secretary were also involved in the leases that William Frederick held as land commander of the Teutonic Order. RDO, 21 (incoming letters of Floris Borre van Amerongen, 1640–64).

52 Compare KHA, WF, VII, C-188 (Correspondence William Frederick with Coenraat Clenck). Coenraat Clenck – son of bailiff Georg Clenck – lived in Amsterdam where he was active in the Russian (Archangel) trade. He also supplied William Frederick with luxury goods, such as tapestries, gold and silver objects, damasks and orange trees. For his career Elias, *De vroedschap*, II, 564–8; Veluwenkamp, *Archangel*, esp. 84–90 and 125–32; Raptschinsky, 'Uit de geschiedenis'; idem, 'Het gezantschap'.

53 A more detailed analysis of William Frederick's news network is offered in Janssen, 'Dutch Clientelism'.

54 KHA, WF, VII, B-III/1a (letters on the stadholdership, 1650); VI, 14 (documents on the field-marshal's rank); Tresoar, SA, 37 (documents on the stadholdership after the death of William II).

55 Van Ruijven's service at the Orange court is evident from NA, ND. 563 (pension for Dirck van Ruijven, 1654). On him see also *NNBW*, I, 1450; De Bruin, *Geheimhouding en verraad*, 444–58; Knevel, *Het Haagse bureau*, 118–19; Nedermeijer, 'Het strafgeding', 195–239.

56 In 1655 Van Ruijven was caught and sentenced to banishment. He received new jobs from William Frederick. Van Ruijven's letters to William Frederick are in, among other places, Tresoar, SA, 38, 367-X; KHA, WF, VII, C-66. Van Ruijven corresponded at the same time with Edward Hyde, Charles II's secretary. Their correspondence in BOX, Rawlinson MS 115, fol. 108r; Clarendon MS 45, fols 459–60. See also KHA, WF, VII, C-218 (Matthijs van Osenbrugge to William Frederick, 13 November 1655, from Arnhem); NA, Johan de Witt, 2777a (letters from Dirck van Ruijven to William Frederick).

57 He had even tried to interest William Frederick in a coup 'that could bring down the pensionary' NA, HvH, 5253.14 (report of the discussions, 18 September 1655); NA, Johan de Witt, 2777a (various documents), hearing of Dirck van Ruijven, 22 and 23 September 1655. The whole affair is discussed in De Bruin, *Geheimhouding en verraad*, 444–58.

58 Cf. Baron, 'The Guises of Dissemination'.

59 KHA, WF, VII, C-206 (letters of Maarten Mazure).

60 KHA, WF, VII, C-236 (letters of Matthias Römer); Tresoar, SA, 48 (letters of Matthias Römer). Other examples: Tresoar, SA, 38. For the official careers of Mazure and Römer see Schutte, *Repertorium*, 94 and 193–4. For a fuller treatment, Janssen, 'Dutch Clientelism'.

61 Tresoar, SA, 38 (letters of Hendrik van Bilderbeek); *Gloria Parendi*, 136. Cf. Lankhorst, 'Newspapers in the Netherlands', 153–4; Stolp, *De eerste couranten*, 36–48.

62 KHA, WF, VIII, 12 (Gerard Schaep Pietersz to Vegelin, 29 July 1650, from Westminster). On Schaep see Groenveld, 'Verdicht verleden', 276–9, and idem, 'Een Schaep in't Schapelandt'. Some other revealing documents about him in: WFG, OAM 1306 (Letters from Gerard Pietersz Schaep to Nicolaas Stellingwerff).

63 KHA, WF, VII, B-III (deed of appointment of Willem Lodewijk van Gramberringen, 1658). Elias, *De vroedschap*, II, 567. Cf. the same phenomenon in the case of Constantijn Huygens: Groenveld, 'C'est le pere'; and also Van Deursen, *Een dorp in de polder*, 31.

64 *Gloria Parendi*, 314 and 484. Some members of the personnel tried to break through this cultivated segregation by marrying daughters of regents, perhaps in the hope of gaining access to the Friesian elite. Gosewijn Wiedenfelt married Lolckje van Aysma, daughter of a Friesian noble family, while Philip Ernst Vegelin married Fockje van Sminia in 1643. Van Nienes and Bruggeman, *Archieven van de Friese stadhouders*, 624–6.

65 Durand, 'Clientèles et fidélités', 3–24; Mousnier, 'Les fidélités et les clientèles', 35–46.

66 The concept of *fidélité* is particularly controversial in Anglo-American historiography: cf. Harding, *Anatomy*, 36–7; Mączak, *Ungleiche Freundschaft*, 60–5; Koenigsberger, 'Patronage, Clientage and Elites', 147–8; Neuschel, *Word of Honor*, 10–16.

67 Dewald, *Aristocratic Experience*, 104–6; Greengrass, 'Noble Affinities', 275–311; Kettering, 'Patronage in Early Modern France', 859; Kooijmans, *Vriendschap*, 132–48; Swann, *Provincial Power*, 9–12.

68 Kettering, 'Clientage During the French Wars of Religion', 239.

Part II

Client at the Orange court, 1640–1650

4

Under the authority of the master

William Frederick spent only a few months of the year in Friesland. For the rest of the time he was mostly to be found in The Hague, 'at court'. By that he did not mean one of his own houses in the town, but the court of the prince of Orange, usually known as the 'stadholder's quarter'. The differences between the two princely households were significant, not least for William Frederick himself. Whenever he left his own house on the Vijverberg to visit that of his cousin, the count entered a different social world, as his diary makes clear. He himself preferred to refer to it as the court of 'His Highness' or simply 'the Boss', a term that leaves us in no doubt of the strict hierarchy that defined the family relationships of the Nassaus, and the place in it that William Frederick believed to be reserved for himself.[1] He might be a patron in Friesland, but in the prince's entourage he was, in his own words, a 'servant'. The use of this vocabulary illustrates how William Frederick incorporated different, competing patronage identities: he developed distinctive roles as patron in his province and at his own court, and had to make a further adjustment to the position of client whenever he exchanged Leeuwarden for The Hague.

The Orange court

The Orange court in The Hague was in every respect larger, wealthier and more distinguished than that of William Frederick. Strictly speaking the House of Orange kept several courts around 1645, for the households of Frederick Henry, his wife Amalia van Solms and their daughter-in-law Mary Stuart were autonomous on paper. In practice, however, there were frequent overlaps between their respective personnel, who also shared many facilities and were largely financed from the same princely fortune. This was also true of certain expenditures and the accommodation of the court of the English Stuarts, which was forced into exile in the Dutch Republic in the later 1640s.[2] The fortune of the House of

Orange was substantial indeed. Its annual revenue amounted to between 700,000 and 1,000,000 guilders from private domain lands, official salaries and emoluments: all in all nearly ten times William Frederick's income.[3]

The Oranges also had much larger resources of patronage than the count of Nassau-Dietz. As captain-general of the United Provinces, stadholder of six of the seven provinces, and owner of extensive private landed estates, the prince had hundreds of administrative, military and household posts directly or indirectly in his gift. Unlike his Friesian cousin, however, Orange was not in a position to control all these various clienteles in person. For his private household and landed estates the prince had a Domain Council, which supervised the running of the estates, the collection of rents and the appointment of office holders. As stadholder, he had no formal body or council to advise him, but nevertheless Frederick Henry built up an extensive informal network of political informants and advisers, just as William Frederick did in Friesland. Some of these clients resided at court in The Hague, while others unofficially represented the stadholder as brokers in the localities.[4]

With about 250 courtiers the noble household of the Oranges was not just larger and wealthier than William Frederick's household, it was also much more international in its composition. This was partly the result of marriage strategies, since the German Amalia van Solms – married to Frederick Henry – and the Englishwoman Mary Stuart – married to William II – were accompanied in The Hague by their own retinues. The presence of Mary – the princess royal and daughter of king Charles I – and her exiled brothers also lent the Orange court a certain royal mystique that William Frederick's household could not match. Its cosmopolitan character was further enhanced by the presence of several high-ranking officers who served in the Dutch States army, but were not uncommonly of German, French or English descent.[5] They often combined their military ranks with more or less permanent posts at court.

Because of this aristocratic and international lustre, the Orange court was also less accessible to outsiders. While William Frederick's court was visited every day by small-town notables from Sloten or IJlst, the threshold for the entrée of civic regents at the court of the prince was undoubtedly higher. At any rate, William Frederick never mentioned their presence in the diary in which he carefully recorded the daily round of visits and dinners.[6] Furthermore, it was less usual for the prince himself to visit these magistrates in their homes, as the Friesian stadholder was accustomed to do in his own province.

Finally, the princely court was more centred in one place than that of William Frederick: The Hague. Although the princes of Orange owned various castles and country houses at Breda, Buren or Dieren, they rarely stayed in them for very long. The continuing war with Spain compelled Frederick Henry to spend every summer in the field. During the rest of the year he had several residences at his disposal in or near The Hague. The 'Oude Hof' on the Noordeinde was used merely as accommodation for guests, while the modern country palaces of Honselaarsdijk and Ter Nieuburg were not far from the town. Huis ten Bosch, built from 1645 and intended for the exclusive use of Amalia van Solms, was more intimate. The heart of the Orange court at The Hague, however, was the stadholder's quarter on the north-west side of the *Binnenhof*. It was not the family's largest or most comfortable residence, or even its own property, for officially it belonged to the States of Holland. Nevertheless, the stadholders preferred to live in this court complex, perhaps because it underlined their status as the first family in the Republic.[7] They could hardly have had a more strategically situated residence, within walking distance of the halls where the States of Holland, the States-General and the Council of State assembled. The modest extent of the stadholder's quarter forced his courtiers to seek accommodation outside the *Binnenhof*. Many of the houses on the Buitenhof, Kneuterdijk, Vijverberg and Voorhout were occupied by the prince's entourage.[8]

The count as client

That entourage included William Frederick, who can undoubtedly be counted as one of Frederick Henry's most prominent clients. Yet the troubles of 1640 already showed the complex nature of their relationship, shaped as it was by family ties, increasing social distance and political rivalry. It was for this reason that William Frederick's mother, Sophia Hedwig, sought to establish a new balance between the two dynasties. On her deathbed in 1642 she had made her only surviving son promise to marry a princess of Orange. Such an alliance would not only improve the relationship between the families, but might also strengthen the Nassau-Dietz claim to the Orange inheritance if Frederick Henry's only son, William II, died without an heir.[9]

Even so, it would be inadequate to attribute William Frederick's loyalty to Orange exclusively to opportunistic calculations. The inequality and growing dependence between the houses of Orange-Nassau and Nassau-Dietz was rather an obvious fact of life for William Frederick. In his diary, he consistently referred to his cousin as 'the Boss' or 'the Chief', and this suggests that his willingness to cast himself in the role of 'servant' was inspired by more than merely pragmatic motives. William Frederick accepted the hierarchy in the family as fundamental on principle, as if the division of roles between patron and client was predicated at birth. Indeed, the count never spoke or wrote of his role as client in terms of his own individual choices or ambitions, but preferred to use such typical language as 'following in the laudable footsteps of our forefathers' to explain his conduct. It was unrealistic to expect one who identified so closely with his family history to break free of what he perceived to be an established inequality. We shall see that William Frederick assumed that this accepted role division rested on a strong religious basis as well. His conviction that a hierarchically organised society was a reflection of God's intentions helped William Frederick to accept that entrenched social differences within the family were essential and had to be respected.[10]

Although William Frederick preferred to define and legitimise his relationship to the prince of Orange in terms of tradition and predestined roles, that did not mean, of course, that their bond was static. On the contrary, after 1641 William Frederick deliberately set up a campaign to restore his damaged reputation at the court and to build up a more confidential relationship with the Orange family. In his diaries he reflected extensively on the strategies used, and on their variable success. A reconstruction of William Frederick's development as a client also makes it clear that the progress he made was simultaneously shaped by profound changes that the Republic as a whole was undergoing.

Frederick Henry

To increase his 'credit' in The Hague, William Frederick developed several strategies. To begin with, he explicitly asked the prince's advice whenever he had a vacancy to fill in the army.[11] In administrative matters too, the failed client kept a sharp eye on Frederick Henry's preferences. In October 1642 he told Johan Veltdriel, a Friesian deputy in the States-General, that any informal 'recommendations' for vacancies made by Frederick Henry must always be honoured.[12] William Frederick even felt obliged to modify the personnel of the Friesian administrative colleges from time to time, to suit the prince. In 1644, for example, a rumour circulated that Frederick Henry thought the same Johan Veltdriel too lightweight as a delegate. William Frederick noted that 'His Highness desired me to urge and advise Mr Roorda to go with me to Friesland, the more so since he had more direction and credit than Veltdriel'.[13] Two years later, however, it was Carel Roorda's turn to fall from grace as a deputy in the States-General. William Frederick heard unofficially that 'they wanted to be rid of Mr Roorda from The Hague, because he will not always yield to the Boss's will'.[14] By following informal instructions of this kind and 'spontaneously' asking the prince's advice, the count explicitly confirmed his role as client. From 1643 he even submitted his letters to the Friesian administrative colleges for Frederick Henry's information before they were sent.[15]

Some of William Frederick's attempts to underline his renewed loyalty were more subtle. The Friesian stadholder followed the prince's daily agenda attentively, and wherever Frederick Henry went, William Frederick also put in an appearance. On 4 May 1643 he noted that he went 'to court assiduously' and 'often went out for a walk with His Highness and Her Highness'. He also made a point of accompanying the Boss and his family, or waiting for them at church services and meals.[16] Ideally, such ostentatious attendance would be sweetened by an exchange of civilities, to make his submission and loyalty even more obvious. William Frederick was flattered when he 'had the honour' of a lengthy conversation with Amalia on 27 December 1643. His hopes were raised because it gave him the chance to assure Frederick Henry personally of 'my obedience and loyalty until death'. He used the opportunity to claim that 'I should not depend on anyone in the world so much as on His and Her Highness, and that I owed them this duty and did it willingly'.[17]

William Frederick might not always manage to gain personal access to Frederick Henry or Amalia, but it was not invariably necessary since, besides his direct contacts, a client could also build up his credit through intermediaries whom he believed to have influence with his patron. The prince's secretary Constantijn Huygens, for example, enjoyed the count's continual attentions in these years, being gratified from time to time by small presents and courtly letters. Other confidants, such as Cornelis van Aerssen or Cornelis Musch, received regular visits from the count in their homes. On these informal occasions William Frederick was careful to be a good listener, but not to say too much himself: 'above all I must refrain from that, and be silent about everything that is happening, and be patient, which is hard, but it must be so'.[18] That was easier said than done, for many a courtier was curious about the tactics of the damaged client from Friesland. In such cases William Frederick felt he had to be constantly on his guard not to put himself in a vulnerable position, or to be over-friendly and too forthcoming. When he heard in the summer of 1646 that 'His Highness thought so much of me, and was very satisfied with me, and spoke of no one so often as he did of me', the count did not feel he could rejoice prematurely. 'Now I must be cautious, manage it well and not let myself be misled by too great boldness and familiarity or presumption.'[19]

William Frederick's patience was put to the test for a long time, but in 1644 he earned some sign of recognition when, with Frederick Henry's approval, he was named colonel of the Walloon regiment, a rank which also made him welcome at the meetings of the general staff.[20] Gradually William Frederick came to feel that the coolness had gone out of their relationship or that 'the worst was over'. Another sign of this was given by several invitations to join the family at Honselaarsdijk in May 1645. The weather was miserable, but on the other hand Amalia was 'very gay and lively'. William Frederick proudly recorded that 'count Heinrich [of Nassau-Siegen], Haulterive and many others were very vexed and jealous that I alone was invited to Honselaarsdijk.'[21] In the count's eyes such an exclusive invitation was a mark of social recognition, and thus a sign of his progress. But at the same time he had to admit that such rapprochements with the prince were followed by moments of renewed coolness. In October 1644 the Friesian stadholder received 'many compliments' from Frederick Henry, 'and he assured me of his friendship'. According to William Frederick it was even whispered that 'I now stood well at court, much better than count Henry'. But when this impression emboldened him to approach the prince about an army vacancy, he was answered as coolly as ever: 'we shall speak to each other again'.[22] The patron appeared to make intensive use of his opportunities to direct his cousin, but would not give William Frederick the credit that he had hoped to gain at court.

Yet the situation was not altogether hopeless. In a certain sense it was the patron himself who unintentionally created new opportunities for his unappreciated client after 1645. From that year Frederick Henry went into a steep physical and mental decline, which William Frederick traced in his diary. During the campaign of 1646 he noticed that the prince 'could hardly stay in the saddle'. That summer it was an open secret in The Hague that the old campaigner 'was quite unable to speak or give a right answer' on official occasions. There were also painful moments when he was not in his right mind, and 'his understanding was quite gone'. The sick man himself no longer hoped for recovery. Though he had occasional better days, he was said to have told his officers that he 'wished he was dead and out of this torment and torture of the world'.[23]

Frederick Henry's failing health had immediate consequences for relationships within the family, as it became clear that his son William would take over his father's task in the near future. The old prince himself, who was said to be rather 'jealous', followed developments with equal keenness and irritation. On 5 June 1644 he was frankly indignant when he saw that some high officers did not come and sit with him in the coach, but with prince William. It struck him that many courtiers were now 'adoring the rising and not the setting sun'.[24] Frederick Henry's analysis was not far wrong. In the spring of 1646 the always well-informed Cornelis van Aerssen advised William Frederick to pay his court to the young prince William.[25] Indeed, the 'rising sun' appeared to be dawning on entirely new prospects for William Frederick.

William II

Frederick Henry died on 17 March 1647. For William Frederick his death meant the loss of a rather distant patron. The accession of William II would bring a great change in his bond with the house of Orange and as a result in his identity as a client. The omens had in fact been good for some years. In the winter of 1643 William had, for example, presented his second cousin with a ring. William

Frederick felt justified in interpreting this as an important sign, which betokened a new phase in his relationship with the House of Orange. He had therefore resolved 'to keep the ring all my life as a memento of his good inclination toward me, in which I hope he will always continue'.[26] This time William Frederick's hopes appeared to be coming true. On 31 May 1646 Cornelis van Aerssen could assure the count 'what a good opinion and sentiment prince William had' of him, an impression confirmed barely a month later by William himself. On 23 June he let it be known that he would regard his second cousin as 'a servant and good friend'.[27]

For his part, William Frederick never missed an opportunity to compliment the young prince and to assure him of his 'subjection and service'. More specifically, he asked William's advice on appointments to military vacancies.[28] In political matters too, he pursued the same line he had taken with Frederick Henry. In 1647, for example, he offered the prince the services of his own Friesian client Joachim Andreae. This was no random choice. In the spring of 1646 William Frederick had managed to secure Andreae's nomination as a member of the States-General, after which the regent had given him 'great promises and assurances of his service and friendship'.[29] William Frederick then used the credit he had amassed with Andreae by nominating him, to offer him to his own patron. He informed the prince of Andreae's 'inclination and affection to the service of Your Highness', and encouraged him to make use of them. At the same time Andreae was instructed to be accommodating to any requests from the stadholder's quarter.[30] In fact in the years 1647–50 the deputy sent reports of his regular talks with the prince. 'I have from day to day discussed with the prince what I should do', Andreae typically reported on 2 April 1650.[31] In a sense the Friesian stadholder's strategy was the same as that employed in Friesland by such burgomasters as Alle van Burum. Just as Van Burum in Leeuwarden had offered his own clientele to William Frederick in the hope of favours from the stadholder, so the latter used his Friesian network in The Hague to reinforce his position as a client of the prince.

William Frederick had learned from experience, however, that caution was always imperative. 'I must go to work cautiously with prince William', he reminded himself, careful to avoid a new fiasco.[32] But unlike his father, William II was prepared to reward the spontaneous services of his second cousin. A year after his inauguration as stadholder he took William Frederick aside for a talk. 'His Highness was very civil to me, very open-hearted, spoke very freely and did me full honour.' The prince gave a more concrete proof of his favour later that year, when he arranged to have the count appointed as general of artillery.[33] He did him even more honour by sending him to Cleves as his representative at the christening of the first child of his sister Louise Henriette in 1648. William Frederick proudly recorded that he had been assigned the place of honour in the church and at table, as the prince's envoy. Even Louise's husband, the elector of Brandenburg, had been willing to treat the count as a prince in Cleves, and 'gave me precedence and his right hand everywhere we went'.[34]

Naturally, after 1647 the private nickname 'the Boss' in William Frederick's diaries passed smoothly from Frederick Henry to William II. Nevertheless, there were considerable differences between the two princes. Frederick Henry had been twenty-nine years older than William Frederick, while William II was thirteen years his junior. Moreover, Frederick Henry was not just of higher rank than the count of Nassau, he had also amassed much more experience and authority as a soldier and statesman. The same could certainly not be said of the 21-year-old William II. Even so, these differences in age and experience do not appear to have influenced William Frederick's judgement of how he ought to refer to his patron in his diaries. By calling Frederick Henry's successor 'the Boss', the count sought to emphasise the continuity and exclusiveness in his relationship to the Oranges.

This usage raises the question of how early modern family relationships related to forms of clientage. Some scholars have argued that kinship must be distinguished from patronage because of its more limited freedom of choice. Others have dismissed such a rigid demarcation as anachronistic and have pointed out that kinsmen were often acknowledged and treated as clients.[35] Simon Groenveld and Luuc Kooijmans have shown that in the Dutch Republic the *paterfamilias* had indeed in practice all the qualities of the classic patron.[36] It could also be argued that the seventeenth-century custom of borrowing the terminology of patronage from that of kinship, and vice versa, indicates that the distinction between families and clienteles was vague and not always regarded as very relevant.[37]

Yet the existence of a logical link between early modern patronage and kinship does not mean that the two relationships were wholly identical. They differed, even in the seventeenth-century context, because the obligation of solidarity and the degree of inequality in the family were fixed by birth. Kinship, that is, was less negotiable – except in case of marriage arrangements. It was therefore much more complicated to switch patrons within family networks. In early modern contexts, kinship could mask patronage, but each had its own origin and its own different consequences. Sharon Kettering has characterised this similarity and connection by arguing that clienteles in a sense 'functioned as artificial kinship groups', and that patron-client relationships thereby created 'a family-like feeling of obligation and commitment'.[38] Perhaps we could also turn that definition on its head, and define family relations among the high nobility as a distinct form of clientage.

A new policy?

The death of Frederick Henry thus transformed William Frederick's position at the Orange court from doubtful client to recognised court favourite, but did not affect the terminology he used to define his relationship with his patron. Moreover, it appears that William Frederick's analyses of his progress were rather one-sided, since his long-hoped-for entrée to the prince's inner circle was in fact not an isolated or incidental phenomenon. In 1647–50 the Orange clientele network as a whole underwent a reorganisation that caused quite a stir. A reconstruction of the events of these years can therefore not only help to clarify the sudden changes in the count of Nassau-Dietz's role, but also reveal the social tensions that they eventually provoked.

The situation at the Orange court in 1647 resembled that at the court of Nassau-Dietz in 1640. Like William Frederick, William II inherited two patronage networks from his predecessor. In the first place he stood at the head of the court personnel and the officials of his domain lands, whose service formally ended on the death of Frederick Henry. Besides this private network there was an extensive second clientele of public office-holders, which the late prince had built up in the provinces. William Frederick's own example in 1640 revealed that at that time the count had simply taken over the personnel of his late brother, and had tried as far as possible to continue his brother's contacts with the Friesian regents. The tendency to continue existing clienteles also had precedents in William II's predecessors, William of Orange, Maurice and Frederick Henry.[39]

Remarkably, however, William II on his accession appeared unwilling to follow the precedent of William Frederick and his own predecessors. 'His Highness wishes to make great changes in his court', so William Frederick summarised William's intentions in June 1648.[40] Some historians have explained this inclination toward personal replacements from the diverging views on international policy between father and son.[41] Unlike Frederick Henry, William II felt that the United Provinces ought to become more deeply involved in the English Civil War, which his royal in-laws were on the point of losing. The young prince was also very distrustful of his father's policy of peace with Spain, fearing that after nearly eighty years of war peace would bring about radical political realignments in the Republic, and perhaps lead to a degradation of the military prestige of the House of Orange. He found evidence for this dismal prospect in the growing eagerness of the province of Holland to restrict the future influence of the stadholder. This policy, clearly visible even in the last years of Frederick Henry, if combined with peace, would block William II's ambition to emulate his illustrious predecessors. 'He has an inordinate passion to win glory by feats of arms', an informant tellingly reported to the French cardinal Mazarin in June 1647.[42]

A possible peace with Spain and the consequent reduction in troops were more than just a personal threat to the prince. Like others in the Republic, he also saw them as a real danger to the future of the Dutch state. William distrusted the promises of the arch-enemy Spain, and allowed his scepticism to be inflamed by French diplomats. Opponents of peace frequently represented the war against the Catholic monarch as the origin and *raison d'être* of the Protestant Dutch Republic, since the foundation stone of the state, the Union of Utrecht, had been intended as a defensive alliance against the Spanish crown.[43] In William's eyes Frederick Henry's close advisers and peacemakers bore the chief blame for that dangerous political line. The new patron therefore felt that it was time for a drastic clear-out of the princely clientele.

Besides, William Frederick's diaries suggest that behind these policy differences between father and son lay a classic conflict of generations. In his later years Frederick Henry had been reluctant to let power slip from his hands, or to initiate his successor into his future duties. William II told William Frederick frankly of his 'jealousy of His Highness', because his father 'always wanted him to leave the room when Their High Mightinesses [the States-General] entered'.[44] There were others who had been critical and worried by Frederick Henry's stubborn refusal to train his son for his future role. Lieuwe van Aitzema related that the old prince was repeatedly urged to 'leave the command of the army to prince William, but neither the princess nor the prince was very inclined to do so'.[45] And so it was that in March 1647 William II took up his tasks as stadholder and captain-general, to his own frustration, with so little experience. The States of Holland even discussed 'whether on this occasion a report ought not to be made to His Highness prince William on the whole state of the country, and chiefly of this province and the finances thereof'.[46]

The relationship between mother and son was similarly troubled. Even in March 1647 Amalia van Solms felt that her son was not yet mature enough to begin an independent career as stadholder. The princess was not very impressed by William's talents, and was convinced that his new political course was damaging for the rather precarious position of the Oranges in the Republic. A reorganisation of Frederick Henry's carefully constructed patronage network was certainly out of the question. Amalia therefore reasoned that she ought to be in control during William's stadholdership. 'She wants to rule with me at any cost', William himself concluded in 1647.[47] But the enforced cooperation between mother and son was not a success. 'Her Highness recommends many things that His Highness cannot do, and then My Lady is vexed, His Highness keeps silent or wants to leave; and then Her Highness blows up', William Frederick recorded.[48] It was even rumoured that the princess intercepted her son's correspondence, and that he was forced to resort to using a cipher.

There were some apparent grounds for Amalia's poor impression of

William's abilities. Cornelis van Aerssen, no friend of the princess, had to admit that the prince was still 'so young' and did not seem very keen 'to do anything, but thought only of his pleasures, hunting, gaming and amours'.[49] William Frederick also noticed that William was to be found mostly in bed or at the gaming table: 'His Highness seldom goes to church, hunts a great deal, sleeps late and plays in the tennis court'. He passed an even more negative verdict in September 1647, describing William as interested only in 'whores, gambling or hunting'.[50] The French ambassador Godefroy d'Estrades wrote at this time that the young prince was 'plunged in pleasures and debauchery'.[51] The pensionary of Holland Jacob Cats visited William in March 1647 and typically reported to the States of Holland that he had found the prince 'sick with a headache and lying in bed, very tired'.[52]

In the older historiography William has often been reproached with his alleged undisciplined and flighty temperament. His biographer J. Eysten described him as 'ardent and energetic, frivolous and passionate', while S.I. van Nooten thought that the young prince sought out 'unbecoming amusements'. Some scholars were willing to find extenuating circumstances: most of William's faults of character could be blamed on his upbringing as an only son in a 'frivolous' milieu of 'luxury and excess', 'often coarse pleasures and trivial diversions'.[53]

Some caution may be appropriate in applying these pseudo-Freudian insights. One may even wonder if William has not led his contemporaries and later historians up the garden path. At any rate, William Frederick's diary for 1647–48 suggests that the picture of the spoiled son permanently at logger-heads with his mother ought to be toned down. One remarkable example is the count's analysis of the alleged quarrels between mother and son in his diary for 5 August 1647. 'They behave as if they are not willing to hear anyone out, and when they have heard him they discuss it with each other, and together fall on the third party.'[54] It was not just family quarrels that might sometimes be staged for tactical reasons; William's visits to brothels were not always what they seemed either. In the summer of 1648 the prince confided to William Frederick that he often visited his secretary Johan Heilersieg at night, 'in whose house he sets about writing, and his people think that he is in the whorehouse, and so he spends whole nights writing'. William even concealed the identity of these secret corre-spondents: 'he often wrote to that man in Dordrecht and to people in Zeeland', according to William Frederick. These observations not only shed a different light on the caricature of the frivolous and hot-headed prince, but also illuminate the methods William II apparently used to implement his new patronage policy. The prince was firmly convinced that, under cover of these diversionary tactics, he could quietly construct a new following and thereby 'get the provinces in his hands' in a short time.[55]

Reorganisation of the court

William's plans 'to make great changes in his court' after Frederick Henry's death suggest in the first place a replacement of the top men in his household. It was relatively easy to replace officials in this private network, since their employment ceased on the death of their employer. Indeed, only a day after his father died, William promptly appointed a new secretary, Johan Heilersieg, a confidant of his youth.[56] Constantijn Huygens did not lose his position, but henceforth he was employed chiefly on private and foreign missions. His correspondence for this period clearly reflects the sinking credit of the former power broker at court.[57]

Huygens was not the only victim of the change at the top in 1647. In October of that year William appointed Frederick Herman Schomberg as first chamberlain, while at the same time he attempted to replace the chief clerk of the domain council, Laurens Buysero. William Frederick reported that William wanted to dismiss him and 'take Ruyl of Haarlem in his place'.[58] In fact, several offers were made to this Albert Ruyl, pensionary of the city of Haarlem. On 11 November 1647 he informed the Haarlem *vroedschap* that 'His Highness the prince of Orange had offered him certain honourable and very profitable terms depending on the disposition of His aforesaid Highness'. The regents of the town were reluctant to let their pensionary go, and immediately raised his salary to 1,000 guilders. Ruyl himself may not have been keen to leave either. When the prince repeated his offer in July 1648, Ruyl was asked to 'excuse himself from the same with all politeness'.[59]

The failed attempt to replace Buysero was not exceptional. On the contrary, in other cases too William was obliged to continue existing officials in their posts. The positions of several prominent members of the domain council, among them Arnould van Beaumont, Nicolaas Verbolt, David de Wilhem and Cornelis Pauw were renewed in November 1647.[60] In the lower ranks of the court personnel changes were equally rare. Perhaps Amalia, who sheltered many loyal old retainers under her wing, managed in practice to prevent her son making a clean sweep of their careers. It is not unthinkable that the young prince himself realised in the end that a true reorganisation of the court would be too risky. One sign of this may be found in his cautious treatment of such prominent courtiers as Huygens. Though Huygens was sidelined, he was kept sweet with presents, and his salary was raised.[61] Finally, it is possible that the prime target of William's reorganisation was not his court clientele, but Frederick Henry's former network in the administrative bodies of the towns and provinces. If so, the choice of a new man to fill the politically crucial post of secretary was indeed William's most urgent concern at court.

A core clientele

That impression is confirmed by the prince's conduct outside the court sphere. In the years 1647–50 William started an ambitious policy to purge Orange's public clientele, causing a political earthquake in the Republic. Hardly surprising, these political replacements mostly concerned men who had supported the peace policy in previous years and who were now thwarting William's military ambitions. It was not a simple matter, however, to remove these former trusted men from office, as the stadholder's rights of appointment were limited in most towns and provinces. It had taken Frederick Henry years to build up these networks of local 'creatures'. It seems that William therefore began by forming a sort of core clientele in The Hague. It was to consist of advisers who had had few ties to the peacemakers in Frederick Henry's network, but who possessed some expertise. Obviously, William Frederick fitted this job description well. In a sense, therefore, his reputation as an outsider recommended him to William II. The count's successes as a client from 1647 thus kept pace with the new political course that the prince had set.

Johan Heilersieg, a key man as the prince's new secretary, was another former outsider who enjoyed William's confidence. The influential clerk of the States-General, Cornelis Musch, was also approached by the prince. Although he had been for years one of the 'creatures' of Frederick Henry as well, the clerk had a rather flexible political agenda and kept up a wide network of political clients on his own, which may have been reason enough for William II to approach him.[62] In October 1648 the prince rather unexpectedly appointed Musch as a chamber councillor, with the official task of putting his finances in order.[63] William also earmarked confidential posts for his half-brother Frederick of Nassau-Zuylestein and Johan Polyander, lord of Heenvliet, who were employed on several missions and appointments of magistrates from 1647.[64] Lastly, Cornelis van Aerssen van Sommelsdijk was given a more leading role in the core clientele. William Frederick's diary indicates that Aerssen had been on good terms with William II even before 1647. The Holland nobleman Philips Jacob van Boetzelaer opined in November 1648 that 'Musch is not alone in the driving seat, but Sommelsdijk sits alongside him'.[65]

Musch, Heenvliet and Van Aerssen had different reasons for joining William's new clientele. Undoubtedly they all hoped to gain incomes and political influence, but Musch probably also acted out of resentment against some of the Holland regents, who had repeatedly exposed his corrupt practices in the States-General. Moreover, many trustees of William at court kept military positions and were irritated by Holland's initiatives to reduce the army. Although the cut in the number of troops had been resolved on a few years earlier, in court circles it was still regarded as a threat to the safety of the Dutch Republic as well as an insult to them. Indignation at the dismissal of troops grew stronger among the war party as the plans took on more definite shape.[66]

It might also be argued that for men like Musch there was no obvious alternative. He and other high civil servants, by definition, needed a patron in The Hague to maintain their position. The same was true of Heenvliet, Heilersieg and to a lesser extent Van Aerssen. The office-holder books of the Nassau domains reveal how dependent these families had grown on the incomes and patronage that the House of Orange offered them. Several of Cornelis van Aerssen's relatives held posts in the barony of Breda, while he himself owed his appointment as a colonel of cavalry to the prince.[67] At Vianden in Luxemburg, a relative of Johan Heilersieg was appointed in 1648; from 1650 this Frans Heilersieg served as bailiff in the Westland. The Orange domain lands were a source of power and income for Heenvliet and his friends as well.[68] It is striking that William II recruited his core clientele largely from men who would barely have had a power base of their own without his protection. Clients who had so much to lose might well be much more willing to transfer their loyalties to the new regime and adjust to the new political set-up.

Selection criteria

With the help of this core clientele, from 1647 William II set about dismantling his father's network in several provinces and installing his own. Some of the letters that the prince received in this period give us an insight into the selection criteria he adopted. Naturally, William bestowed special favours on regents who had been sceptical about the Münster peace settlement and who had not opposed his war policy.[69] Ideally, such a political profile would be matched by other social characteristics. Like William Frederick, the prince generally preferred candidates with 'good means' – that is, with ample financial resources. His counsellor Johan Dedel advised him in 1650 against nominating the Dordrecht regent Antony de Rou, 'who is a smith, said to be very dirty and not respectable'.[70] Forebears who had been on the 'wrong' side could also damage a candidate's chances. Cornelis Musch advised the prince to refuse Leendert Sypestein because 'his nearest relative … was put to death by the sword here in The Hague about fifty years ago, on the occasion of a plot by him to betray the town and island of Tholen, a design to be executed with Spanish assistance'.[71]

In his confessional preferences William II, like William Frederick, was formally bound by the requirement for office-holders to belong to the Reformed Church. Frederick Henry, however, had applied this test rather flexibly. To broaden his political base and to calm political-religious passions, such as those over the Arminian controversies in 1618, he had always kept a balance between orthodox and more 'libertine' Calvinists. On a few occasions he had even promoted Catho-lics to the magisterial benches.[72] William II does not appear to have shared his father's preference for a broad-based clientele, and clearly intended to seek closer links with the orthodox Reformed community. This group generally shared William's scepticism about peace with Catholic Spain and reduction of the army, and so became the prince's natural allies.

Some within that Calvinist circle therefore saw William's policy as a revival of the old quarrel between Arminians and Contra-Remonstrants, which had split the political landscape of the Republic during the Twelve Years' Truce (1609–1621). The court preacher Johan Goethals was one of these, and welcomed the tightening of the ties that bound Orange to the orthodox. In a conversation with William Frederick, Goethals formulated these shared fortunes in negative terms, stigmatising the prince's opponents as 'Arminians, who were therefore enemies of religion and of the fatherland'.[73] The count agreed with this interpretation: 'His Highness does not like Arminians, and in time he will root them out and bring them down', he concluded in May 1647.[74] Many Reformed preachers were delighted when, immediately after his accession, William issued instructions to expel Catholic priests from the Orange domain lands and to strip the churches there of any remaining Catholic symbols.[75]

But that did not mean that Calvinist doctrine and the prince's political agenda were as closely intertwined as Goethals wished to believe. There was indeed an overlap between the more orthodox in the Reformed Church and the advocates of continuing the Spanish war under Orange's leadership.[76] From William's own point of view, on the other hand, his decision to associate himself with the Calvinist community was above all a response to the political problems of the time. The prince himself showed little sign of any religious interests, and none at all of puritanical opinions. His aversion to the so-called 'Arminians' was probably not inspired by confessional preferences, but by their association in his mind with the political views of several of the Holland regents. William's personal political agenda was not linked to a 'libertine' or orthodox interpreta-tion of Calvinist doctrine.

This is borne out by William's actual appointments. Unlike William Frederick, the prince certainly did select for urban magistracies potential clients who had little or no connection with the Reformed Church. In 1647 he appointed the former Mennonite Hendrik Willemsz Nobel in Rotterdam, and in 1650 his choice fell on Christian Prins, who came from a family with pronounced Arminian sympathies.[77] Closer inspection reveals that William's religious patronage policies in his domain lands were equally ambiguous. There was some commotion in the council of 's Gravenzande in 1649 because 'the first alderman on His Highness's list was of the Romish religion'.[78] A Calvinist background, in short, was not an absolute precondition for administrative office.

It was not a man's religious allegiances as such, but their potential implications for his politics, that guided William in deciding when confessional backgrounds should be a bar to public office. This meant that the clientele he built up from 1647 was in the end more diverse in its religious allegiances than that of William Frederick in Friesland.

Finally, the prince attached less weight to political credit than his second cousin, the count. In the towns of Friesland William Frederick generally sought contact with regents who already had local clienteles of their own. By relying on these local heavyweights he hoped to give his nascent patronage network more stability. William II's advisers, on the other hand, reasoned in precisely the opposite sense. The Zeeland regent Hendrick Thibaut advised the prince to choose candidates 'who had no support, power or authority'.[79] It would be more effective to appoint such men, because they could only rise to office through 'Your Highness's singular favour', and their loyalty and dependence would be guaranteed. Cornelis Musch recommended François Granier in Middelburg for the same reason: 'he was born in Ghent, and not attached to anyone in the government'.[80] In Friesland William Frederick had always been reluctant to promote such *homines novi*. The career of William II would indeed expose the tensions that could result from such an unorthodox patronage policy.

Old and new networks

Holland and Zeeland

The success of the new course that William II intended to steer would depend above all on the powers of appointment he had accumulated as stadholder of six provinces. They were not equally extensive in all of them, and in some there was not even an instruction that explicitly defined the stadholder's rights.[81] The habits and privileges that had grown up over time in the localities meant that appointment procedures differed from place to place. If he was to form a new personal clientele, therefore, William II needed to be well informed about these local arrangements. His archives contain several government regulations in which, significantly, the stadholder underlined in pencil the passages that described the system of appointment to offices.[82]

William's powers were greatest in the western provinces of Holland and Zeeland. In this urbanised region the stadholder had the right to appoint members of the magistracy each year in most of the towns. Still, according to Frederick Henry, the possibilities for patronage in Holland were limited in practice. The prince had once pessimistically claimed to William Frederick that 'there was nothing to be done with Holland', because of the large number of regents, whose continual comings and goings in the administrative colleges made it difficult for him to get a grip on them.[83] What's more, unlike the practice in Friesland, the magistrates in each of the Holland towns were appointed at different times of the year, and the number of members that the stadholder could appoint also varied from town to town. In eight of the ten largest towns William was allowed to choose the new burgomasters and aldermen from a duplicate list submitted to him; but in Amsterdam and Leiden he could choose only the aldermen. In the eight smaller towns the number of offices at his disposal also varied.[84]

Finally, an old privilege that dated from Habsburg times required the stadholder to act in conjunction with the Court of Holland when choosing the magistrates. In practice the Court seems to have given advice, which the stadholder generally followed. In the prince's absence the Court even took on responsibility for the whole appointment procedure.[85] On 20 October 1649 Cornelis Musch therefore warned William II to cut short his stay in Dieren, since the elections in Dordrecht were imminent: 'may it please Your Highness to consider that the nomination of the men of the Eight will undoubtedly be made on Sunday the 24th of this month after noon, here in The Hague'.[86] Apparently the prince could not always manage to be in the province in time. In Haarlem, for example, in 1647, 1648 and 1649 both burgomasters and aldermen were appointed by the president and counsellors of the Court of Holland 'in the absence of His Highness'.[87]

The prince's absence could not be blamed on lack of interest. The Holland towns had a large majority in the provincial States, where the supporters of a peace policy had the upper hand. The prince told his second cousin that he too drew up summary tables, as William Frederick did in Friesland, to keep himself up to date on the shifting balance of power in the towns. 'He said he had a list of all the *vroedschappen* in the Holland towns, marked A, B, C. A was against him, B was in between, C was for him. The As were in the majority, the Bs quite a few and the Cs the fewest. He will do his best to help his men come to the top.' Because the prince wished to keep his plans for political change secret, he and Heilersieg also wrote 'to many people in his own hand and in cipher'.[88] The need for confidentiality also explained why William preferred to use private messengers rather than the regular postal service. Incoming letters were burned after they had been read, to prevent leaks.[89] These precautions have made it almost impossible to reconstruct William's networks of correspondents and potential brokers today.

The registers of magistrates in the southern quarter of Holland, however, do reveal how often the stadholder declined to take the advice of the Court of Holland.[90] In twenty two years as stadholder Frederick Henry had done so only twenty seven times.[91] In the three years of his stadholdership, on the other hand, William turned down the Court's advice on nine occasions, especially in the turbulent year 1650.[92] It seems that the prince also made attempts to influence the Court itself, by intervening in vacancies in its membership and secretly recruiting its president Johan Dedel as one of his informants. In 1650 Cornelis Musch mentioned that in the forthcoming elections in Dordrecht Dedel would 'direct and guide matters in such a way that only wolf cubs are thrown into the nest'.[93] This cryptic phrase undoubtedly alluded to the nomination or election of favourable candidates in the city. Dedel himself hinted that the stadholder had instructed him 'to keep an eye on the renewal of the men on the council of Eight'. In his own words, he was to try to guide the preferences of the other councillors in the Court, naturally after 'communication' with Musch.[94]

At the same time William disposed of other resources of patronage. William Frederick was told that the prince had 'four times obliged' the pensionary of Hoorn, Nanning Keyser, 'with a company of foot and a ship's captaincy and two other benefits, so that he hopes to win Keyser over'. He even held out the prospect of a vice-admiralty for the pensionary.[95] The office of *drost* (sheriff) of Muiden, vacant since the death of the poet and historian Pieter C. Hooft, was made to serve William's Amsterdam patronage policy. The stadholder had the right to choose the new *drost* from a list of three candidates submitted by the States of Holland. The Rotterdammer Johan van der Meyden soon dropped out, leaving the choice between the respective nominees of Adriaan Pauw and Andries Bicker. Because the former appeared to be losing influence in Amsterdam, William Frederick recommended the prince to nominate the latter's candidate: 'I advised him to win Bicker over'. This Andries Bicker had until then been among the proponents of a reduction in the army, and was also known as the leader of the governing 'Bicker League' in the city. In 1649 the prince did indeed appoint Andries's son Gerard as *drost* of Muiden.[96] Apparently the stadholder hoped that the favour of this office would persuade his old adversary to change his political line.

If building up a clientele of his own in Holland was a rather laborious process, William's chances looked brighter in Zeeland, in part because the stadholder was entitled to appoint the burgomasters and aldermen of Middelburg, Zierikzee and Tholen each year. More important, the towns of Flushing and Veere were the personal property of the Oranges, as parts of the marquisate of Veere, which had belonged to them since the time of William of Orange. In that sense William II's appointment of their magistrates could be seen as a case of 'private' patronage. All in all, of the six towns that had a vote in the States of Zeeland, it was in Goes alone that William had no right to appoint either as stadholder or as prince. Finally, the dignity of First Noble, which he bore as prince of Orange, made it a relatively simple matter for William to assert his dominance in the States.[97]

The young stadholder therefore had good reason to assume that he would soon have things his own way in Zeeland. The first step was to remove Johan de Knuyt, who had represented Frederick Henry as First Noble and was also Zeeland's delegate to the peace conference in Münster. His hold on these top positions was now seriously threatened. In William's eyes the regent stood for all the unreliable advisers who had induced Frederick Henry to seek peace. As early as 1646 William Frederick had confided to his diary that 'prince William blamed Knuyt and was not well pleased with him'. Two years later the prince 'abused him as a scoundrel and a traitor': Knuyt's dismissal appeared to be only a matter of time.[98] Remarkably enough, in 1647–50, Frederick Henry's former provincial power broker managed to retain his offices, probably thanks to the support of Amalia.[99] In practice, however, William II stripped him of all influence, systematically rejecting his recommendations and deliberately keeping his friends out of office.[100] Cornelis Musch rejoiced at De Knuyt's public humiliation and did not conceal his delight. Joachim Andreae reported to William Frederick how 'the clerk said to Knuyt in my presence that he was like a man who had fallen through the ice, and had got his arms above the ice, struggling to lift himself out of the ice again'.[101]

In the meantime William had found a new broker in Zeeland. It is not quite clear when he first made contact with the Middelburg regent Hendrik Thibaut, but it was probably Thibaut himself who offered his services to the prince.[102] In any case, from 1648 he was giving William advice on whom to appoint, where and when. As the colleges were thus purged of De Knuyt's 'wily old birds', the new broker proceeded to recommend his friends to the prince, promising him that by appointing them he would soon make himself 'absolute master' in Zeeland.[103] This prospect was not unrealistic. In 1649 William Frederick for one felt that his second cousin had 'Middelburg, Thibaut and the whole of Zeeland, and can do what he likes there, and Thibaut must depend absolutely on His Highness'.[104] The prince even rubbed salt in De Knuyt's wounds by publicly speaking of Thibaut as 'the first man in Zeeland'.[105]

Gelderland, Utrecht, Overijssel and Groningen

In the eastern provinces of the Dutch Republic William II's patronage tactics were bound to differ from those he employed in the urbanised west. In most 'eastern' towns the magistrates were chosen by the so-called *gemeente*, which was supposed to represent the local population.[106] Moreover, the local nobility had long wielded great influence in these more rural provinces. William's best hope of attaching these noblemen to himself was to use his powers as captain-general to bestow military commissions on them. There are indications, however, that William felt less need to replace his father's contacts among the provincial nobility. Many nobles were alarmed by the prospect of a reduction in the army and therefore tended to support William's war ambitions. Moreover, both the urban and the noble elites in the eastern provinces distrusted the growing dominance of Holland in the Generality. In the years 1647–50 William II could usually count on their support in the States-General.

In the province of Gelderland, William therefore continued to stay on good terms with the most powerful nobles by rewarding them with commissions in the army. Alexander van der Capellen was one of them and presented himself to the prince in October 1650, with a 'humble petition for one of my three sons ... for a cornet's place', promising his 'loyal and zealous services'.[107] Cornelis Musch counted Alexander and his brother Hendrik van der Capellen among 'the good party' in the States-General. Joachim Andreae too suspected in 1650 that with Alexander in the assembly 'more manly language will be used in that quarter, to all appearances'.[108] Unsurprisingly Alexander was one of the members of William's delegation to the towns of Holland in June of that year.[109]

More complicated for the prince were matters in Gelderland's biggest town, Nijmegen. In this garrison city Holland's peace policy could count on much sympathy, and the local magistrates had already put forward a plan to abolish the stadholder's rights of appointment in their town after peace was made, on the grounds that they only belonged to him in wartime. After an unsuccessful first attempt to mediate made by Frederick of Nassau-Zuylestein, Musch urged the prince to take a tougher line.[110] In 1649 William, accompanied by 'most of the high officers and no fewer than ninety wagons', set off for Nijmegen, where he appointed his favourite candidates as burgomasters, simply ignoring the official nominations.[111]

There was no need for such tactics of intimidation in Utrecht, where the stadholder's prerogatives were limited anyway. In the city itself he could only appoint magistrates if he was present in person, whereas in the other towns the States of Utrecht decided and then 'presented or sent their choices for approval'.[112] It seems that William II never criticised the States' choices, for while he was stadholder there were hardly any changes in the city's bodies, and the political elite in the rest of the province also remained intact.[113] Johan van Reede van Renswoude, the former confidant and provincial broker of Frederick Henry, was able to continue his advisory role with William's approval after 1647. Van Reede had several talks with William about administrative appointments in the city, and remarkably frequent discussions with him whenever he sat in the States-General.[114]

In Overijssel too William invested above all in his contacts with the political heavyweights in the nobility. In 1649 he appointed the 6-year-old son of the influential Boldewijn Mulert as a cornet, and admitted members of Mulert's family to his household.[115] Rutger and Anthony van Haersolte emulated Renswoude in Utrecht, by making the transition from Frederick Henry's clientele to William's. Rutger became treasurer of the Orange domains in Lingen, while Anthony, who had been a page at court until 1647, made a career as an army officer. In 1649 Anthony confidently told Huygens that he was eager to know 'His Highness's intention ... so that I shall not make a false move' in politics.[116] Finally in Groningen political conditions had long been unstable, and the stadholder's opportunities for patronage were few. There is no sign that the prince made any attempt to change this, and the prince's efforts to mediate between the city and the Ommelanden nobles in 1648 do not reveal an active policy of building up a clientele in Groningen.[117]

Public and private circuits

A comparison between William II's patronage strategies and those of William Frederick in Friesland sheds some revealing light on the use and limits of clientage in the republican body politic and shows some remarkable differences between the two men. The most striking contrast was perhaps the greater personal connection between Orange's private and public patronage circuits. While William Frederick had never recruited his court clientele from the provinces where he served as stadholder, and had thus kept his two networks separate, the prince's republican and princely clienteles were more likely to overlap. For instance, the despised Johan de Knuyt was a member of the Orange Domain Council as well as Zeeland's delegate to the States-General. His colleague on the Domain Council Cornelis Pauw, the son of a burgomaster of Amsterdam, had had an earlier career as the States-General's envoy. Rutger van Haersolte combined membership of the Overijssel States with a post as treasurer of several Nassau domains. Such high urban officials as the pensionary of Haarlem (Albert Ruyl) and the clerk of the States-General (Cornelis Musch) were offered posts at court as well.[118]

This linkage did not originate in William's patronage policy, but went back to Frederick Henry. As De Knuyt's case indicates, several of these clients had already combined 'public' and 'private' service before 1647. In that respect William II made changes in the composition of his father's clientele but not in Frederick Henry's strategies of patronage: he too deployed his private patronage resources to reinforce his republican clientele. The same strategy was later pursued more often and more systematically by William III and his eighteenth-century successors.[119] As a result, the government of the republican state was more and more brought into the private sphere of the princely court. Even so, the events of 1647–50 reveal that the ambition to connect 'public' and 'private' administrations in the Republic could easily destabilise clienteles when the patron lacked insight and tact.

Reactions

William II did not foresee the tensions that his rearrangements would cause. On the contrary, in the summer of 1648 he had no doubt that he was making progress, and was confident that he had brought six of the Holland towns and the nobles into his direct sphere of influence. William Frederick heard that Zeeland too was 'wholly in the prince's hands', and that things were going 'well' or 'passably' in the eastern provinces. 'In Gelderland he has ... more than half or almost the whole province', the Friesian stadholder recorded.[120] But William Frederick himself was less optimistic and suspected that 'it will turn out badly for him, for he has no credit or respect'.[121] This analysis was shared by Alexander van der Capellen, who wrote to his brother Hendrik in March 1647 that 'respect for the young upcoming prince is too weak'.[122]

Indeed, William's efforts to build up his patronage were not going as well as the patron himself assumed. At court the rumours of his plans for reorganisation had been very badly received. Many courtiers regarded a possible dismissal as a personal slight after years of loyalty to the family, and even when it appeared that the prince would simply continue most of his courtiers in their employment, the suspicion aroused would not die down. William's financial mismanagement caused further friction. The equerry Anthony des Champs voiced the general discontent in November 1648, when he expressed the hope that 'His Highness would put his household affairs in order, for he is ruining himself, and nobody is being paid'.[123] William Frederick also found it remarkable 'how His Highness pays no attention to his house'.[124] The count noticed that many of the prince's personnel felt that they were not appreciated by their new patron. The first chamberlain Schomberg and his family even felt insulted by the prince's dishonourable treatment. On 2 June 1648 William Frederick recorded a visit to Mrs Schomberg, 'who told me that His Highness had never spoken to her'. Her husband found such social neglect unacceptable. A year later Amalia remarked that 'Schomberg too complains of His Highness and wants to leave'.[125] The princess was constantly irritated by her son's lack of social skills and sense of responsibility. 'He did not give an audience and fell short of his obligations to himself and the officers and all his dependants', she told William Frederick.[126]

In a sense these complaints were symptomatic of William's conduct in the republican sphere. Cornelis van Aerssen told William Frederick in November 1648 that 'His Highness was not affable and did not caress people enough, which they took very badly'. William of Nassau-Odijk also thought it was unreasonable of the prince to have kept someone as important as the chairman of the States-General waiting several days for an audience.[127] Clients who had been dismissed found it even harder to conceal their indignation. Cornelis van Beveren of Dordrecht, who claimed 'always to have been His late Highness's servant on all occasions', was shocked to find that the new patron requited his years of service with ingratitude and opposition.[128] His Zeeland colleague Johan de Knuyt undoubtedly had far more to lose by William's purge, and on 19 October 1650 he wrote to the prince reminding him of all the services he had performed for the House of Orange 'during the time of around 30 or 40 years'. De Knuyt slyly remarked that, just before his death, Frederick Henry had entrusted him with some letters 'of weight and consideration'; he did not rule out the possibility that he might be compelled to reveal this sensitive correspondence, which would be seriously embarrassing for the Orange family.[129]

De Knuyt's attempted blackmail luridly revealed the despair felt by many clients who had been shown the door. But even the new favourites were worried, in their case by the precarious stability of the prince's clientele. Cornelis van Aerssen, for one, doubted that the prince's tactics of intimidation in Nijmegen would be effective.[130] William Frederick was another who feared the consequences of William's over-hasty reorganisation and misplaced self-confidence. As long as the loyalty of new clients had not been put to the test, the count felt that caution was still required in dealing with the old ones. In the winter of 1649 William Frederick thought that things were going from bad to worse and doubted that William's attentions to Bicker, Ruyl or Keyser would earn him their political loyalty. The Friesian stadholder believed that effective management of one's relations demanded more than handing out posts and exchanging letters in cipher: 'he must see them more often, speak to them and eat with them and caress them, that is how it should be'. Regular attendance at church was also required, 'which the commonalty has very much in view'.[131] It was in fact the self-image that William Frederick himself tried to project as patron, which he found lacking in his own Boss. To his own disappointment, William Frederick also had to admit that he had little influence on his patron's habits.

The dilemmas of the client

William Frederick's reflective comments on William's conduct show that his new status at the Orange court did not inspire him with greater self-confidence. The count knew from experience that relationships at court were always in flux, and he never regarded his restored contacts with Orange as guaranteed. William Frederick therefore acted with extreme caution when he sought to guide or advise 'the Boss'. Very occasionally he tried to strengthen his position as broker by, for example, praising Andries Bicker and submitting vacancies to William.[132] This prudence did not always produce the desired effect. 'His Highness will not follow any advice', he wrote on 4 November 1648, 'and if one tries to tell him anything, he gets angry and says "I shall manage"'.[133] The count of Nassau was also struck by the fact that other prominent men were having more success as brokers; and that he was repeatedly losing in competition with Musch or Thibaut, men whom he did not consider valuable acquisitions for the prince's clientele. At a dinner with Amalia he gave vent to his frustrations: 'I ate there and told Her Highness once again what a lightweight Thibaut was, how he deceived people with oaths, promises and good words, that he was His Highness's greatest enemy, and would betray His Highness'.[134]

The competitive atmosphere that William II's patronage policies generated at court was hard for William Frederick to cope with. Interestingly, in his diary notes he sought mainly external causes for his lack of success, blaming the 'inconstancy' of others for his own failure to get a grip on the situation. 'So one cannot count on the things of this world, especially at court', he concluded, 'one must provide for oneself in this world, take one's chance where it presents itself, and manage it well, for people's humours are changeable'. William Frederick lamented his own bad experiences in terms that echoed the general criticism of courtly morality encountered in many early modern texts.[135] Characteristically, he was particularly convinced that the presence of women made the situation at court less easy to control. At his own court in Leeuwarden, where as patron he had a more stable position, there were hardly any noble ladies, but in the household of the Oranges at The Hague they held several prominent positions. William Frederick therefore thought it was not unlikely that the disorder and uncertainty he experienced at the Orange court could be explained by the presence of women. 'Fickleness' and instability were after all characteristic where women ruled, 'for they are capricious, bizarre and choleric'.[136] William Frederick's analysis of his problems perfectly fitted with more general seventeenth-century assumptions that women were by nature less restrained, more unstable and more unpredictable than men.[137]

Yet at the same time these sexual stereotypes suggest that it was merely William Frederick himself who found it difficult to cope with the constant changes in his social roles, especially that of client. In his capacity as patron he had found clientage a useful tool to guarantee a certain harmony and clearly defined social relationships. But paradoxically enough his experience as a client was that patronage could generate opposite effects as well. At the court of the Oranges clientage practices appeared to bring confusion and competition above all.[138] William Frederick's preoccupation with order and stability therefore repeatedly came back to haunt him in The Hague. As the frustrations he expressed make clear, the count found it tiresome to deal with these conflicting experiences, and wrestled with the consequences of his ever-changing social roles.

The switch between his position as patron in Friesland and client in The Hague caused some other complications as well. As his remarks on Thibaut reveal, William Frederick was regularly irritated by certain social habits in Orange circles, and saw the intrigues of Thibaut or Musch as signs of moral decay. He detected similar symptoms in the frivolous behaviour of Zuylestein, who often sang 'godless ditties' at meals.[139] In short, the moral standards at the prince's court were not those of William Frederick. The count thus became a member of a clientele whose forms of social conduct and religious experience were in many respects very different from his own. As a client he sometimes found it difficult to decide how far he should adjust his own conduct to that of his patron and his surroundings. At any rate he never contemplated the possibility of detaching himself from these undesirable consequences of his client status, for his relationship with Orange was probably too much a part of his own aristocratic identity. William Frederick's conviction that he must be a loyal servant of 'the Boss' rested chiefly on his perception that his forebears had played the same part. His sense of his duty to follow 'in their footsteps' and to marry a princess of Orange, made it impossible for William Frederick to distance himself from his natural patron.

This frame of reference and the dilemmas in which it placed him were perhaps also responsible for William Frederick's failure to be aware of the objections that his own Friesian clients could have raised against him. In themselves, there were many points of resemblance between the problems with which William Frederick struggled as a client, and those of his own 'creatures' in Friesland. They too had to weigh how far they should adjust their religious and social standards to their patron's desires. Yet William Frederick was either unable or unwilling to remark on this possible parallel in his diaries. The count saw himself as a client of Orange, but his identity as a high nobleman was apparently too well-ingrained to allow him to recognise reflections of his own problems in those of other clients. The result was that in his diaries, in which William Frederick recorded his ambivalent feelings, the difference between these two types of clientship is largely suggested by the way in which he structured and made sense of his own experiences.

Notes

1 Cf. *Gloria Parendi*, 17, 213 (Frederick Henry), and 583, 706–7 (William II).
2 Eysten, *Het leven*, 99–100; Groenveld, 'Willem II en de Stuarts', 169–70; Veeze, *De raad van de prinsen*, 69–75.
3 The prince's debts, however, kept pace with his assets. In 1647 they were said to amount to 3,000,000 guilders: Veeze, *De raad van de prinsen*, 9–12 and 69ff. For William Frederick, see the survey in chapter 3.
4 Groenveld, 'Frederik Hendrik', 20–33; Israel, 'Frederick Henry', 10–27, and 'The Holland Towns', 41–69; Poelhekke, *Frederik Hendrik*, inter alia 336–8, 423–7, 507–16.
5 Tiethoff-Spliethoff, 'De hofhouding van Frederik Hendrik', 43–61; Mörke, *'Stadtholder' oder 'Staetholder'*, 183–91.
6 See also Frijhoff, 'Het Haagse hof', 10–17; Israel, 'The Courts', 119–30; Mörke, 'Sovereignty and Authority', 455–80; Schilling, 'The Orange Court', 441–54; Zijlmans, 'Aan het Haagse hof', 30–2. Things were probably different in the army when the prince was on campaign with the field-deputies. Maurice too is known to have invited the regents to dine with him. For these customs cf. Zandvliet, 'Het hof'.

7 Jansen, 'Het stadhouderlijk kwartier', 57–69; Morren, *Het huis Honselaarsdijk*, 11–45; Mörke, 'Stadtholder' oder 'Staetholder', 216–36; Ottenheym, 'Van Bouw-lust soo beseten', 105–25.

8 Van Diepen, 'Een historisch plekje', 66–122; Jansen, 'Het stadhouderlijk kwartier', 57–69; Kossmann, *De boekverkoopers*, 61–122; Ter Meer Derval, 'Namen van de opeenvolgende eigenaars', 123–42; Mensonides, 'De geschiedenis van de huizen', 205–33; Tiethoff-Spliethoff, 'De hofhouding van Frederik Hendrik', 43–61; Wijsenbeek, *Het Lange Voorhout*, 45–62; Zijlmans, 'Aan het Haagse hof', 320–4.

9 Sophia Hedwig had previously urged the same policy on Henry Casimir. For this marriage policy see Kooijmans, *Liefde in opdracht*, inter alia 37–42.

10 Cf. Adamson, 'The Aristocracy', 173–4; Dewald, *Aristocratic Experience*, 72–5.

11 Tresoar, SA, 30, bundle 1 (William Frederick to the Delegated States, 22 July – 1 August 1642, from the army camp). Other examples: Tresoar, SA, 30, bundle 3 (William Frederick to the Delegated States, 6–16 October 1644); KHA, WF, VII, A, 1–15 (letters of Frederick Henry to William Frederick, 1641–5). Cf. chapter 1.

12 UBL, MSS, HUG 37 (William Frederick to Johannes Veltdriel, 5 October 1642, from the army camp).

13 *Gloria Parendi*, 89. See also Groenveld, 'Nassau contra Oranje', 32–3.

14 *Gloria Parendi*, 213.

15 For example in 1645, 'I let H.H. see my letters to the gentlemen, with which he was pleased; wrote in particular to messrs Roorda, Sminia, Veltdriel.' Two years earlier the diary states '[I] often communicated to H.H. letters from Friesland'. *Gloria Parendi*, 5. See also Groenveld, 'Nassau contra Oranje', 33.

16 *Gloria Parendi*, 5 and 70.

17 Ibid., 92, 137 and 177.

18 *Gloria Parendi*, 16.

19 Ibid., 255.

20 Groenveld, 'Nassau contra Oranje', 40.

21 *Gloria Parendi*, 137–8.

22 Ibid., 80–2.

23 Ibid., 234, 257, 260 and 303. For descriptions of his last years and deathbed see Poelhekke, *Frederik Hendrik*, and Kooijmans, *Liefde in opdracht*, 42–60 and 74–105.

24 *Gloria Parendi*, 47.

25 Ibid., 239.

26 Ibid., 36.

27 Ibid., 239 and 246.

28 KHA, WF, VII, A-III (correspondence of William II with William Frederick, 1642–49).

29 *Gloria Parendi*, 218 and 246.

30 Groen, *Archives*, IV, 320–2. See also KHA, WF, VII, C-64 (Joachim Andreae to William Frederick, 8–18 December 1649, from The Hague); *Gloria Parendi*, 407. The deputy Willem van Haren was also recommended to William II in this way: Groen, *Archives*, IV, 350–2.

31 KHA, WF, VII, C-64 (Joachim Andreae to William Frederick, 2 April 1650, from The Hague). On 7 March the same year he wrote: 'Today at about 8 o' clock receiving all the resolutions with the missive from their Lordships the States, I immediately waited on His Highness and read them to the same from beginning to end'.

32 *Gloria Parendi*, 351.

33 NA, Aitzema, 10 (Letter book 5–15 December 1648). Cf. *Gloria Parendi*, 606.

34 *Gloria Parendi*, 529 and 544.

35 Compare analyses in Blok, *The Mafia*, 179–82; Kettering, 'Patronage and Kinship', 408–35; Kooijmans, *Vriendschap*, inter alia 132–48; Greengrass, 'Noble Affinities', 283; Harding, *Anatomy*, 21–31; Reinhard, 'Oligarchische Verflechtung', 49–50; Wolf, 'Kinship, Friendship, and Patron-Client Relations', 167–77.

36 Groenveld, 'C'est le pere'; Kooijmans, *Vriendschap*, 132–48. Cf. Kettering, 'Patronage and Kinship', 409.

37 Cf. Davis, *The Gift*, 56–72; Kettering, *Patrons, Brokers and Clients*, 12–18; Wootton, 'Francis Bacon', 184–204.

38 Kettering, 'Patronage and Kinship', 430–1.

39 Cf. chapter 1.

40 *Gloria Parendi*, 528.

41 Groenveld, 'Willem II en de Stuarts', 158–63; Kernkamp, *Prins Willem II*, 64–118; Kluiver, *De souvereine en independente staat Zeeland*, 227–54; Price, *Holland and the Dutch Republic*, 134–48; Rowen, *The Princes of Orange*, 77–80.

42 Groen, *Archives*, IV, 233.

43 Cf. Price, *Holland and the Dutch Republic*, 248–9; Troost, *William III*, 12–19.

44 *Gloria Parendi*, 532.

45 Aitzema, *Saken van staet en oorlogh*, VI, 236. See also Groenveld, 'Een out ende getrouw dienaer', and idem, 'C'est le pere'; Kernkamp, *Prins Willem II*, 48.

46 ING, Notulen Schot, Tuesday 19 March 1647.

47 Cited in Kooijmans, *Liefde in opdracht*, 104.

48 *Gloria Parendi*, 528 and 697. See also Groen, *Archives*, IV, 234.

49 *Gloria Parendi*, 299.

50 Ibid., 389–90, 433 and 468–9.

51 Groen, *Archives*, IV, 260. See also the reaction of David de Wilhem in Worp, *Briefwisseling*, IV, 431 and 438.

52 ING, Notulen Schot, 28 March 1647.

53 Eysten, *Het leven*, 38–40; Van Nooten, *Prins Willem II*, 99–101; Geyl, *Orange and Stuart*, 42; Kernkamp, *Prins Willem II*, 67–72.

54 *Gloria Parendi*, 417.

55 Ibid., 534.

56 NA, ND 563 (appointment of Johan Heilersieg on 15 March 1647, with a salary of 1,000 guilders). See also Groenveld, 'Een out ende getrouw dienaer', 16–18; Kernkamp, *Prins Willem II*, 65.

57 Huygens was still in a position to mediate in appointments to vacancies in the Orange domain lands, but he was excluded from political appointments in the towns and provinces. Cf. Worp, *Briefwisseling*, IV, xi–xvi; V, vii–x; Groenveld, 'C'est le pere', 70–1, and 'Een out ende getrouw dienaer', 16–18; also Kluiver, 'Brieven'.

58 NA, ND, 563 (appointment of Schomberg (Schönberg), 16 October 1647); *Gloria Parendi*, 528.

59 ADK, Stadsarchief Haarlem, *vroedschap* resolutions, fols 13v–15r (11 November 1647), fol. 49 (6 July 1648); fol. 50v (13 July 1648).

60 NA, ND, 563 (appointments of Beaumont, 4 November 1647, De Wilhem, 4 November 1647, Verbolt, 2 July 1647, Pauw, 4 November 1647).

61 NA, ND (deed of annuity of 1,200 guilders for Huygens, 18 March 1647). Similar payments were made to Charles Lanoij (24 May 1647), David Marlot (21 December 1647) and Quirijn van Strijen (20 March 1648).

62 There is a good survey of Musch's career in Knevel, *Het Haagse bureau*, 123–44. See also Japikse, 'Cornelis Musch'; Wildeman, *Elisabeth Musch*, 3 ff.

63 NA, ND, 563 (order of 7 June 1653 to pay the estate of the late Cornelis Musch 3,000 guilders on the basis of the commission of 22 October 1648).

64 KHA, WII, IV, 5 (William II to the burgomasters of Amsterdam, 5/6 March 1650, with instructions for Heenvliet); VIII, 2 and 156 (William II's notes on missions of Heenvliet and Zuylestein). Also in Krämer, 'Journalen', 452. For Heenvliet see Groenveld, 'Verdicht verleden', 305–6; 't Hart, *Historische beschrijving*, 207–14.

65 *Gloria Parendi*, 592. Van Aerssen's place in the prince's confidence is also evident from *Gloria Parendi*, 386, 563, 586, 589, 599 and 722. Amalia complained repeatedly of Van Aerssen, because he 'gave His Highness such bad advice'.

66 Knevel, *Het Haagse bureau*, 142. Cf. Geyl, *Orange and Stuart*, 55–66.

67 NA, ND, office-holder books of Breda. This was a relative of Cornelis, also called Cornelis van Aerssen.

68 NA, ND, office-holder books of Breda, Westland and Luxembourg.

69 Cf. for example LAD, Oranienbaum, A7b, fols 19r–22r and 47r–48v (Cornelis Musch to William II, 8 and 11 January 1650, from The Hague). See also the examples in Kluiver, 'Brieven'.

70 KHA, WII, XI, C-3 (Johan Dedel to William II, 27 October 1650, from The Hague). Cf. Roorda, *Partij en factie*, 40–4; Van Deursen, *Een dorp in de polder*, 164 ff.; Price, *Holland and the Dutch Republic*, 49–51.

71 LAD, Oranienbaum, A7b, 116 fols 19r–22r (Cornelis Musch to William II, 11 January 1650 from The Hague). The same example in Kluiver, 'Brieven', 54. See also Van der Bijl, *Idee en interest*, 16–21; Kluiver, *De souvereine en independente staat Zeeland*, 118–20.

72 Israel, *The Dutch Republic*, 595–600.

73 *Gloria Parendi*, 720.

74 Ibid., 391 and 479.

75 Israel, *The Dutch Republic*, 600; Knuttel, *Acta*, III, 76. This concerned the domains of Breda and Lingen.

76 See also Geyl, *Orange and Stuart*, 63; Groenveld, *De prins voor Amsterdam*, 93–8. More generally see Van der Bijl, *Idee en interest*, 166–95; Israel, *The Dutch Republic*, 392 and 758–9; Price, *Holland and the Dutch Republic*, 57–69.

77 LAD, Oranienbaum, A7b, 90 fol. 275r.; Worp, *Briefwisseling*, IV, 438. Nobel was known as a Mennonite, but after 1618 he seems to have attended the Reformed church. See also Engelbrecht, *De vroedschap*, 94–6; Bijlsma, *Rotterdams welvaren*, 183–4.

78 NA, ND (minutes of the Domain Council, 27 and 28 July 1649).

79 Kluiver, 'Brieven', 53.

80 LAD, Oranienbaum, A7b, 116, fols 19r–22r (Cornelis Musch to William II, 11 January 1650, from The Hague).

81 Fruin and Colenbrander, *Staatsinstellingen*, 221–2. Cf. KHA, WII, VI, 25 to 32. This includes the commissions of Gelderland, Holland, Utrecht, Overijssel and Groningen. Only the last two contain a fuller instruction that describes the powers of the stadholder. A Utrecht instruction can be found in UA, SvU, 364-11-188 (instruction for William II, 10 March 1647).

82 LAD, Oranienbaum, A7b, 86 (on Middelburg, Dordrecht, Brielle and the Generality); 90 (on Holland, Dordrecht, Rotterdam and Gorinchem).

83 Cited in Groenveld, *Verlopend getij*, 83.

84 The *vroedschap* decided whose names went on the duplicate list, and recruited its own members by co-option (with the possible exception of Rotterdam and Schiedam). NA, HvH, 5981; LAD, Oranienbaum, A7b, 86 and 90. Cf. also Engelbrecht, *De vroedschap*; Groenveld, *Evidente factiën*; Gabriëls, *De heren als dienaren*.

85 As appears from the registers of magistrates of the Court of Holland; NA, HvH, 5981. See also the remarks in Aitzema, *Saken van staet en oorlogh*, III, 391. Cf. Fockema Andreae, *De Nederlandse staat*, 42–50; Groenveld, *Evidente factiën*, esp. 34; Price, *Holland and the Dutch Republic*, 23–4.

86 LAD, Oranienbaum, A7b, 116 fol. 6r–v. (Cornelis Musch to William II, 20 October 1649, from The Hague). Musch gave the same warning a year later: ibid., fols 36r–38v (Cornelis Musch to William II, 18 October 1650, from The Hague).

87 ADK, Stadsarchief Haarlem, *vroedschap* resolutions, 7 and 11 September 1647, 7 and 11 September 1648, and 7 and 11 September 1649.

88 *Gloria Parendi*, 391 and 534.

89 As appears from William's correspondence with the Zeelander Hendrick Thibaut, which, exceptionally, escaped destruction. See Kluiver, 'Brieven', 41 and 60.

90 NA, HvH, 5981.

91 For this analysis see Groenveld, *Evidente factiën*, 34.

92 NA, HvH, 5981; Aitzema, *Saken van staet en oorlogh*, III, 391.

93 LAD, Oranienbaum, A7b, 90 fol. 162r; 116, fols 36r–38v. (Cornelis Musch to William II, 24

October 1650, from The Hague). See also Kluiver, *De souvereine en independente staat Zeeland*, 247.

94 KHA, WII, XI, C-3 (Johan Dedel to William II, 27 October 1650, from The Hague). Dedel and Musch were well known to each other. 'Councillor Dedel' was a witness at the baptism of Cornelis's daughter Anna Catharina in 1641. Wildeman, *Elisabeth Musch*, 5.

95 *Gloria Parendi*, 397 and 534. Cf. also Keyser's own account in Kernkamp, 'Memorie van Nanning Keyser', 348–9 and 361–5.

96 GAA, Burgemeestersarchief, 113 (Adriaan Pauw to the magistrates of Amsterdam, 18 July 1647, from The Hague); *Gloria Parendi*, 397, 399, 404, 599, 603 and 659; Elias, *De vroedschap*, I, xciv. Adriaan Pauw had also hinted to William's steward that he would be willing to pay 20,000 guilders for the office.

97 Van der Bijl, *Idee en interest*, 16–21; Kluiver, *De souvereine en independente staat Zeeland*, 15–22 and 116–20.

98 *Gloria Parendi*, 268, 386 and 529.

99 NA, ND, 563 (commission for Johan de Knuyt, 4 November 1647); *Gloria Parendi*, 626 and 713–14. Cf. Krämer, 'Journalen', 435. For the close relationship between Amalia and De Knuyt see also KHA, WF, VII, C-203 (Johan de Mauregnault to William Frederick, 5 September 1652, from Middelburg); Groenveld, 'Willem II en de Stuarts', 160–2; Kluiver, 'Brieven', 36–9.

100 Compare William Frederick's reports in *Gloria Parendi*, 526 and 626.

101 KHA, WF, VII, C-64 (Joachim Andreae to William Frederick, 16–26 March 1650, from The Hague).

102 Cf. Kluiver, 'Brieven.'

103 Kluiver, 'Brieven', 68 and 83. Cf. also UA, Des Tombes, 1175 (documents on appointments of William II in Zierikzee, 1647).

104 *Gloria Parendi*, 697. LAD, Oranienbaum, A7b, 122 fol. 161 (unknown to 'My Lord', 12 June? 1648, from Middelburg).

105 Kluiver, 'Brieven', 36.

106 For this distinction cf. also Gabriëls, *De heren als dienaren*.

107 RAG, Van der Capellen, 89 (Alexander van der Capellen to William II, 26 October 1650, from Zutphen). Later Alexander again referred explicitly to the promises that William had made him. NA, Collectie aanwinsten, 1617 (Alexander van der Capellen to Constantijn Huygens, 12–22 September 1653, from Budelhof). See also ibid., his letter to Huygens of 16–26 October 1648, from The Hague, with another request to the prince.

108 Van der Capellen, *Gedenkschriften*, II, 263. LAD, Oranienbaum, A7b, 86, fols 452r–453v; 88, fol. 23. Also KHA, WF, VII, C-64 (Joachim Andreae to William Frederick, 18 April 1650, from The Hague). Musch too was satisfied with Alexander's presence on several committees: LAD Oranienbaum, A7b, 116, fols 24r–30v (Cornelis Musch to William II, 13 February 1650, from The Hague).

109 Compare RAG, Van der Capellen, 89 (Alexander van der Capellen to Hendrik van der Capellen, 13–23 February 1652, from Arnhem). In the times that followed the death of William II in 1650 Van der Capellen denied that he had been an intimate of the prince. Cf. Poelhekke, *Geen blijder maer*, 62–70; Worp, *Briefwisseling*, IV, 462.

110 LAD, Oranienbaum, A7b, 116, fols 3r–4v (Cornelis Musch to William II, 10 June 1648, from The Hague). Krämer, 'Journalen', 452 and 499ff; Kernkamp, *Prins Willem II*, 96–7.

111 NA, Van Aitzema, 10 (letterbook, 8 January 1649). See also Aitzema, *Saken van staet en oorlogh*, III, 294; Jenniskens, *De magistraat*, 23–5.

112 UA, SvU, 364-11-188 (Instruction of William II, 10 March 1647).

113 UA, Stadsarchief, 110 (list of members of the magistracy). Cf. also Worp, *Briefwisseling*, IV, 498–9; Perlot, *De Staten van Utrecht*, 7–19; Faber and De Bruin, 'Tegen de Vrede', 107–34.

114 UA, Hardenbroek, 1529 (Johan van Reede to Adam van Lockhorst, 19 February 1649, from The Hague); UA, SvU, 278 (William II to the States, 27 July 1647, from The Hague); LAD, Oranienbaum, A7b, 88 fols 60r–461r (various visits of Van Reede to the prince); 92, fols 2r–5v (Johan van Reede to William II, 7 September 1650, from Utrecht); 122 fol. 274r–v (Johan van

Reede to William II, 10 February 1650, from Utrecht).

115 NA, ND, 563 ('List of noblemen of H.H. who have been paid up to anno 1650 inclusive'). They include a 'jonkheer Mulert'. Bussemaker, *Geschiedenis van Overijssel*, I, 15. Cf. also Fruin, *Brieven aan De Witt*, I, 41.

116 HCO, Van Haersolte, 336 (Anthony van Haersolte to Constantijn Huygens, 9 October 1649, from Deventer); NA, ND, 563 (list of appointments, 5 July 1647); LAD Oranienbaum, A7b, 115, fols 10r–11r (Rutger van Haersolte to William II, 8–18 October 1650, from Lingen). For the role of the Van Haersoltes in Overijssel see Streng, *Stemme in staat*, 342–4, and *NNBW*, VI, 674.

117 LAD, Oranienbaum, A7b, 106, fols 8r–9r (letters and notes of William II on disputes in Groningen).

118 For De Knuyt and Pauw see Mörke, '*Stadholder*' oder '*Staetholder*', 126–7, and Elias, *De vroed-schap*, I, 198–9. For Ruyl, ADK, Stadsarchief Haarlem, resolutions, fols 13v–15r (11 November 1647); fol. 48 (6 July 1648); fol. 50v (13 July 1648). For Haersolte: NA, ND, 563 (list of appointments, 5 July 1647); LAD, Oranienbaum, A7b, 115, fols 10r–11r (Rutger van Haersolte to William II, 8–18 October 1650, from Lingen). For Musch: NA, ND, 563 (ordinance of 7 June 1653, in which the estate of the late Cornelis Musch is paid 3,000 guilders on the basis of the commission of 22 October 1648).

119 Gabriëls, *De heren als dienaren*, 99–135; Mörke, '*Stadholder*' oder '*Staetholder*', esp. 140–51; Price, *Holland and the Dutch Republic*, 247–59; Roorda, 'Le Secret du prince', 172–89; Rowen, *The Princes of Orange*, 87 ff.

120 *Gloria Parendi*, 534. See also LAD, Oranienbaum, A7b, 115, fols 4r–5v (Herbert van Beaumont to William II, 15 October 1649, from The Hague); LAD, Oranienbaum, A7b, 86, fol. 182r, 116, fols 6r–15v.

121 *Gloria Parendi*, 289.

122 RAG, Van der Capellen, 70 (Alexander van der Capellen to Hendrik van der Capellen, 1–17 March 1647, from Budelhof).

123 *Gloria Parendi*, 585.

124 Cited by Kooijmans, *Liefde in opdracht*, 110.

125 *Gloria Parendi*, 526 and 701.

126 Ibid., 586.

127 Ibid., 590 and 378. See also 469, 516 and 519.

128 Ibid., 594.

129 KHA, WII, XI, C-4 (Johan de Knuyt to William II, 19 October 1650, from Middelburg).

130 *Gloria Parendi*, 533.

131 Ibid., 720.

132 Examples ibid., 352, 358, 388, 391 and 594.

133 Ibid., 585.

134 Ibid., 577. For Hendrik Thibaut's later career see Van der Bijl, *Idee en interest*, 18–21.

135 Uhlig, *Hofkritik im England*, 170–223.

136 *Gloria Parendi*, 279 and 423–5.

137 Cf. Davis, *Women on the Margins*; Harris, 'Women and Politics', 259–81; Kloek, 'De vrouw', 250–6.

138 Cf. Kettering, *Patrons, Brokers and Clients*, 185–6.

139 *Gloria Parendi*, 151.

5

The fall of the Boss

In the spring of 1651 a commemorative medal was struck in Amsterdam, depicting the mythological Phaeton, the son of Helios the sun-god. The obverse illustrates the moment at which Zeus' thunderbolts hurled him from his father's chariot. Phaeton is shown falling to earth in the midst of a funeral procession alongside the *Binnenhof* in The Hague. Around the border are the words 'Magnis excidit ausis'.[1] Remarkably these words from Ovid are also to be found as the epigraph to a poem written in the same year by Joost van den Vondel. In his text the Amsterdam poet made the relationship between Phaeton and the funeral in The Hague even more explicit:

> Thus Orange falls like Phaeton,
> who could not follow in his father's traces
> and was not to be restrained by any reason.
> How the earth shuddered at that headlong career;
> How the lightning from the heavens struck
> Those who trusted in that rash adventurer.
> When a gambler's throw fails
> Pride goes before a fall.

Vondel's poem removes any doubt that the reckless Phaeton on the medal must symbolise the late prince William II of Orange. The mythological fable was an apt metaphor for the dramatic responses that William's sudden death in 1650 provoked in the United Provinces. His proverbial fall on 6 November of that year left the House of Orange without an adult heir, and also inaugurated the first stadholderless period in the Dutch Republic since the revolt of the sixteenth century. William's death thus caused a political earthquake, which for the time being put an end to the political and military dignities of the House of Orange.

Those who had thrown in their lot with William II suffered equally far-reaching consequences from his death. Courtiers and regents who had relied on the patronage of Orange lost the source of their incomes, power and prestige on 6 November 1650. The absence of an adult successor meant that the implications of the event were both acute and chronic. Seen in this light, the metaphor of Phaeton's fall could apply just as well to William's numerous clients as to the prince himself. The sudden loss of their old security forced many clients to look for new patrons and to redefine their relationship with the House of Orange. As we shall see, the way in which they did so was strongly influenced by the crisis that had preceded William's death during the summer of 1650.

Crisis

The summer crisis grew out of the events of the previous years. William Frederick had initially followed the growing tensions from a distance, since in the spring of 1650 he had remained longer than usual in Friesland. Normally the count returned from Leeuwarden to The Hague around March each year, but at the beginning of April 1650 he apologised to William II for his absence on the grounds that Friesian administrative matters had delayed him longer than he had planned; it would be the end of the month before he expected to see his patron again.[3] As usual while in Leeuwarden the count kept himself informed of events in The Hague through weekly reports sent by the Friesian deputy Joachim Andreae.[4] Because of his absence, therefore, William Frederick's archives contain a very full correspondence, in which the mounting tension between the prince and several of the Holland regents is carefully described.

Andreae's letters show that the long-running dispute between William II and the States of Holland was now focused on the proposed reduction of the army. William Frederick's correspondent reported that the gap remaining between the parties did not appear unbridgeable: the Hollanders proposed to dismiss only 600 more troops than William and the Council of State.[5] Yet it was not easy to find a solution that would satisfy both parties, for the real interests at stake were far more important than a few hundred demobilised soldiers. Andreae suggested that the ostensible questions at issue masked a struggle for prestige between the prince and the towns of Holland.

No exceptional political insight was needed to arrive at this analysis. In the previous two years William had had to look on as all his attempts to frustrate the peace negotiations with Spain and to assist his Stuart in-laws in England ended in failure. He was quite right to attribute the thwarting of his ambitions to the machinations of a few prominent Holland regents, and to see the reduction of the troops as the tactic the Hollanders were using to curtail his powers as stadholder as far as possible. This process had in fact begun in the last days of Frederick Henry, but it was William's fierce opposition to it after 1647 that brought the prince and the regents into open confrontation. The real conflict in the spring of 1650 therefore revolved around the question of principle: who should wield political power in the Republic in peacetime? Should the informal authority of the prince of Orange be maintained after the peace of Münster of 1648, or should the initiative in future lie with the urban patricians of Holland?[6]

When William Frederick finally arrived in The Hague in May 1650, he saw that the conflict had grown into a serious political crisis. Like his second cousin he blamed the Hollanders. After venturing to make independent diplomatic overtures to the English republicans in January, in April the States of Holland let it be known that they would proceed to dismiss troops on their own authority. Holland believed that it was within its rights in both measures, a view that William Frederick did not share.[7] The count considered the autonomous action of the States of Holland dangerous and provocative. In his opinion the regents of the most powerful province were twisting the terms of the Union of Utrecht to suit themselves, and thereby ratcheting up the tension even further.

There were those in the other provinces who also saw Holland's policy as a threat to the balance of power in the Republic, and even to the continued existence of the Union, a fear that was not altogether unfounded.[8] The Union of Utrecht of 1579 had been intended at the time as a defensive military alliance, and was not at all suited to a peacetime situation. The Hollanders saw an opportunity, after the Peace of Münster, to reinterpret some of the principles of the Union to their own advantage. This policy irritated the other provinces and at the same time threw the political authority of the prince of Orange open for discussion. Thanks to his combination of six stadholderships, the prince had formerly been able to act as arbiter between the provinces and thereby to pose as the symbol and upholder of the Union. It was hardly surprising, therefore, that William II saw in Holland's independent line a threat to his own position in the Republic, which called for a decisive response.

Yet this potential threat to the Union was probably only a partial explanation of William's motives to frustrate Holland's policy. The turmoil of 1650 was equally the result of his unsuccessful patronage policy in the previous years. At the time the prince had hoped, by investing in a new clientele, to be able to turn Holland's peace policy into a more aggressive course. As we saw, the prince at first was fairly hopeful of success for this approach, but his own leading clients were a good deal less optimistic. From the autumn of 1649 the patron himself began to realise that his ambitious patronage strategy was not working. The offices, gifts and favours he had showered on the Holland regents in particular did not appear to be having the desired effect in practice. On the contrary, it was precisely such potential clients as Andries Bicker, Nanning Keyser or Albert Ruyl who were now among the most ardent advocates of a reduction in the army. 'His Highness complains much of Ruyl, who was good [but] has changed', William Frederick remarked in November 1649. Keyser was another who, for all the favours heaped on him, felt no obligation to adjust the voting behaviour of his town of Hoorn to suit the prince's preferences. The worst offender in William's eyes was one of the burgomasters of Amsterdam, Andries Bicker. The prince was scandalised that Bicker should have accepted the office of *drost* of Muiden for his son and then refused to repay this favour with his political support. According to William Frederick the prince felt duped and insulted by Bicker's failure to live up to his expectations. 'Every day he is deceived by those to whom he does a good turn', William Frederick wrote in his diary, 'once they have enjoyed it, they change their tune in the meeting, allow themselves to be outvoted or absent themselves altogether, so that one cannot rely on those people.'[9]

William Frederick's diary makes it clear that this was the point at which William II decided that forcible intervention in Holland was the only remedy for the persistent opposition and growing discord.[10] In other words, once the prince saw that his strategy of patronage had failed, he resorted to blackmail and intimidation. Seen in this light, the negotiations in the spring of 1650 were no more than a front; and, contrary to Andreae's suspicions, William probably had no intention of reaching a compromise with the Hollanders. Rather, he contrived the breakdown of dialogue as a pretext for drastic intervention. On Good Friday 1650, just after the States of Holland had voted to stop paying some units of the army, William appeared unexpectedly in person in the assembly of the States-General. He must have known that few deputies would be present that day, and he used the thin attendance to make a very unusual proposal to send 'a very notable deputation to all the towns and members of the province of Holland, to move the same to refrain from all separate or independent cashiering, reduction or change of the men of war'. William managed to force the resolution through, and even to procure an instruction for himself to decide 'on what footing and through what persons the aforesaid deputation shall be sent'. The very next day it became clear that he as stadholder would personally accompany the commission he had orchestrated.[11]

The legality of the special deputation to the towns of Holland was, to say the least, highly debatable. It was not a success, but William had never meant it to be. In such 'Orangist' cities as Leiden and Enkhuizen the stadholder was certainly 'received by the citizenry in arms and greeted with all respect', while in the more neutral towns of Rotterdam and Den Briel 'people had been sent beforehand to intimidate the leading citizens or to tempt them by promises'.[12] In Dordrecht and Amsterdam, however, where opposition to William was strongest, his reception, as might be expected, was unusually cool. The *vroedschap* in Dordrecht did not bother to conceal its indignation at the 'very sharp, bitter and intolerable words' in which the deputation had presented its message to the city.[13] In Amsterdam the visit produced some even more painful moments. Because William arrived 'about two hours before the appointed time' on 23 June, the militia and the reception committee were not yet ready. The prince was given a hurried welcome 'on the Dam square, on a creaking and unfinished bridge, which alarmed the burgomasters and made people fear that it would break'.[14] The prince then rejected an invitation to dine with the notables, alleging that he 'could not eat with those who would not hear him speak'. Indeed the Amsterdam *vroedschap* had refused to grant William an audience in their council chamber, and he left the city on the following day.[15]

Now that he had been given such an unfortunate welcome in Amsterdam and Dordrecht, and the States of Holland had stuck to their policy on the army, William hoped that he had done enough to justify recourse to the more drastic measures he had been secretly planning for some time. These involved the seizure of the city of Amsterdam, the arrest of his most important opponents in Holland, and a pamphlet campaign to win over public opinion.[16] As early as the autumn of 1649 William had begun to draw up lists of the men to be detained. Their number and names varied from list to list, but in each case they were all regents who had refused to be bought by William's patronage: Bicker, Ruyl and Keyser, together with the burgomasters of Haarlem, Delft and Dordrecht: Jan de Waal, Johan Duyst van Voorhout and Jacob de Witt. The pensionary of Medemblik Nicolaas Stellingwerff was also one of the candidates, and some versions added the names of Nicolaas Ruysch and Cornelis van Beveren of Dordrecht, Adriaan Pauw, Cornelis Bicker and Anthony Oetgens of Amsterdam, Frans Meerman of Delft and Willem Nieuwpoort of Schiedam. It is not clear in all cases why they were on these blacklists, but William may well have made some of them secret offers of money and office, without gaining the support he expected in return. It may be also that pensionaries such as Ruysch and Stellingwerff were treated as spokesmen of the towns that were most intransigently opposed to William's policy in the States of Holland.[17]

The obedient client

William Frederick's reference to these lists in his diary shows that he was involved in William's secret plans from an early stage. Significantly, he underlined the names of potential detainees, in Andreae's letters. The Friesian stadholder was not the only one whom the prince took into his confidence; other members of the core clientele, including Van Aerssen, Musch and Heilersieg, were also aware of the prince's intentions, perhaps even earlier than the count.[18] Yet William Frederick's involvement was particularly remarkable, because he had previously advocated a more cautious approach, believing that there was nothing to be gained by taking a hard line. In Friesland too, he had always been a model of caution as a patron.[19] How did William Frederick, as a client, find himself in the hawkish camp?

As we saw, the count certainly had reservations about his patron's political agenda and patronage tactics, but he subordinated these differences of opinion to his belief in his role as that of a servant. His duty to marry a princess of Orange and thus place himself in line to inherit if William II should die without an heir, gave him a further incentive to conform as far as possible to his patron's standards. As a loyal client of the prince, William Frederick was even willing to adopt his patron's political ideals. Between 1649 and 1650 William Frederick came to be convinced that force was indeed the solution to what had at first appeared to be William II's problem and not his own. It is doubtful, however, that the client saw this change in his attitude as a new insight; rather, he came to feel that the change was not in him but in the world around him.

William Frederick's ideas about a peace with Spain may serve as a case in point. At the Friesian *Landdag* of 1647 the stadholder had still supported peace negotations, but his doubts about the treaty grew more serious in the following years. In 1649 he feared that Spain 'will make itself master through our own disunity, which it could not do by force'. In short, the count saw the growing political division between the prince and the towns of Holland as a new danger for the Republic. He blamed these discords on the behaviour of the prince's critics in Holland, and not on the prince himself. William Frederick regarded the refusal of 'that scoundrel Bicker' to cooperate with William in return for the prince's favours as insulting and irresponsible conduct, which threw suspicion on Bicker and his followers. In 1649 William Frederick became convinced that those Hollanders were playing the game of the Catholics and Spaniards. 'So this country will be lost through the bad government of the regents, through Holland and its pensionaries', he argued in October of that year, 'and furthermore all the Catholics in our country, who are bold and powerful ... and if we get rid of the soldiers, it is to be feared that they will seize their opportunity and seek to overthrow the government.' He had heard from a reliable source that these Hollanders were 'led by Spanish money'.[20] This appeared even more plausible when William Frederick discovered a striking parallel with the advice that the humanist scholar Justus Lipsius had given the Spanish governor Fuentes fifty years earlier, namely 'to use soft measures to draw us into disunity'.[21]

In December 1649 William Frederick found further confirmation of these bad omens in rumours he had heard that 'there were some who wished to murder His Highness', although this scheme failed.[22] Nevertheless the Friesian stadholder was amazed that others in his entourage took these signs of treason less seriously or even dismissed them altogether. In the same month, when the Friesian deputy Eelco van Glinstra appeared to be wavering over the reduction in the troops, William Frederick made an impassioned speech about the 'intentions of Holland, of Amsterdam and of Bicker'. Was it not obvious that 'those rogues want to change our religion and hand us over to the Spaniards'? When Cornelis van Aerssen hinted that he 'did not wish to take such a hard line', William Frederick replied that drastic action was exactly what was needed. The time would be ripe in March or April of the new year, 'when the moon was between Mars and Saturn, which means a change of government'.[23]

William Frederick did not seek legitimacy for William II's plans in the stars alone; he also looked for historical parallels, and found them above all in Maurice's coup in 1618. Then too there had been 'treachery and delivery of the country to the Spaniards', he argued. Bicker and his supporters undoubtedly intended to 'chase us out of the country', just as the former Holland pensionary Johan van Oldenbarnevelt had argued that 'as long as that rabble and the bald counts of Nassau are in the country, it will be no good, they have to be thrown out of the country'. William Frederick detected more and more similarities between the present crisis and that of thirty years earlier. 'It is a work like 1618', he concluded in his diary in late October 1649, while in February 1650 he wrote to the prince that 'the Hollanders have the same design as Oldenbarnevelt and the Arminians had in the year 1618, to make themselves masters of the other provinces.'[24] Once he had found this historical frame of reference it became also easier for William Frederick to identify himself with his revered uncle William Louis. Just as William Louis had supported Maurice in 1618, so he as William Louis's successor would stand by the Boss in word and deed. William Frederick thought he was on the right track.

For a long time historians used to brand William Frederick as the instigator of the assault on Amsterdam, but since the discovery of his diaries in the 1980s he has no longer been cast in the role of William II's evil genius.[25] His notes in fact show that it was not he but the prince who took the initiative for the attack on the city. This new factual material has helped to deconstruct the old picture, but a clientelistic perspective on the events can take the process even further, since it reveals that the count was never in a position to act as the architect of the assault. In fact the situation was quite the reverse: William Frederick's opportunities to influence his patron prove to have been limited, while William II was utterly successful in pushing his client in the direction he wanted. Indeed, the Friesian stadholder himself saw his part in the attack as a duty imposed on him from above. The night before the enterprise he wrote a final justification 'in the name of the All-Highest, since by the command of His Highness I am to go to Amsterdam'. This political testament shows that William Frederick, in the last analysis, knew that he was risking his life in the assault. In that case the count was firmly convinced that he would die 'to maintain religion, in the service of the country, and for His Highness, after the example of my parents and forebears, who gladly gave their lives for the common fatherland'.[26]

William Frederick's testament is interesting because it shows how inseparable the welfare of the Dutch Republic, the position of the Reformed religion and the history of the House of Nassau had become in his mind. The pietist tone of the text further suggests that the testament was not so much intended to make William Frederick's acts appear legitimate in the eyes of the outside world as to justify himself before God. William Frederick sought that justification in the unmistakable parallels he saw with the behaviour of his forebears. By inter- preting the current crisis in terms of precedents from his family history, he could represent the whole undertaking as a duty to which he was called as a scion of the House of Nassau-Dietz. That conviction also explains why William Frederick finally decided to bequeath his property in the Netherlands, if he should die, to Albertine, the intended bride whom his mother had chosen for him.[27]

The coup

After the deputation of June 1650, William II felt that the time had come to put his plans into action. Because of the objections they might raise, he found it more practical not to ask the other provinces for their support until after the event. To begin with, a pamphlet campaign was launched in July 1650, with the publica- tion of a fictitious military treaty supposed to have been made between the city of Amsterdam and the English republicans. Heilersieg would later be unmasked as the most likely author of this document, and it was secretly printed by Willem Breeckevelt in The Hague.[28] The imaginary plot was part of a stream of 'booklets and pasquils' that began to pour from the presses in that month, though it is not always possible to prove that William II bore personal responsibility for them. In any case the pamphlets, which appeared under such titles as 'Bicker's Fall' or the 'Bicker Troubles', all took much the same line: they made all kinds of accusations against Amsterdam, while presenting an ideologically tinged argument that the stadholder was the upholder of the Union and of religion.[29] The suggestion of this natural trinity was not altogether new, and had been put forward in the past by pro-Orangist preachers. The timeliness of having William's intervention legit- imised by the Calvinist Church elite must not be underestimated. An irritated Englishman wrote from Leiden of 'how profitable it is for him to have an Orator in every Church to lead the people by the ears, to serve him in his interest, he gratifies them upon all occasions with what is in his power, either by donation or intercession'.[30]

The second stage of William's campaign was the arrest of his opponents in Holland. On the morning of Saturday 30 July Nanning Keyser, Nicolaas Stelling- werff, Jan de Waal, Albert Ruyl, Johan Duyst van Voorhout and Jacob de Witt were summoned to the stadholder's quarter in The Hague, where they were arrested by the captain of the guard and then conveyed to the fortress of Loevestein.[31] The surprise assault on Amsterdam, the third stage of the plan, began the same day. A few days earlier, William had mustered his troops on the heath at Wageningen, ostensibly to hold a review for his wife Mary Stuart. He then ordered William Frederick to march on Amsterdam that night with the assembled company, and to secure the city 'in the best and mildest way he can'. The obedient client was therefore put in charge of the most dangerous part of William's coup. The other officers were also among the prince's most loyal clients. Besides Cornelis van Aerssen and Frederick of Nassau-Zuylestein, they included members of the court or army commanders of foreign descent, who owed their positions to Orange appointment, and whose loyalty and discretion were not in doubt.[32]

Yet even these precautions were not enough to guarantee success. Nature threw a spanner in the works in the night of 30–31 July, when a thunderstorm broke out, and many of the troops lost their way in the neighbourhood of Hilversum. For good measure, a postboy who happened to be riding by en route from Hamburg noticed the soldiers and informed the magistrates of Amsterdam of his discovery when he arrived in the city early in the morning. Even before William Frederick arrived at the Amstel river, the bridges had been raised and cannons placed on the city walls.[33] The surprise attack had failed. The count could do little but surround the city and wait for new orders from the prince. These arrived very quickly, for as soon as the first reports of the fiasco at Amsterdam reached The Hague later that day, William II decided to take command on the spot in person. When he arrived at nearby Amstelveen on 1 August the magistrates intimated that they were willing to negotiate. The *vroedschap* was ready to talk, because a blockade of the city would have disastrous commercial consequences. The prince also knew that there had been frictions within the *vroedschap* for some time, caused by the authoritarian behaviour of the Bicker brothers and their faction. These critics, who included Cornelis de Graaf, Nicolaas Tulp and Anthony Oetgens, may well have been willing to use the assault to undermine the Bickers, and would therefore have been potential allies of the prince.[34]

William's plan succeeded wonderfully well. On 3 August both parties agreed that Amsterdam would end its support for the reduction of the army, in return for William's withdrawal with his forces. In a separate article it was further agreed that 'for the service of the country' Andries and Cornelis Bicker would henceforth 'withdraw from all further government of the city'.[35] Later in the month the prince was able to exact the same promise from his Holland prisoners. William thus returned to The Hague in apparent triumph, claiming victory.

Success?

Yet William's victory was obviously not a brilliant one, and opinions on the success of his coup varied widely. In fact, it has never ceased to be a matter of debate among historians. Recently Gees van der Plaat argued that the assault must

certainly be regarded as a triumph for the prince. In her support she cited chronicler Lieuwe van Aitzema, who described William's intervention as a successful
step toward consolidating the stadholder's authority. Previously Herbert Rowen
had defended the thesis that, on the whole, the prince's coup worked to his advantage.[36] Most historians, however, have not shared their view of 1650. Pieter Geyl
and G.W. Kernkamp saw it as a downright failure, because it did not achieve its
original goal, the replacement of the magistracies in all the opposition towns in
Holland. Simon Groenveld found further confirmation of this view in the defeat
that the prince suffered in the States-General only three weeks after the assault.
William had proposed that the Dutch Republic should mediate between between
France and Spain in their ongoing war, but the text of this so-called 'mediation
proposal' was in fact an ultimatum to the Spaniards, which only made the chance
of a renewed war greater. The members of the Committee Council of the States
of Holland refused to agree to the prince's explosive proposal, even though the
assault on Amsterdam was fresh in their memory.[37]

In fact, as early as 1650 doubts about the success of William's campaign
were being voiced in unimpeachable quarters, in the first place by William
Frederick himself. The count concluded that the coup 'had been a completely
useless, bad and miserable failure'.[38] Gerlach van der Capellen passed a more
cautious verdict on it in early August, when he wrote that in Zutphen there was
'great discontent about this work of Amsterdam', and that the Gelderland *jonkers*
(nobles) had begun to doubt William's integrity.[39] After the prince's defeat in the
States-General in the same month, Johan van Reede van Renswoude was forced
to admit that many regents in Utrecht openly deplored the assault. Even the
removal of the Bickers from the government in Amsterdam was, in his view, a
Pyrrhic victory. Van Reede had heard from a reliable source that 'they still speak
very ill of Your Highness there, and that the resolutions are framed in the house
of the Bickers'.[40] The lukewarm response even in Orangist circles was revealed
in the obligatory but rather neutral congratulations that William received from
the other provinces.[41] Even the hoped-for ratification after the event was not
forthcoming.

J. L. Price has argued that William's action in a sense demonstrated what
could go wrong 'when [the] delicate system of power and patronage was misused'
by the stadholder.[42] Indeed, the prince's intervention could not be regarded as
a great success from the point of view of patronage either. Whereas Maurice's
coup in 1618 had enabled him to strengthen his own clientele, William II only
exacerbated the bad feeling between himself and his clients. As the letters of
Van der Capellen and Van Reede make clear, Orange lost considerable prestige
in the summer of 1650, and even his sympathisers began to lose confidence in
him. They evidently interpreted his resort to force without a clear mandate as a
message of weakness from a failed patron.

It was more important, however, that the discussion of William's success or failure became completely irrelevant a few months later. On 6 November the prince died suddenly after a short illness, 'whereby that work that was done this summer goes for nothing, and will do more harm than good', as William Frederick wrote.[43] Indeed, the effects of the assault entirely rebounded against Orange from that moment. The events of that summer left many regents wondering if it might not be better to leave the stadholdership vacant for the time being.

The full extent of this scepticism about a new stadholdership under a prince of Orange began to be revealed eight days after William's death. On 14 November Mary Stuart gave birth to her first and only child; prince William III. In his chronicle Lieuwe van Aitzema claimed that the event caused much rejoicing in The Hague, 'thereby letting it be known that they had no other idea, but that the prince was Sovereign and hereditary lord of the country', but this suggestion of dynastic and political continuity was utterly unrealistic. Holland immediately left it in no doubt, after the birth of the prince, that it would not install him as stadholder and captain-general.[44] Deputations had already been sent from Holland to the other provinces to persuade their States to leave the offices vacant. On this occasion the Holland pensionary Jacob Cats compared the Republic to a church or great palace, the provinces and their States being the pillars that must support it. The stadholder was merely a 'crown or great chandelier, which served for light and ornament but which could be easily replaced if lost'.[45]

The full enormity of the damage that William's death had inflicted on the House of Orange only became clear in the weeks after 14 November. The Holland deputations achieved their aims with brilliant success in all but a few cases. Gelderland, Zeeland, Utrecht and Overijssel decided to leave the stadholdership vacant for the time being, and the respective provincial States took back control of all the stadholder's functions, such as the appointment of magistrates and officers. At the same time they agreed to a 'Great Assembly', in which the future of the Union, religion and the army would be discussed. Only Groningen and Drenthe took a different line, by appointing William Frederick as their stadholder in December. Even that election, in a sense, only made the eclipse of the House of Orange more obvious. The dynasty of William of Orange, Maurice and Frederick Henry lost a great deal of its prestige in 1650. 'Men have nothing else on their lips now but the freedom of the States, and everyone wants to appear zealous for it', the Dordrecht regent Johan de Witt wrote to his father Jacob on 8 November.[46] The age of True Freedom had dawned.

Clients in a time of crisis

Historians may regret the premature death of William II, because it prevents them from determining how his unorthodox patronage strategy would ultimately have turned out. At the same time, however, the fall of the patron offers an opportunity to examine the strength and durability of Orange's networks in the crisis years 1650–51. For instance, did Orange's clients all disappear from the political stage after that year, did they look for new patrons, or were they able to continue their careers independently? In other words, which forms of clientage would prove durable and which would not?

The resilience of patronage relationships in periods of crisis has already been studied in another context. The French wars of religion of the sixteenth century offered a test-case of the permanence of aristocratic clienteles in turbulent times. Robert Harding claimed that many of these networks fell apart when local patrons found their own patronage resources or those of the crown dwindling because of the fortunes of war.[47] His conclusion was not shared by Mark Greengrass, who believed that many noble clienteles did indeed survive the religious civil wars, and felt that Harding had understated the emotional dimension of many patron-client relationships. He argued that some clienteles were not based on material interests alone, but on what he called 'affinities', emotional loyalties that could help to guarantee the longevity of patronage.[48] Sharon Kettering combined these two hypotheses when she showed that the French nobility suffered a dramatic falling-off in its clienteles in the sixteenth and seventeenth centuries because of a decline in patronage resources; but that a hard core of *fidèles* persisted inside these networks. This balanced conclusion, however, does not explain precisely what causes enabled some clienteles to survive while others did not.[49]

Other historians too have found it difficult to identify the considerations that guided the behaviour of clients in a time of crisis. Even before the publications of Greengrass and Kettering, Henk van Nierop had argued that the clienteles of William of Orange did not survive the crisis of the Dutch Revolt. He believed that 'although patronage certainly played a part in political life, the bonds it forged were less durable than has been assumed'.[50] Such a view, however, seems to be at odds with the fact that William Frederick's household clientele was recruited partly from men whose ancestors had been in the service of the Nassaus in the sixteenth century. Their relationship with the family had apparently survived two or three generations and eighty years of war and crisis. The persistence of these *fidèles* and the decline of the clienteles that Van Nierop investigated, suggest that the social environment in which these relationships had been formed influenced the success with which they were able to cope with crises. In other words, the durability of a patron-client relationship in the Dutch Republic varied depending on its republican (public) or princely (private) environment.

Orange's private clientele

To test this hypothesis we must compare the transformations in Orange's private and public networks after November 1650. At first sight the implications of William's death might appear to be most far-reaching for his courtiers and domain officials, but as William Frederick's case has already shown, in practice they could often appeal to the patronage of their patron's successor. Court and domains, after all, continued to need administrators after the death of the lord. In that sense the death of a patron was not necessarily a threat to the private clientele. Yet the situation at the Orange court in 1650 was rather different from that in Friesland in 1640. In the first place the family was weighed down by an enormous burden of debt left by William II. The need for drastic economies was made more pressing by the loss of the income from his official and military salaries. These ceased on 6 November, while the prospect of new offices and emoluments in the United Provinces was poor. The 'unemployment' of William's heir had both acute political and financial implications.[51]

The Domain Council therefore decided as early as December to undertake a thorough reorganisation, which included compulsory redundancies. Dirck van Ruijven wrote to William Frederick the day before that there were plans 'to redress the affairs of the household and to abolish the kitchen, hunt and stables, apart from the horses that will be needed for the funeral, and all other unnecessary things', saving 600,000 guilders.[52] This was followed on 31 December by an instruction to the equerry to 'cause the expenses of the household to cease and to tell all the officers under his authority that it is understood that their salaries shall come to cease'. Mass dismissals would follow the next day. Only a handful could still count on payment up to the day of William's funeral. Mary Stuart therefore thought it desirable to have the funeral in the New Church at Delft held as quickly as possible; and meals were not to be served at court with effect from 3 January.[53]

The actual result of these measures was that five chamber servants, thirteen lackeys and trumpeters, forty servants and cooks, and a dancing master were forced to leave on 1 January, not counting the seventeen nobles who were also dismissed. On 6 July 1651 a new wave of redundancies removed a further thirty-four personnel.[54] These were not just kitchen boys or undercooks, but high noble officials who kept personnel of their own. Only in the domains did the network of *drosts*, treasurers and bailiffs remain largely intact. Some months after William's death, the decimated Orange court had thus lost most of its servants and much of its lustre.[55]

Even the handful who were allowed to remain could not look forward to a rosy future. In practice the success of their future career at court would depend on keeping on good terms with Amalia or Mary. Secretary Heilersieg, as a relative newcomer, had not had time to win the favour of either and therefore had a hard job to maintain himself in office, all the more so as he bore much of the blame for the objectionable pamphlet campaign. Heilersieg's rapid rise under the prince's patronage in 1647 was matched by his abrupt fall into disfavour after December 1650.[56] His colleague Huygens, on the other hand, had better luck thanks to the protection of Amalia. Though he lost his post as secretary, unlike Heilersieg he kept his seat on the Domain Council.[57] Even so, William's death meant that Huygens, who had been experiencing a loss of favour in recent years, now lost much of his remaining credit within government circles. In December 1650 he was nominated to succeed the chief clerk of the States-General Musch, but in the end the removal of the Oranges from the political scene frustrated his hopes of advancement. It was not Huygens but the pensionary of Dordrecht, Nicolaas Ruysch, 'an enemy of the House of Nassau', who was promoted to become Musch's successor.[58]

Johan de Knuyt had to swallow an even bitterer pill. Ironically, the death of his hated patron dealt him another blow in Zeeland. Though he looked forward to a speedy reappointment to the Domain Council, his position in the province was far from secure. The new commission as representative of the First Noble, which the Domain Council granted him in November, was simply rejected by the States of Zeeland. They claimed that the dignity of First Noble could only be conferred by them, and they refused to 'admit [De Knuyt] or give him a seat in their assembly, so that Mr Knuyt was left a private citizen without employment'.[59] The Zeelanders rubbed salt in his wounds in March 1651 by letting it be known that the ex-member of the States 'will have to provide himself with another house by May, or at the latest by All Saints' Day, and vacate the residence of the States of Zeeland'.[60]

The disintegration of the Orange's court clientele was not caused by the economy measures alone; it was accelerated by persistent internal tensions. Because William had not left an adult heir, his death on 6 November created a power vacuum that had to be filled by his widow Mary. Amalia van Solms, however, had no intention of humbly submitting to her daughter-in-law's leadership. The two princesses had been on bad terms for years, and the crisis of 1650 only made matters worse. Their struggle for power from that moment revolved around the guardianship of the young prince. Mary and Amalia actively sought allies among the remaining courtiers, who were thus forced to make a choice between them.[61]

On 6 January 1651 Dirck van Ruijven sent William Frederick a report on the complicated situation at court. 'Your Grace would be surprised', he wrote, 'if he were here and saw these jealous dealings, how people speak ill of one another, or are suspect.'[62] Meanwhile the Court of Holland had been asked to mediate and to interpret William's will in favour of one party or the other. According to Van Ruijven, ill-intentioned clients were exploiting the chaos for their own profit. Heenvliet, who was married to Mary's lady-in-waiting Catherine Wotton, had already put himself forward spontaneously in November as Mary's agent, to reorganise the household. The Domain Council asked him to consider 'if it would not be proper to prevent further disorders' by limiting the mass dismissals, but the self-appointed 'superintendent' was not going to lose this chance to get rid of troublesome rivals.[63]

The power vacuum at the Orange court ultimately led to the formation of two rival factions. Mary associated with, among others, Frederick of Nassau-Zuylestein (the husband of another of her ladies-in-waiting, Mary Killegrew), Louis of Nassau-Beverweert, Willem van Crommon and her secretary Nicolaas Oudaart. Other prominent persons, including Huygens and De Knuyt, chose to side with Amalia, who also had the backing of her son-in-law, the elector of Brandenburg.[64] This family schism further crippled the House of Orange as a political force in December 1650. Even at the prince's baptism 'the two great Ladies' openly quarrelled over his baptismal name. In the event Mary's preference for Charles had to yield to Amalia's choice of William.[65]

Orange's public clientele

The struggle for power at court cast its shadow in advance over the consequences of William's death in the republican scene. Inevitably, the former peace factions in the towns of Holland turned this hopeless discord to their advantage. Their arguments in favour of a stadholderless regime naturally gained strength in December 1650. In its impact on Orange's patronage resources, the ultimate decision of Gelderland, Holland, Zeeland, Utrecht and Overijssel to leave the stadholdership vacant was even more devastating than the enforced economies at court.

Because the powers of the stadholder and captain-general varied from province to province, the consequences of the States' decision to leave both offices vacant also differed. In the largely urbanised provinces of Holland and Zeeland, the loss of the annual opportunities to select the magistrates dealt a serious blow to the House of Orange, while in Utrecht and Gelderland relatively few civic offices were affected.[66] In every province, however, the family lost a substantial fund of military patronage which was particularly damaging to Orange's ability to manage relations with the nobility.[67] A further consequence of this loss of powers of appointment was that office-seekers could no longer use the court as the central clearing house for their applications, as the centre of the traffic in offices migrated from the stadholder's quarter to the council chambers of provincal States and the local *vroedschappen*.

These radical changes forced sitting magistrates to look for new alliances. In the Vollenhoven quarter of Overijssel the most important regents promptly concluded a 'contract of correspondence', to prevent the shift in power weakening their own position.[68] But the need for reorientation was most urgent in the towns and provincial colleges of Holland, where the stadholder had previously held numerous rights of appointment. In that province many regents displayed a remarkable adaptability in 1650. In December field-marshal Johan Wolfert van Brederode, who was a member of Orange's family, spontaneously approached the former Holland peacemakers. To avoid becoming a victim of Orange's political degradation and the disunity at court, the field-marshal was even willing to help Cornelis van Beveren and Hieronymus van Beverningk to organise the anti-stadholder lobby in Utrecht.[69] In that province the former broker Johan van Reede van Renswoude also managed to land on his political feet by associating himself with Brederode and other Holland notables.[70]

The informal influence of the Holland deputies could be felt elsewhere. The peace factions, which in the summer of 1650 had appeared to be overthrown by William's coup, completely regained the political initiative in December of that year. Under the appropriate name of 'the Loevestein faction' they were the moving spirits behind the lobbying campaigns in the other provinces. In the rural eastern provinces these Hollanders tried to win the States for their cause by dispensing the military patronage that had fallen into their hands when the States of Holland had gained control of the stadholder's strategic army appointments. Because Holland paid nearly 58 per cent of the tax revenue, it had the right to appoint by far the greatest number of army officers. This trump card gave the Hollanders the chance to attach to themselves the nobles who had previously been predominantly followers of Orange. In December 1650 some Gelderland *jonkers* promised to leave the stadholdership vacant 'in the hope of obtaining benefits or companies'. Alexander van der Capellen believed the tactic was utterly successful:

> And those of Holland worked by all manner of means to bring the people of the country over to their side, accusing those whom they believed to be working to counter their designs, and feeding others with hopes of freedom and advancement to companies, promised to several *jonkers* who sided with them.[71]

Dirck van Ruijven indeed noted in December 1650 that many Gelderlanders were now talking 'Holland's language'.[72]

At first sight, therefore, it may appear that the composition of the urban and provincial colleges did not change very much, but that at most Orange lost influence over its former clienteles. After November 1650 most regents simply exchanged the old alliance for a new one. As Johan de Witt's remark suggested, many magistrates who had risen to office through Orange were now willing to attach themselves to the Holland peace faction. Their personal survival and local priorities were much more important than the loyalties that Orange had tried to foster. Thus, it seems as if clientage from the centre did not form genuinely lasting attachments in the republican system. As soon as the stadholder's patronage resources were in other hands, the unwritten obligations assumed vanished without trace. This picture of opportunist regents, whose political motives were rooted in their families and localities, has been dominant in Dutch historiography since the studies of D.J. Roorda.

Yet this impression of continuity and of weak patronage allegiances was partly a façade, behind which far-reaching changes were certainly concealed. Those who had openly supported the assault on Amsterdam were most at risk of being swept away in Orange's wake. In the spring of 1651 Holland was even pressing for the prosecution of the men who had plotted the coup. Urged on by William Frederick, the Friesian delegates in the Great Assembly succesfully called for a general amnesty. For Cornelis van Aerssen, however, the Hollanders made it a condition that he should 'absent himself' permanently from the nobility assembly in the States of Holland.[73] Cornelis Musch would also have faced a political reckoning if he had not died suddenly in December 1650. Rumours that the death of his patron had driven him to suicide immediately began to circulate in The Hague.[74] Finally Hendrik Thibaut's power in Zeeland was at an end for the time being. While De Knuyt lost his post as representative of the First Noble in December, William's broker was forced out in early 1651. In May Joachim Andreae wrote that 'there have been rumours about Thibaut for several weeks, that he and his party were overthrown', a portent of the serious disturbances that broke out in Middelburg later that month, in which Thibaut's windows were broken. The opposition to his rule had a local background, but it was the loss of his patron which gave his enemies their chance to get rid of him.[75]

Several pamphlets and satires of 1650 also referred to this collective fall of William's core clients:

> After the band of rogues broke into pieces on the prince's death
> Musch went to Hell to sneak on Aerssen,
> Thibaut and Renswoude, Van Noortwijck and Capel
> when they should descend to Hell.[76]

The coming of the 'True Freedom' simultaneously improved the career prospects of those who had been held back under Orange. In Dordrecht Jacob de Witt was invited to resume his seat in the council 'immediately after the prince's death'. The promise exacted from him and his fellow prisoners, to refuse government offices for evermore, was evidently a dead letter after 6 November. All the Loevesteiners returned to their seats in the *vroedschappen* in the following weeks.[77]

The settlements that followed William's death reveal the dramatic changes that came with the fall of the Orangist patronage system. These were reinforced by the ideological debate that was raging in the United Provinces on the future of the Republic and the role of the stadholder.[78] In a sense, the prince's death had given the long-running theoretical discussion on the form of the republican state an immediate relevance. For the first time since the Revolt of the sixteenth century the fundamental question of the need for an 'Eminent Head' urgently required a practical answer. Many saw in the recent conduct of William II and his clientele a reason to reconsider the stadholdership. It is therefore not very satisfactory to ascribe the reactions to William's death and the fall of his core clientele exclusively to pragmatism, and to define the conduct of regents in terms of opportunism and material interests.[79] The magistrates of Leiden, for example, felt obliged to reject Holland's new course on principle. Even after the States had resolved to leave the stadholdership vacant, the city continued to hammer home the point that 'the high merits of the illustrious House of Nassau ought to be taken into consideration, and therefore its posterity ought not to be absolutely deprived of all dignities'. As a more fundamental argument they added that without a stadholder the conferring of offices would probably degenerate into 'trafficking and other dirty practices'.[80] On this reasoning a stadholderless regime would lead to 'corrupt' practices and threaten unity and stability.

The fall of their patron thus provoked different reactions among clients in the public and private spheres. In both, William's death brought radical changes, but while at court the patron's successors were compelled to cut back the clientele, in the republican bodies the initiative to break the old ties came from the clients themselves. The consequences of William's death differed in the two circuits because patronage in them had grown up under different conditions. As the crises of 1640 and 1650 show, the division between patronage spheres that the republican system created had profound implications for the form and durability of patron-client relationship in Dutch society.

Losing the patron

For William Frederick the death of William II was a mental shock. 'My best friend is gone', he wrote in January 1651, 'and for his sake I have lost many friends and made myself many enemies'. The count was equally sombre about the possible long-term repercussions of his association with the prince. 'No one has lost more by this than I have', William Frederick assumed, 'for I keep all my enemies and gain new ones every day in Holland.'[81]

This was a prophetic analysis. On 23 January William Frederick was already hearing rumours in Leeuwarden of how 'the Hollanders [were making] me black and hateful among the commonalty'. They had also 'taken information wherever they could in and around Amsterdam, to see what they could find against me, to blame me with'. Those in the know, however, admitted that the count had just been a willing tool of his former patron. Brederode confided in him that it was 'my misfortune to have been used therein, and if His Highness had used him or another, they would have done the same'.[82] William Frederick kept notes of these conversations, because they bore out his consciousness of having been no more than the faithful instrument of the Boss's orders. His conviction of his own rectitude made it difficult for the count to accept that he would have to pay for his loyalty by losing his credit. Now that he no longer had a patron to protect him, he seemed to have been handed over to the mercies of the rancorous Holland regents. In July 1651 he prayed God to 'redeem me from the hands of my enemies who are so hateful to me and who disfavour and scorn me'.[83] In the humble phrasing of this prayer William Frederick was inspired by the Psalms, texts from which he paraphrased, modelling his recent experiences on biblical precedents.[84]

The attack on Amsterdam and the death of William II continued to haunt the count in later years. He himself contributed to this by consistently attributing new reverses in his life to the catastrophe of 1650. This preoccupation with the events of that year also prevented him from taking a more realistic view of the developments in the Republic. William Frederick regularly reflected on his relations with Amsterdam, and in December 1651 felt that he could detect signs of an improvement after a delegation from the city had personally come to congratulate him on his forthcoming marriage. But a few years later the count again had the impression that the Amsterdammers were still very bitter toward him for his role in the assault on their city. In 1659 there were new grounds for relief: 'the Lord has preserved me from harm in Amsterdam. Now I stand on better terms with the city'.[85] To confirm these impressions William Frederick often asked his court purveyor in Amsterdam, Coenraat Clenck, to find out what people in the city thought of him.[86] Yet in the years that followed his patron's death William Frederick would ultimately be forced to adjust to the new realities of power and formulate a new answer to the challenges that confronted him as former client of Orange.

Notes

1 'Through his bold deeds he fell'. On the reverse of the medal is a riderless horse. Below, the river Amstel is represented with two blockhouses, while in the background the city of Amsterdam can be recognised. Obverse and reverse of the medal were also illustrated in a print, beneath a portrait of William II. Van Rijn, *Atlas van Stolk*, II, 323. Cf. Rijksprentenkabinet Amsterdam, Frederik Muller, 1997 (twenty medals struck in memory of William II).

2 The poem opens 'In November of the Golden Year, the setting sun saw how the sixth day closed the days of the second William, who tried to plague our country, where peace and freedom were planted, with the burdens of war'. Bergsma, *Hekeldichten*, 118. Vondel's poem is said to have been pasted on the boxes in which the medal was sold. Van Nooten, *Prins Willem II*, 169.

3 Groen, *Archives*, IV, 358.

4 KHA, WF, VII, C-64 (letters from Joachim Andreae to William Frederick, December 1649 to May 1650, from The Hague).

5 Kernkamp, *Prins Willem II*, 117; Wijnne, *De geschillen*, lxxxi.

6 Groenveld, 'Unie, religie en militie', 79–81.

7 On the embassy, Groenveld, 'Een schaep in 't schapelandt', 187–8. For the dismissal of the troops, Wijnne, *De geschillen*, xliv–xlvi. Also Kernkamp, *Prins Willem II*, 107.

8 Frijhoff and Spiess, *Dutch Culture in European Context*, 75–8; Van der Plaat, *Eenheid als opdracht*, esp. 155–73. Geyl saw it rather differently: Geyl, *Orange and Stuart*, 59–60.

9 *Gloria Parendi*, 704, 715, and 720–1.

10 From the end of October 1649; ibid., 707–8 and 722–4.

11 NA, SG, Resolutions of the States-General, 5 and 6 June 1650. The commission that was appointed on 6 June consisted mainly of confidants of the prince: Johan Mauregnault, Johan van Reede van Renswoude and Adriaan Clant. Alexander van der Capellen was chairman. The commission was completed by three members of the Council of State, Philips Jacob van Boetzelaer, Willem Lucas and the treasurer-general Govert Brasser.

12 Aitzema, *Herstelde leeuw*, 64. See also Groenveld, *Evidente factiën*, 41.

13 SAD, Stadsarchief, Resoluties Oud-Raad, 1643–52, fols 129r–33r.

14 Van der Capellen, *Gedenkschriften*, II, 308; Wagenaar, *Amsterdam*, V, 84. In this connection Wagenaar confused Andries and Cornelis Bicker. The latter was burgomaster in 1650. For the deputation see also Poelhekke, *Geen blijder maer*, 87–103.

15 GAA, Burgemeestersarchief, 5029-14 (Coenraad van Beuningen to the deputies in the States of Holland, 25 June 1650, from Amsterdam); Wagenaar, *Amsterdam*, V, 84–6. In many towns the decision whether or not to admit William to an audience in the *vroedschap* hinged on the capacity in which he would appear: as stadholder or as a commissioner from the States-General.

16 Groenveld, 'Een enckel valsch ende lasterlijck verdichtsel'.

17 KHA, WII, VIII, 4 (notes of William II on possible detainees, 1650); KHA, WF, VII, C-64 (Joachim Andreae to William Frederick, 2 April 1650, from The Hague); *Gloria Parendi*, 707 and 729; Groen, *Archives*, IV, 395 and 432. It is also striking that several of them had formerly been involved in William's financial affairs: Cornelis Bicker as burgomaster of Amsterdam, which had made a large secured loan to William in April 1650, De Witt and Duyst van Voorhout because they had bought several Orange estates, which William II had been forced to sell because of his burden of debts. There was a rumour in 1650 that the prince wanted to seize the funds of the Amsterdam Bank. NA, ND (notes of 7 April 1648 and 4 March 1649). Other motives for the choice of the regents named are given by Eysten, *Het leven*, 141–2, Kernkamp, *Prins Willem II*, 151–4, and Wijnne, *De geschillen*, 145–6.

18 KHA, WF, VII, C-64 (including the letters of Joachim Andreae to William Frederick, 7 April 1650, from The Hague); *Gloria Parendi*, 722; Kluiver, 'Brieven', 42.

19 William Frederick rarely used force in his provinces. In 1662, with powers from the States, he suppressed guild riots in Groningen. During the troubles of 1640 a few rioters were arrested. See chapter 1 and Tonckens, 'Het proces-Schulenborgh', 66–93.

20 *Gloria Parendi*, 369, 699, 704 and 719.

21 Ibid., 570 and 683. The letter from Lipsius to Fuentes is in Bor, *Oorsprongk*, IV, 607. William Frederick had several copies of Bor's history in his library (NA, ND, 893).

22 *Gloria Parendi*, 735. There were stubbornly persistent rumours of this assassination scheme; LAD, Oranienbaum, A7b, 115, fol. 37r. (statements of one 'Bouman' about the plan to 'do away with' William II).

23 *Gloria Parendi*, 722–3 and 734. Cf. Egmond, 'De aansprakelijkheid van God', 11–27.

24 Groen, *Archives*, IV, 354; *Gloria Parendi*, 707–8; the citation from Oldenbarnevelt is in Kooijmans, *Liefde in opdracht*, 145.

25 Groenveld, 'Een enckel valsch ende lasterlijck verdichtsel', 113–14.

26 LAD, Oranienbaum, A7b, 172, fol. 4r. (testament of William Frederick, 'being of sound mind, in my chamber at The Hague, the 17–27 July 1650, Wednesday afternoon').

27 LAD, Oranienbaum, A7b, 172, fol. 4r (statement of William Frederick). William Frederick expressed the hope 'that princess Albertine will always wear something I owned, a diamond or pearls, all her life long, every day as long as that sweet princess and fair angel lives'. Two days later he also wrote her a personal letter, 'que je ne may jamais ose dire a Vostre Altesse par grand respect que je vous ay toejours porte.' LAD, Oranienbaum, A7b, 172, fol. 3r. Cf. Groenveld. 'Gemengde gevoelens', 34.

28 This scheme only came to light in December 1650, after the arrest of Breeckevelt and his brother. See references to it in KHA, WF, VII, B-III/1a (Reinier Casembroot to William Frederick, 18 December 1650, from The Hague); Tresoar, SA, 367-X (Dirck van Ruijven to William Frederick, 24 December 1650, from The Hague). Cornelis van Aerssen was also in the secret of the plan. On 30 July 1650 he spread the rumour around Haarlem that Amsterdam had concluded a treaty with the English, and that he would therefore proceed to attack the city. ADK, Stadsarchief Haarlem, vroedschap resolutions, fols 147v–149v (30 July 1650). For more detail on the affair see Groenveld, 'Een enckel valsch ende lasterlijck verdichtsel'.

29 Groenveld, De prins voor Amsterdam, 42–53; Israel, The Dutch Republic, 605–8; Van de Klashorst, 'Metten schijn van monarchie getempert', 96ff; Van der Plaat, Eenheid als opdracht, 161–71.

30 Geyl, 'Een engelsch republikein', 83. Cf. Gloria Parendi, 723 and 738.

31 See the account of Nanning Keyser: Kernkamp, 'Memorie van Nanning Keyser', 342–406.

32 Christian von Dohna was attached to William's court, while Gosewijn Wiedenfelt and Doeke van Hemmema were members of William Frederick's. Other army officers were Pellnitz, Bax and Hume. Tresoar, SA, 367-E (letters of William II to William Frederick, 29 July 1650, from The Hague); KHA, WII, IX, 2 (statement of William II, n.d.).

33 GAA, Burgemeestersarchief, 5025-19 (vroedschap resolution, 30 July 1650). There is a detailed account of the assault in De Beaufort, 'De aanslag', 66–101.

34 William II explicitly asked Cornelis de Graaf to negotiate for him. The other negotiators were Nicolaas Tulp, Pieter Cloeck and Simon van der Does. GAA, Burgemeestersarchief, 5025-19 (vroedschap resolutions, 1–2 August 1650); Kernkamp, Prins Willem II, 135. In the meantime Amsterdam tried to approach the other towns of Holland about negotiations: LAD, Oranienbaum, A7b, 92, fol. 109r (secretary Gerard Hulst to the magistrates of Leiden, 31 July 1650, from Amsterdam); NA, Raadpensionaris, 136 (Gerard Simonsz Schaep to the deputies in the States of Holland, 1 August 1650, from Amsterdam).

35 KHA, WII, IX, 2. Also printed as Verdragh, Ghemaeckt tusschen sijn Hoocheyt aen d'eene zyde: ende de Heeren Burgemeesteren ende xxvj Raden der Stadt Amstelredamme ...

36 Van der Plaat, Eenheid als opdracht, 155–6; Rowen, The Princes of Orange, 91; Geyl, Orange and Stuart, 64–5; Kernkamp, Prins Willem II, 186. Cf. also Israel, The Dutch Republic, 607–9; Troost, William III, 12–19; Price, Holland and the Dutch Republic, 137.

37 Groenveld, De prins voor Amsterdam, 30–1; Poelhekke, Geen blijder maer, 163–79.

38 Gloria Parendi, 738.

39 RAG, Van der Capellen, 89 (Gerlach van der Capellen to Alexander van der Capellen, 26 July – 5 August 1650, from Budelhof).

40 LAD, Oranienbaum, A7b, 92, fols 2r–5v (Johan van Reede to William II, 7 September 1650, from Utrecht).

41 'Felicitations' are in LAD, Oranienbaum, 92; Aitzema, Herstelde leeuw, 126–30; Wijnne, De geschillen, 178–9 and 189. In Utrecht the meeting about the letter was a lengthy one because the city was unwilling to show 'appreciation' of the coup. UA, SvU, 232-24 (resolutions of 30 August and 5 September 1650).

42 Price, Holland and the Dutch Republic, 137 and 147.

43 Gloria Parendi, 738. William II died of smallpox. Rumours that the prince had been poisoned began to circulate immediately, but no convincing proof of this has ever been produced. Cf. De Beaufort, 'De dood', 102–14; Schoon, 'Het vermoeden', 7–15; Polyander, 'Journaal van Johan van Kerckhoven', 544.

44 Aitzema, Herstelde leeuw, 143.

45 Ibid.

46 Fruin, *Brieven aan De Witt*, I, 11.

47 Harding, *Anatomy*, 68–87 and 106–7.

48 Greengrass, 'Noble Affinities', 285–300.

49 Kettering, 'Clientage during the French Wars of Religion', 221–39. Other examples of clienteles in periods of crisis in Mączak, 'From Aristocratic Household', 321–4; Kettering, *Patrons, Brokers and Clients*, 185–91.

50 Van Nierop, 'Willem van Oranje', 675.

51 Veeze, *De raad van de prinsen*, 72–9.

52 Tresoar, SA, 367-X (Dirck van Ruijven to William Frederick, 30 December 1650, from The Hague).

53 NA, ND, 7 (notes of the Domain Council, 31 December 1650). Free meals were part of the working conditions of many courtiers.

54 NA, ND, 563 (list of nobles paid until 31 December, 17 April 1652; list of officers and servants who were dismissed after 31 December, n.d.).

55 Frijhoff, 'Het Haagse hof', 10–16; Israel, 'The Courts', 130–1; Mörke, 'Stadtholder' oder 'Staetholder', 91–151; Veeze, *De raad van de prinsen*, 73–106; Wijsenbeek, *Het Lange Voorhout*, 45.

56 Tresoar, SA, 367-X (Dirck van Ruijven to William Frederick, 24 December 1650, from The Hague). After 1651 William Frederick still kept in touch with the ex-secretary. *Gloria Parendi*, 747; KHA, WF, VII, C-146 (Johan Goethals to William Frederick, 19–29 July 1661, from Delft).

57 NA, ND, 563 (appointment of Huygens, 29 November 1651).

58 KHA, WF, VII, B-III/1a (Reinier Casembroot to William Frederick, 18 December 1650, from The Hague); Tresoar, SA, 367-X (Dirck van Ruijven to William Frederick, 16 December 1650, from The Hague); Groen, *Archives*, V, 24; Groenveld, 'Een out ende getrouw dienaer', 19–20.

59 NA, Aitzema, 10 (letterbook, 22 November 1650); NA, ND, 7 (minutes of the council 10, 11 November and 5 December 1650; Aitzema, *Saken van staet en oorlogh*, III, 461.

60 GAA, Burgemeestersarchief, 5026–55 (Jacob Bas to the burgomasters of Amsterdam, 31 March 1651, from Middelburg).

61 NA, Aitzema, 95 (documents on the House of Orange with notarised deeds, 1650–51); Polyander, 'Journaal van Johan van Kerckhoven', 553–644.

62 Tresoar, SA, 367-X (Dirck van Ruijven to William Frederick, 6 January 1651, from The Hague).

63 NA, ND (minutes, 29 December 1650); Polyander, 'Journaal van Johan van Kerckhoven', 553–644. Cf. Groenveld, 'Verdicht verleden', 305–6.

64 NA, Aitzema, 95 (documents on the House of Orange and notarised deeds of both parties, 1650–51); Worp, *Briefwisseling*, V, xi; Geyl, *Orange and Stuart*, 146. The guiding role of Frederick William of Hohenzollern – the elector of Brandenburg – in Amalia's faction is not entirely clear. Cf. NA, Aitzema, 95 (notarised statements of the elector on the guardianship, 1651).

65 Fuller accounts of the conflict in Geyl, *Orange and Stuart*, and Veeze, *De raad van de prinsen*.

66 Aitzema, *Saken van staet en oorlogh*, III, 461, and *Herstelde leeuw*, especially 150–2 and 310–13; Fruin and Colenbrander, *Staatsinstellingen*, 275–7; Groenveld, *Evidente factiën*, 46. In the Zeeland towns of Veere and Flushing Orange retained his rights of appointment because these places were personal possessions of the family.

67 Price, 'The Dutch Nobility', 95–102; Poelhekke, *Geen blijder maer*, 205–46.

68 Streng, 'Le métier du noble', 65–6.

69 Aitzema, *Herstelde leeuw*, 143; Koenheim, *Johan Wolfert van Brederode*, 34–5. See also Otterspeer, *Groepsportret*, I, 376. Brederode also nourished hopes of becoming stadholder or captain-general of Utrecht himself. See chapter 6.

70 Perlot, *De Staten van Utrecht*, 14–17. Meanwhile Van Reede did not neglect his relations with Orange: in 1653 his son became a page to William III. Cf. Groenveld, *Evidente factiën*, 54.

71 Van der Capellen, *Gedenkschriften*, II, 349 and 354. Cf. Poelhekke et al., *Geschiedenis van Gelderland*, 205, and *Geen blijder maer*, 245; Rowen, *John de Witt*, 154–69.

72 Tresoar, SA, 367-X (Dirck van Ruijven to William Frederick, 24 December 1650, from The Hague); Israel, *The Dutch Republic*, 706.

73 NA, Raadpensionaris, 65 (documents and votes on the amnesty 1651); 66 and 124 (reports on the amnesty); Aitzema, *Herstelde leeuw*, 680ff.; Groen, *Archives*, V, 42–7. Van Aerssen had feared a political day of reckoning as early as 1649. *Gloria Parendi*, 701. He formally remained a member of the nobility, but agreed to no longer attend its meetings.

74 NA, Aitzema, 10 (letterbook, 20 December 1650). The well-informed Dirck van Ruijven described Musch's death as natural: Tresoar, SA, 367-X (Dirck van Ruijven to William Frederick, 16 December 1650, from The Hague). The most recent analysis of Musch's career and death is in Knevel, *Het Haagse bureau*, 123–44.

75 KHA, WF, VII, C-64 (Joachim Andreae to William Frederick, 17 May 1651, from The Hague); GAA, Burgemeestersarchief, 5026–55 (Frans Oetgens van Waveren to the burgomasters, 7 June 1651, from Zeeland); Fruin, *Brieven aan De Witt*, I, 19 and 25. Cf. 't Hart, 'Autonoom maar kwetsbaar'. Ten years later Thibaut made a political comeback in Middelburg. Van der Bijl, *Idee en interest*, 17–20.

76 This text is found in manuscript in the archives of William II. KHA, WII, XII, 2. For a survey of the pamphlets see Geyl, 'Het stadhouderschap in de partij-literatuur'; Groenveld, *De prins voor Amsterdam*; Van de Klashorst, 'Metten schijn van monarchie getempert'. A more complete picture is in Knuttel, *Catalogus van de pamfletten-verzameling*, II-1, 113–38.

77 Aitzema, *Herstelde leeuw*, 159; Elias, *De vroedschap*, I, ci; GAA, Burgemeestersarchief, 5025–19 (*vroedschap* resolution, 8 November 1650).

78 Groenveld, *De prins voor Amsterdam*, 32–75; idem, *Evidente factiën*, 42–3; Van de Klashorst, 'Metten schijn van monarchie getempert', 93–136; Van der Plaat, *Eenheid als opdracht*, 143–73.

79 Compare Kossmann, *Political Thought*. See also Geyl, 'Het stadhouderschap in de partij-literatuur'; Van de Klashorst, 'Metten schijn van monarchie getempert'. For the significance of these idealistic motives see Van der Bijl, *Idee en interest*, 166–95; Israel, *The Dutch Republic*, 702–7; Price, *Holland and the Dutch Republic*, 161.

80 ING, Notulen Schot, 7 December 1650; WFG, OAM, 1305 (Nicolaas Stellingwerff and Jacob Acker to the burgomasters, 14 December 1650, from The Hague).

81 *Gloria Parendi*, 738.

82 Ibid., 747.

83 KHA, WF, VIII, 3-I (note of 4–14 July 1651).

84 Cf. Psalms 59 and 69.

85 KHA, WF, VIII, 3-I (notes of 10–20 December 1651; 1–11 January 1651, 6–16 September 1658, 1–11 January 1659). Also compare Bontemantel, *De regeeringe*, I, 217. Thurloe, *A Collection*, I, 318.

86 KHA, WF, VI, 14; VII, C-188; Tresoar, SA, 30, 31, 32.

Part III
Without a patron, 1650–1664

6

New relationships

As was his habit every year, on 1 January 1651 William Frederick looked back in his diary on the events of the last twelve months. All in all, the balance sheet was favourable: although 1650 had been a year of disaster, the stadholder had to admit that he himself had been spared the worst of its ill effects. William Frederick thought he had good reason to see his 'prosperity' as an example and a further confirmation of God's particular design for him and his family. 'No one', he wrote, 'owes the Lord more gratitude than I do.'[1]

When William Frederick wrote these words of thanks, his life had just taken a radically new course. The death of William II had overturned relationships within the family, and its consequences had dramatically transformed the political landscape in the Republic. In the years that followed the death of the Boss, William Frederick found himself compelled to adjust to the new political order. That meant rethinking his role as a patron and also redefining his relations with the House of Orange.

Discord

In itself such a political and social reorientation was not new for William Frederick. In the years before 1650 the count had more than once had to adjust his roles as patron or client to suit the circumstances in Friesland or The Hague. Yet after the death of his patron, William Frederick was forced to be much more flexible than ever before, because the political degradation of Orange and the absence of an adult head of the family had removed all the familiar hierarchical landmarks. Before 1650 his patronage roles had helped him to interpret his own experiences by the example of his predecessors. The count, as a client, had tried to emulate his uncle William Louis, whose relations with Maurice he took as his pattern. For one who constantly sought historical parallels to help him define and legitimise his own position and conduct, the events of 1650 were extraordinarily challenging. His predicament after William's death, in which he was left without a patron, was one for which William Frederick could find no precedents to guide him. 'If His Highness had not died, all would have been well', he wrote in one of his almanacs for the 1650s.[2] In such a situation, where the old bonds seemed to be broken, the count was forced to look for a new role model.

This need for reorientation was made more urgent by the continuing discord within the family itself. Like other court clients in the winter of 1650–51, the count of Nassau-Dietz was in fact obliged to choose between the rival factions that had emerged in the House of his late patron. William Frederick was reluctant to make such a choice; or at least in the months after William's death he preferred not to associate himself too explicitly with either of the princesses. Neither Mary nor Amalia appreciated this neutral attitude.[3] 'Her Highness ... is very ill-pleased with me, speaks ill of me, and will not write to me', he recorded in January 1651.[4] Amalia's suspicions were fed by William Frederick's solicitations for office in several stadholderless provinces at this time. It was clear to her by now that this Friesian cousin was trying to exploit William's death for his own advantage. The English courtier Sir Edward Nicholas inferred from the count's refusal to align himself with either princess 'that count William was so intent on his own advantage' that he was not to be relied on:

> I continue sometimes on occasion to correspond with count William, albeit I have no great confidence in him, having heard and observed him to be so avaricious and ambitious as that he will for his own ends and advantage do that which I cannot understand to become a person of his quality to do.[5]

This picture of the count's attitude sketched by those concerned has prevailed until recently among historians, but it is doubtful if it is entirely accurate. At any rate the count would not have recognised himself in it. He felt that the mistrust aroused by his applications in Groningen and Drenthe was particularly unjustified. Since the stadholderships of those provinces had formerly been held by his brother, father and uncle, William Frederick believed it was his plain duty to keep these posts in the family. He saw no contradiction between his bids to become stadholder of the provinces where his 'forebears' had held the same office, and his undiminished loyalty to the House of Orange. Therefore he was indignant when Amalia openly doubted his integrity: 'But it seems that woman cannot stand me, and always tries to put me down, though unreasonably, for I have always served, honoured, waited on and respected her more than anyone has done'.[6] In his letters to Cornelis van Aerssen and Constantijn Huygens, William Frederick also reiterated his undiminished 'obéissance et service' to the House of Orange.[7]

William Frederick's policy in the winter of 1651 was indeed more influenced by doubts and concerns than courtiers such as Nicholas suggested. The count was convinced that the family ought above all to reflect unity and for that reason he found it difficult over the winter of 1650–51 to take sides. He did not regard his reluctance to side with Mary or Amalia as disloyalty, but as part of his effort to prevent the further disintegration of the House. Torn between conflicting interests, William Frederick looked for inspiration in the bible, which he read intensively at this time. The prayers he wrote down express the same hope for divine guidance. 'I pray to your divine majesty for the support of your holy spirit, for alone I can do and think no good.'[8] In his day-to-day notes William Frederick often repeated his attachment to the House of Nassau and his reverence for Orange. 'I prayed the Lord', he wrote in July 1651, 'that the amnesty may proceed ... so that it may be settled for His Highness's honour and reputation with unity, good correspondence and the preservation of the country and the good inhabitants.' When there was still no improvement two years later, he again asked God 'not to allow His Highness, our House or me to be harshly oppressed, but Lord arouse pious hearts and good patriots to maintain my continued existence and to keep me in honour and consideration'. William Frederick was even willing to endure Amalia's reproaches, if that would preserve peace. He resolved to be 'on good terms with Her Highness and to keep in her good favour and graces, even if I have to force myself, if she does me wrong, to let it go unnoticed, without being indignant at it or opposing her when she is in the wrong, which she cannot bear'.[9]

These passages display a striking resemblance to the reflections that William Frederick had committed to paper the night before the attack on Amsterdam.[10] It seems, therefore, that the count had seen no reason to change his perception of the bonds that bound him to the House of Orange. To underscore his unbroken loyalty, he also expressed his constant care for the family in his letters to Mary's brother, the pretender to the English throne, Charles II. From 1652 William Frederick made repeated appeals to Charles 'to work as hard as it is possible for him for a good correspondence and union of their Highnesses'. He argued that continual disorder within the family would profit no one but the prince's enemies.[11] As we shall see, this rhetorical emphasis on unity and continuity was also William Frederick's personal response to the feelings of instability with which he was continually wrestling. In practice his course of action was bound to be less straightforward than the rhetoric and principles he noted in his diary would suggest.

Rivals

It was, after all, not William Frederick's often repeated calls for 'unity' in the family that kept the quarrel alive, but the question of who should embody this unity. Like those of all the other candidates, the count of Nassau's answer to this question was rather egocentric. As the sole surviving stadholder he considered himself the proper person to represent the young William III in the provinces for the time being. This self-imposed task led him to put himself forward success-fully as stadholder in Groningen and Drenthe, and then to try to establish his claim to a role as 'lieutenant-stadholder' in the other stadholderless provinces.

It is not altogether clear if the idea of the lieutenant-stadholdership was entirely his own, but at any rate it was an attractive solution from his point of view, for it offered a new yet honourable manifestation of his bond with Orange, which could appeal to certain precedents. William Louis and Ernst Casimir had been lieutenant-stadholders in Friesland and Gelderland, albeit in rather different circumstances.[12] William Frederick found these historical parallels good enough grounds to justify his new role as representative of the prince. In December 1650 he reminded several of the provincial States of 'the unforget-table good services of the highly praiseworthy House of Orange', hoping thereby to hasten the appointment of the young William III. 'But since in this unusual conjuncture and these tempestuous times, the youth of the aforesaid prince does not permit him to steer the ship of this state, crewed and filled with so many interests, divisions and religions, by himself', it made sense to appoint him, William Frederick, as the provisional lieutenant of this 'young shoot'.[13] Ambition and a sense of duty could go hand in hand.

Unfortunately not everyone in Orange circles was convinced by William Frederick's rhetoric. The doubters naturally included the infant prince's rival guardians, Mary and Amalia, but William Frederick's path as the protector of his future patron was also barred by his cousin, John Maurice of Nassau-Siegen, and Amalia's brother-in-law, Johan Wolfert van Brederode. When the Friesian stadholder solicited the lieutenant-stadholdership of the other provinces at the end of 1650, he was surprised to find two competitors there before him. Reinier Casembroot wrote to William Frederick that field-marshal Brederode had got in first in Utrecht with an application for the post of captain-general. Although this military office was independent on paper, Brederode's applica-tion certainly competed with William Frederick's ambitions.[14] John Maurice, the former governor of Dutch Brazil, also announced his candidacy in Utrecht in the same month. He reminded the States that he was 'currently the eldest in the eldest branch of the House of Nassau'. Besides his seniority he claimed to be the most eligible candidate on the grounds of experience, for, he wrote, 'it should be recalled that both here and overseas I have served the United Provinces in various high capacities and charges for thirty years in all faithfulness'.[15]

The presence of three rival candidates in Utrecht revealed just how hopelessly divided the House of Nassau had become since William's death. There had been squabbles within the family under Frederick Henry and William II, but now, without a central Orange patron to hold the ring, they got out of hand. Even Frederick William of Hohenzollern, the elector of Brandenburg, ruled himself out as a possible mediator by explicitly aligning himself with his mother-in-law Amalia.[16] The situation hardly improved in the following years. Mary and Amalia remained openly at loggerheads until Mary's death in 1660, and John Maurice refused to submit to William Frederick's claims to the ad hoc leadership of the family. When Brederode died in 1655 and William Frederick claimed his field-marshal's rank, he again found John Maurice 'working hard against this'. 'We had hoped in vain', wrote a disappointed William Frederick, 'that our cousin the prince Maurice, for various pregnant reasons, would have allowed himself to be moved not to pursue his initial pretension to the vacant field-marshal's office.'[17] But the interest of unity could not prevail against individual ambition. Quarrels about seniority and prestige flared up time and again throughout the 1650s and 1660s. William Frederick's authority in the army was further undermined by Louis of Nassau-Beverweert, who as a son, if only a natural one, of a prince of Orange simply refused to serve under a count of Nassau-Dietz.[18]

The power of the broker

Lack of leadership was not the family's only misfortune; the loss of its sources of patronage further complicated matters. As long as the young prince of Orange lacked the authority and the powers to present himself as a new patron, the family members had to look for other ways to maintain themselves and their friends. Only a few could realistically hope to find them. Many of Orange's relatives and courtiers had had hardly any power base of their own that would give them access to the sources of patronage in the republican system. The more dependent on the prince they had been, the more dramatic was their fall from high position during the stadholderless period.

William Frederick's own prospects were not unpromising. His combined stadholderships gave him a significant patronage fund of his own, which made him less vulnerable to the loss of influence from the Oranges. Indeed, besides allowing him to maintain his own clientele, these resources gave him an opportunity to mediate on behalf of relatives. William Frederick had distributed his Friesian patronage funds at the Orange court earlier to please his patrons Frederick Henry and William II, but after 1650 he was in a relatively stronger position. Mary and Amalia could use the domain lands to provide several courtiers with administrative offices, but William Frederick was the only member of the family who could satisfy the urgent demand for military appointments.[19]

That explains the extremely respectful letters he received from, among others, Elizabeth Stuart of Bohemia. In February 1651, she recommended several of her courtiers for military posts.[20] Her nephew, the exiled Charles II, also repeatedly solicited the help of his Friesian 'cousin' in these years in securing military positions for his English protégés.[21] Constantijn Huygens and other courtiers were equally dependent on William Frederick's favour, especially since these well-known Orangists were unable to obtain a military post in stadholder-less Holland.[22] Above all it was Amalia van Solms who appealed most successfully to her 'beau fils' William Frederick when military vacancies had to be filled. In 1656, for example, Frederick Henry's widow procured an officer's post in a Friesian regiment for her servant Jan Martijn.[23]

During the 1650s William Frederick became very practised in steering military appointments toward his family. He manoeuvred himself into a strategic position as broker by being of service now to one faction, now to another in the House of Orange. Thanks to this, he enhanced his standing in the family, and also made himself a much more attractive prospect to Amalia as a potential son-in-law. Her eventual decision in 1651 to grant him Albertine's hand in marriage can be explained by these shifts in political and military influence. The widow herself left it in no doubt that it was not the count of Nassau-Dietz, but the stadholder of Friesland and Groningen, whom she desired as her son-in-law.[24]

Success in Groningen and Drenthe

In a sense, William Frederick profited from Orange's loss of patronage resources, and his marriage was by no means his only success in this field. He also seized the opportunity to draw some of the prince's former sources of patronage into his own hands. His first step was to right a painful wrong done him ten years earlier. In December 1650 he made a new bid to secure the stadholderships of the provinces of Groningen and Drenthe, which Frederick Henry had secured for Orange in 1640.

Only two weeks after William's death, William Frederick's first letters soliciting his appointment were on their way to the north.[25] At the same time he tried to add weight to his candidacy by urging the States of Friesland to send a deputation to the city and Ommelanden of Groningen. Naturally those official lobbyists were not chosen at random, but belonged without exception to his most loyal clients in Friesland, including Cornelis Haubois and Johan van Aylva.[26] Interestingly, Frederick Henry had adopted much the same approach in 1640. William Frederick seems to have learned the lesson of his failed lobbying ten years earlier, and repeated the tried and tested strategy of the prince in 1650. The new approach bore witness to the insight he had gained over the years and to the greater flexibility he could display, not least in financial inducements. 'We had to spend notable sums', Vegelin wrote later in his autobiography, 'and the steward Wiedenfelt was sent express to Groningen.'[27]

Wiedenfelt indeed received orders from William Frederick to make overtures to some of the political heavyweights in Groningen, among them the *jonker* Osebrand Jan Rengers of the Ommelanden. Unfortunately it is not clear who took the initiative for this alliance, but in any case it was the nobleman who wrote to William Frederick on 28 November about 'certain clients of Your Excellency' whom he had lately met. He had also had meetings with 'those who, as we well knew, are well affectioned to this business'. Rengers proved willing to support the stadholder's application, and believed that his own network of 'clients and obedient servants' could bring the election to a speedy and successful conclusion.[28] By so explicitly offering his own local clientele to the stadholder, the *jonker* positioned himself to become a provincial broker in future. It was a familiar strategy, and one which the burgomaster of Leeuwarden Alle van Burum had already employed in Friesland.

William Frederick, however, did not wish to be exclusively dependent on Rengers and his following, for his Friesian experience had taught him that operating through brokers involved all kinds of risks. At the same time, therefore, he approached some gentlemen in Groningen directly. The Friesian deputy in The Hague, Joachim Andreae, helped him in this and was ordered to pay calls on several Groningen deputies in The Hague, among them burgomaster Pieter Eyssinga 'in his own house'. During these visits Andreae could drop hints that the stadholder would be willing to 'do them agreeable services on occasion' if they supported his candidacy.[29] William Frederick himself also asked several Groningen regents to discuss the matter with their 'sons and other gentlemen, their correspondents and friends', so that they could join forces and 'help to direct matters so that I am chosen stadholder at the next *Landdag*'.[30] The would-be stadholder was willing to reward the help received, even with money: 'And because I know very well that the freeholders cannot be led except by some means, I shall assure your honours and promise to pay the freeholders the sum of twenty thousand guilders, if the stadholdership of the Ommelanden is conferred on me'.[31] This time William Frederick's campaign succeeded, and on 9 December 1650 he was at last able to call himself stadholder of Groningen.

It is hard to say whether the inducements he offered were decisive. Probably the political constellation in the province and the absence of a serious opponent contributed as much to his early and successful nomination. In 1650 William Frederick seems to have been a less controversial candidate than he had been in 1640. There was hardly any factional rivalry, or as Vegelin put it: 'This time the parties were not so hard'. Moreover, the Groningers had not gained the benefits they had expected in 1640 from ten years of their connection with Orange, so that a renewed alliance with Nassau-Dietz appeared attractive to the various factions. It has also been pointed out that there was a noticeable anti-Holland sentiment in the city and the Ommelanden, from which William Frederick could also profit.[32]

The count's success in Groningen foreshadowed a similar success in Drenthe, where his campaign followed almost the same pattern. After their visit to Groningen the Friesian deputies moved on to Assen, to convince their colleagues in Drenthe of the value of sharing a stadholder. Gosewijn Wiedenfelt was again one of the deputies, sent 'to direct the affair', as he himself said. The steward did not not go to Drenthe empty-handed; his baggage included 'three ewers with accessories and three pairs of candlesticks ... worth about six hundred guilders each', which he was to distribute in the corridors of power, 'on His Excellency's instructions'.[33] Prominent Drenthe notables were shown favourable consideration. The *drost* Rutger van den Boetzelaer was honoured by a visit in his house, where he was promised the command of a company of soldiers, 'from good sincere inclination and affection', if he would support William Frederick's application.[34]

In the meantime the role of broker that Rengers had played in Groningen was assumed in Assen by Johan Struuck, the secretary of the States of Drenthe. He offered to visit his friends 'at the inn here' on William Frederick's behalf, and also to recommend them to Wiedenfelt and the Friesian deputies. But just as in Groningen William Frederick was wary of depending exclusively on local brokers, and on occasion he approached the regents directly, without going through Struuck. On 15 November Joost van Welvelde was asked 'to be willing to help direct and promote the cause with his brothers and other good friends, with the greatest secrecy possible'.[35] Another obvious parallel with the election in Groningen was the absence of factional strife, for in Assen too William Frederick's candidacy in 1650 enjoyed the backing of the most prominent families.[36]

William Frederick's successes in Groningen and Drenthe were thus the result of a favourable political mood, but also of his years of experience as patron and client. This time he managed with remarkable ease to win the support of the local political stars for his candidacy. William Frederick's instructions to Wiedenfelt and Andreae illustrate that he was keenly aware of the hopes and expectations of his future clients. As the construction of his network of clients in Friesland had already revealed, the inexperienced candidate stadholder of 1640 had grown in ten years into a capable strategist of patronage.

Stadholder in Groningen

Yet William Frederick's improved political skills did not guarantee a successful career in Groningen. In fact the prospects were far from promising from the beginning. Just as in Friesland, William Frederick as stadholder and captain-general received a formal job description from the States. The Groningen version took twenty-one articles to summarise the rights and duties of the highest official of the province.[37] Some of them were fairly general, such as his obligation to maintain the 'true religion' or the 'sovereignty of the province', but the stadhold-er's right to appoint to offices was defined in very precise terms, and his authority by comparison with that in Friesland was very limited. The magistrates of the city of Groningen were not appointed by the stadholder, nor did he bestow offices in the Ommelanden. As stadholder William Frederick was only entitled to take the chair of the college of Delegated States when he was in the city.

There were a few army ranks to which he could promote men in his capacity as captain-general. The count underlined this fifteenth article in his own copy of the instruction.[38] He might commission 'troop-captains, captains, lieutenants, cornets and ensigns', it stated, on condition that the vacancies occurred in the field and William Frederick was present in person. In all other cases 'appointments to military rank were at the disposition of the States'. In parenthesis, it added that this rule did not apply to colonels, first lieutenants, majors and quarter-masters, whose appointments by definition were reserved to the States. With his authority so narrowly defined the stadholder of Groningen was not much more than a muzzled top official. Even so, his Friesian experience had taught William Frederick that stadholder's instructions often had gaps in them, which in practice allowed him more room for manoeuvre than the rules suggested. It is quite possible that William Frederick may have tried in Groningen as in Friesland to interpret such ambiguities to his own advantage.

In the spring of 1651, however, it soon became clear that the distribution of power in Groningen was very different from that in Friesland. During the Great Assembly in The Hague, William Frederick was amazed to find that the Groningen deputies had no intention of allowing their votes to be guided by the stadholder. Osebrand Jan Rengers himself refused to be bound by William Frederick's guidelines and began openly to associate with some of the Holland regents.[39] The explanation was probably not William Frederick's lack of capacity, but the rivalries between the Groningers themselves. There was a long-running feud over competence in the provincial government between the city and the Ommelanden, and administrative stability was further weakened by factions, which cut across the two regions.[40]

In these unstable circumstances the stadholder's role was bound to be limited. In 1652 William Frederick was forced to note 'with dismay, that our good and true-hearted intention about the holding of a new conference and settle-ment of two outstanding points, was fruitless and without effect'. Could not the regents learn from the example of their Friesian counterparts? In Leeuwarden, as William Frederick pointed out eloquently, the *Landdag* had ended 'in peace, calm and without the least difficulty'.[41] It is doubtful that this exhortation from Fries-land cut any ice in Groningen. Two years later the situation had barely improved: 'Since recently some new disputes have arisen between the members of the Ommelanden', William Frederick was obliged to set off again for Groningen in an attempt 'if possible, to promote peace, calm and good correspondence among the aforesaid persons.'[42]

In 1655 the unrest got so out of hand that William Frederick called in external assistance. He asked the States-General to send a delegation to the province, and requested the pensionary of Holland Johan de Witt to mediate on their behalf.[43] Two years later there was renewed disorder, and the stadholder was forced to send in troops during guild riots in the city.[44] In 1662 armed force again had to be used in the city of Groningen, reminding William Frederick of the attack on Amsterdam twelve years earlier.[45] His stadholdership in the northern province was ending in factional quarrels, riots and harsh repression. William Frederick tried to get a grip on the always divided administration by cooperating now with one faction, now with another, but he was not enthusiastic about this strategy, which was forced on him by circumstances.[46]

Unstable political systems clearly did not offer fertile soil for the kind of clientage that William Frederick hoped to develop. Despite the chronic instability and the stadholder's limited powers, there are signs that William Frederick tried to form a certain clientele among the Ommelanden *jonkers* by tempting them with military appointments, and to some extent he managed to strengthen his privileges in that context. By putting pressure on the nomination of officers, he succeeded on several occasions in getting commissions in the army for his favourites. Admitting their sons as pages at his court could sometimes help to win the loyalty of the Ommelanden nobles as well.[47] With these modest resources William Frederick hoped in the first place to attach a few central figures to his cause, Rengers among them. In 1660, for example, he promised Osebrand Jan's young son 'the first company of horse that we shall have to dispose of in the province of the city and the Ommelanden'. In return, Rengers assured him that he would 'help obtain' for William Frederick's own son the reversion or right to succeed his father as stadholder.[48]

Even so, all these attempts to play the patron had only a limited effect. Rengers, as a broker in the Ommelanden, enjoyed more freedom than such Friesian counterparts as Haubois. In Friesland, it was the stadholder who offered the brokers the chance to consolidate their own position in the towns, but in Groningen the initiative came from Rengers, who placed his own existing network at William Frederick's service in exchange for certain favours. Because Rengers was in a stronger bargaining position, his relationship with the count was less asymmetrical than that of Haubois. It was also much less permanent, for once he had got his company and supported the reversion, the *jonker* had no further need to act as William Frederick's intermediary.[49] William Frederick simply lacked the means to retain a broker such as Rengers for very long, and as a result his patronage in Groningen was less intensive and less durable than that in Friesland.

Stadholder in Drenthe

Assen, the capital of Drenthe, was not William Frederick's town either. In general his stadholdership in Drenthe left little trace in the archives, a fact that says a great deal about it. The so-called *Landschap* of Drenthe was the odd man out in the Republic of the United Provinces, for as the 'eighth province' it played no part in the Generality.[50] Nevertheless, it had its own administration and stadholder, who, like his colleagues in Friesland and Groningen, was formally bound by an instruction from the States.[51] The emphasis in this document was very heavily on the duties of the captain-general, who had to supervise the maintenance and provisioning of the frontier fortifications. William Frederick himself was allowed to appoint the commander of the important fortress of Coevorden, but the burgomaster of the village was chosen by the *drost* of Drenthe. There were no real towns in Drenthe, so that the question of appointments to civic magistracies did not arise. The States themselves appointed the other office holders, the *drost*, treasurers and receivers of taxes. Finally, William Frederick had the privilege of appointing some army officers, but only by choosing one name from a list of three presented to him by the States.

Given the weak position of the stadholder in Drenthe and the *Landschap*'s unimportance in the Republic, it is not surprising that William Frederick rarely put in an appearance in Assen. His contribution to local politics seems to have been confined to preserving the administrative status quo by bestowing incidental favours on the clan around the *drost* Rutger van den Boetzelaer and the secretary Johan Struuck. By accepting Van den Boetzelaer's nominees for army commissions William Frederick assured himself of the *drost*'s backing, and so felt no need to disturb the internal structures of power.[52] When William Frederick wanted to secure the reversion of the stadholdership for his son Henry Casimir II in 1661, it was Van den Boetzelaer and Struuck whom he approached. On this occasion he repeated his tactics of eleven years earlier, honouring both gentlemen with unspecified 'advantages'.[53] Although Van den Boetzelaer and Struuck were powerful locally, they never became important clients at William Frederick's court.

Thwarted ambitions

The developments of 1650–51 illustrate how William Frederick was forced to adjust to the new balance of power in the Republic, and how the eclipse of Orange in fact offered him some new opportunities. As a client he lost much by the death of his former patron, but paradoxically as a patron he was free to draw on a wider range of resources. Backed by the successes in Groningen and

Drenthe, William Frederick even tried to put himself in a position as 'lieutenant-stadholder' – on behalf of the young prince of Orange – in the other, stadholderless provinces.[54]

This last ambitious strategy however, was doomed to fail. As in Groningen and Drenthe, William Frederick's plans in December 1650 involved canvassing the most prominent regents in Gelderland, Utrecht, Zeeland, Overijssel and even Holland, either in person or through intermediaries. He began by assembling a core group of reliable 'creatures' or clients: Vegelin, Wiedenfelt and Casembroot from his household, and Joachim Andreae from the Friesian network. Andreae was to visit his fellow deputies in The Hague, while the courtiers were to deliver William Frederick's letters soliciting office in the provinces. They also received lists of names of local regents, whom they had to visit in their homes.[55] In his letters William Frederick appealed to the local elites' loyalty to the prince of Orange, the patron whose place he would take for the time being.[56]

This appeal, however, was problematical as long as the House of Orange itself was not united in backing William Frederick's campaign. The result was that the count of Nassau-Dietz could make hardly any use of the contacts formed by Frederick Henry and William II. To be sure, in December 1650 the count received handsome promises and letters, but he could not be certain of wide support anywhere.[57] The Holland deputations that visited the provinces at the same time were persuasive enough to prevent a hard core of William Frederick's supporters forcing his appointment through the States. Not one of the five stadholderless provinces appointed a new stadholder or even a lieutenant that December.

Even so, William Frederick did not give up hope of acquiring further offices. In the politically unstable 1650s the debate on the stadholdership and the captain-generalship flared up from time to time.[58] Local factional struggles, combined with the protests of pro-Orangist citizens, might turn the political situation upside down at any moment. William Frederick was therefore careful to keep his relationships in the stadholderless provinces in good repair, sometimes by promoting Gelderland or Utrecht nobles to army commissions on Friesland's payroll, sometimes by instructing the Friesian deputies how to vote when there was a military or political office to be disposed of by the States-General or the Council of State.[59] The stadholder also kept a close eye on the mood among Orangist preachers, who could be used to put pressure on the sitting regents by inflaming public opinion against them.[60]

The best time to draw on this credit balance, of course, was when political life was disturbed. In 1652, when the Republic went to war with Cromwell's England, Zeeland seemed to offer a good springboard for a renewed bid for the captain-generalship. The province had been the scene of several minor disturbances, in which local issues of discontent were coupled with a call for the appointment of an army commander from the House of Nassau. Although William Frederick and his supporters managed to present a draft resolution in the States of Zeeland on 21 September, that 'the young prince of Orange may be declared captain- and admiral-general, and during his minority count William of Friesland as his lieutenant', the Zeelanders eventually yielded to pressure from Holland, which prevented the implementation of the resolution.[61]

Meanwhile the Friesian stadholder was accused of fishing in troubled waters. The criticism, especially from Holland quarters, did not prevent William Frederick from risking a new bid for the lieutenancy in Overijssel in 1654. As elsewhere, the occasion was supplied by local factional rivalry. In April of that year the appointment of Rutger van Haersolte as *drost* of Twente split the States of Overijssel: Kampen, Zwolle and most of the nobles supported the appointment, while Deventer and the nobles of Twente opposed it. When the Haersolte camp also pronounced in favour of the stadholdership and approached like-minded factions in Gelderland, Zeeland and Utrecht, their opponents promptly appealed to Johan de Witt, so that a local conflict grew into a rivalry of pro- and anti-stadholder factions in the province. In October, with the support of the Haersoltes, William III was indeed named stadholder and William Frederick his lieutenant, though the resolution was backed by only two-thirds of the States.[62]

Such weak support was bound to lead to complications.[63] Johan de Witt did everything in his power to induce William Frederick to resign the lieutenancy. The death of field-marshal Brederode in September 1655 played into the pensionary's hands. The highest military rank in the Dutch Republic was now vacant, and since it had once been held by his father, William Frederick had a personal motive to regain it for the House of Nassau-Dietz. In the same year the stadholder made an agreement with De Witt, the 'Harmony' as it was called.[64] William Frederick resigned his lieutenancy in Overijssel, in the hope of being named field-marshal soon.

William Frederick's move provoked much criticism, not least in Orangist circles. What's more, it does not seem that De Witt ever really intended to allow his Nassau opponent to hold the field-marshal's rank.[65] The count definitively resigned his lieutenant-stadholdership in October 1657, but the pensionary never gave him more than lukewarm support in his bid for the highest military rank in the following years. Later William Frederick wrote the word 'deceit' alongside the paragraphs in his diaries where the Harmony was mentioned, and drew up a lengthy list of the tricks De Witt had played on him.[66] In fact the vacancy was not filled until 17 January 1668, three years after William Frederick's death, when John Maurice was appointed.[67]

All of William Frederick's bids for the lieutenancy and the rank of field-marshal thus ended in failure. This fiasco has done his already rather doubtful reputation no good among historians. Bilderdijk, Fruin, Poelhekke and Rogier dismissed him as a 'useless worm', a 'second- or third-rate figure', whose 'gibberish' and 'conceit' were completely outclassed by the cunning statecraft of Johan de Witt.[68] But was William Frederick's failure really the result of his own ineptitude or, rather, of the circumstances in which he had to operate? We can at least regard his bids for office in the 1650s as foiled attempts to give his self-defined role as lieutenant of Orange a real content and to take over the former clienteles of Frederick Henry and William II. Three causes offer a more convincing explanation of his failure than the analyses of Fruin or Rogier.

His unsuccessful quest for office in the stadholderless provinces shows, first of all, that William Frederick's patronage resources were simply too meagre for him to build up or take over local clienteles outside Friesland. A stadholder who lacked even the means to win the support of the local political heavyweights in his own province of Groningen could hardly be expected to succeed in provinces where he had no powers of his own.[69] William Frederick had far too few military commissions in his gift or within his influence to retain the loyalty of the noble elite for very long.

Secondly, his power was weakened by the drastic changes in the methods of appointment which had taken place since 1650. After the death of William II the count's opponents, the regents of the wealthiest province Holland, had captured the greatest fund of military patronage in the Republic for themselves. Johan de Witt's correspondence reveals how the pensionary made continual use of these army commissions to keep the nobles in the rural provinces out of William Frederick's sphere of influence. Similarly, De Witt regularly used appointments to administrative posts in Holland and the Generality as opportunities to expand his own clientele. Because the provincial States either retained the former stadholder's rights of appointment in their own hands or left them to local authorities, after 1650 power was slowly transferred into the hands of the Holland regents.[70] Patron-client relations as such did not disappear as a result, but the number of patronage centres as well as potential patrons increased significantly after 1650. The French ambassador Pierre Chanut described the situation in the early 1650s: 'In the present state it is impossible to assure oneself, by any benefits, of persons sufficiently powerful to get a resolution passed'. Things had been very different, he believed, when there had been one patron at the centre, the Orange court, 'who distributed charges and favours, and who kept authority fixed in certain persons'.[71] This process of fragmentation made it difficult for William Frederick to get a hold on the local elites, who had been able to develop positions as patrons in their own right.[72]

Finally, the third reason for William Frederick's failure lay in the hopeless division of the family itself. Hardly an important vacancy occurred in which William Frederick did not find himself opposed by John Maurice or his other relatives. There was no one at court with the authority to call the competing family members to order. The House of his former patron thus itself undermined the influence and prestige that had taken it decades to acquire. This dissipation of trust and authority built up over the years naturally played into the hands of Nassau's enemies. Critics of rule by a stadholder could point to the public quarrels of Amalia, Mary, John Maurice and William Frederick to prove their case.

Affairs in The Hague

William Frederick's dealings in the 1650s do not just point to the changing political landscape in the Republic, but also to some of the long-term effects of his patronage policy in Friesland. For it was during these years that the patron exploited his Friesian power base to defend his interests at the central institutions of the Republic in The Hague.

Within the republican state system, the meetings of the States-General were not formally open to the stadholders, who served as 'servants of the States'. Yet from the 1640s onward, William Frederick had managed to draw the Friesian delegates to the States-General from his most loyal clients.[73] By choosing such men as Andreae, Haubois or Bootsma, the stadholder followed a deliberate policy of placing his own men at the meeting table. This did not go unremarked in The Hague. In February 1651 Alle van Burum, the burgomaster of Leeuwarden, observed that the Friesland delegates were derided as William Frederick's lackeys, because 'they did not dare do anything that did not please' the stadholder. Johan de Witt dismissed them in unflattering terms as the 'creatures of His Lordship count William'.[74]

Indeed, although on paper the deputies from Friesland represented only their sovereign, the provincial States, in practice they received their informal instructions from William Frederick. He required his appointees to keep him regularly informed of political news by sending him weekly reports of the debates.[75] Information was also exchanged orally. 'Mr Andreae was with me twice and gave me a report on everything that has happened in The Hague', William Frederick wrote in May 1648.[76] Probably the stadholder was often better, or at least earlier, informed than the States of Friesland themselves. On 20 February 1650, for example, Andreae asked his patron 'not to communicate the enclosed news until those for the province have followed'.[77] These reports usually enclosed copies of one or more resolutions, and even secret resolutions and minutes were leaked to William Frederick, at his explicit request. On 21 August 1652 Johan van Aylva sent him 'an extract from my notes of the secret business' of 20 August 1652, including strategic information on the States' navy. His colleague Andreae did something similar on 5 May 1646, when he visited the stadholder and discussed what 'he had done on Sunday with the French ambassador' and 'what took place on Monday'.[78]

William Frederick's instructions to the deputies required more from them than regular reports. Between the lines he made it clear enough that he wanted a say in how the Friesian delegates were to vote, for example when political and military vacancies occurred. In February 1654 he asked Johan Aylva in a friendly way to 'favour the case of Doecke Hennema in the assembly', so that this *jonker* might 'be designated by their High Mightinesses to sit in the East India Chamber at Amsterdam'. A month later Aylva was told to 'favour with his vote' the application of Johan Panhuys for a place in the Council of Brabant.[79] The stadholder kept a similarly watchful eye on the Friesian contribution in other areas of policy, sometimes holding preliminary discussions with the delegates in one of his residences in The Hague.[80] Occasionally the deputies themselves took the initiative. In March 1650, for instance, Andreae asked the stadholder 'to advise me in secret of his wise considerations [so that I] can direct my actions and advices more freely accordingly'. He even let William Frederick 'correct' his papers, so that he could 'regulate' himself by the stadholder's comments.[81]

William Frederick intervened more actively in the conduct of the Friesian delegation in the States-General whenever it was Friesland's turn to take the chair for the week, since the chairmanship offered an opportunity to put sensitive topics such as the stadholdership on the agenda, or to influence the wording of resolutions.[82] For this reason Cornelis Haubois wrote to the stadholder in April 1652 that he had passed on William Frederick's instructions 'to Mr Wijckel as president'.[83] Of course the effectiveness of such guidelines depended on the skill and experience of the chairman. In March 1655 William Frederick asked Johan van Aylva to come to The Hague, since 'I believe Your Honour would gladly do Mr Bootsma a service, for His Honour has never presided before'.[84]

William Frederick's meddling in the States-General's business, both invited and uninvited, lacked any constitutional basis.[85] William Frederick therefore asked the deputies to keep their intensive discussions with him secret. But they could hardly be concealed, especially from the deputies of the other provinces. As Johan de Witt's disparaging reference to his 'creatures' suggests, William Frederick's practices were an open secret in The Hague. The pensionary therefore tried as far as possible to exclude Friesian deputies from the most important committees and embassies. William Frederick, for his part, insisted 'that the province of Friesland should always seek to have someone in an embassy', and all in all he got his way remarkably often.[86] The stadholder received regular letters from Matthias Vierssen in Copenhagen in the 1650s, from Allard Jongestall in London during the first Anglo-Dutch War, and from Philips van Humalda in Madrid in the 1660s.[87]

An ideological dimension

The shifts in political power after 1650 presented challenges not only for the networks that William Frederick had to manage but also for those of his competitors. As we saw, the stadholderless regime gradually allowed several new patrons to emerge in the Republic, not least Johan de Witt. As clienteles fragmented, it seems that they also began to assume more clear-cut profiles and develop an ideological vocabulary. Confessional or political ideology had rarely characterised William Frederick's patronage before 1650, but in his correspondence from the 1650s and 1660s the dividing lines between the supporters and opponents of the stadholdership, were much more sharply drawn than they had been before. The development is not strange in itself, for since the death of William II the choice between the alternative forms of government had come to be the question of the hour. Political factions therefore tended to crystallise around different views of the stadholdership. Clientage and political ideology thus became more closely intertwined than they had been in the 1640s.[88]

This ideological conflict of 'republicans' and 'Orangists' also became entangled with the confessional agenda of part of the elite in the Reformed Church. In particular, those preachers with pietist tendencies published numerous pamphlets in the 1650s and 1660s, in which they combined a plea for a stadholder as 'eminent head' of the 'Dutch Israel' with a call to set a more orthodox and pietistic stamp on the Reformed Church. After 1650 William Frederick seems to have identified himself increasingly with this confessional-political programme. His diaries leave no doubt that in his eyes the opposition between 'Holland' and the anti-stadholder regents on the one hand and the 'good party' of Orange on the other had become the central controversy in Dutch politics. William Frederick resorted to this antithesis more and more often in this period to label local, provincial and national divisions. He continually found confirmations of his own generalisations: 'One sees very well nowadays that Holland merchants do not make good politicians', he wrote triumphantly on the outbreak of the First Anglo-Dutch War.[89] At the Orange court too, the name of 'Holland' began to stand for everything that was suspect. A lady of the court, Van Varijck, wrote that 'those of Holland seek nothing but to plunge this afflicted House further into ruin, and to crush it underfoot'.[90]

William Frederick articulated his ideas on the political system of the Republic in more public ways as well. When the 2-year-old William III was made a knight of the Garter in 1653, the Friesian stadholder promptly had the civic militia of The Hague march past his residence on the Vijverberg. Meanwhile a trumpeter provocatively blared out the *Wilhelmus*, the Orange anthem, across the Hofvijver toward the debating chambers of the States-General and States of Holland, where the 'republican' factions of Johan de Witt now had the upper hand.[91] A year later the stadholder pushed through a resolution that required Friesian preachers to pray for the prince of Orange in services in future.[92] This reflected his conviction that the divide between supporters and opponents of Orange ran parallel to that between 'libertines' and orthodox Reformed Protestants, a conviction he underlined time and again in his correspondence with such preachers as Johan Goethals and Maximiliaan Teellinck. Goethals also tried to enlist William Frederick's support in spreading his Reformed and Orangist message in pamphlets. Because he could hardly get them published in Holland any longer, Goethals asked the stadholder if his publications could not be printed in Friesland.[93]

Feelings ran just as high at the other end of the political spectrum. In August 1654 the burgomasters of Amsterdam summoned the keeper of the 'Count William of Friesland' tavern in the Kapelsteeg before them, to demand the immediate removal of his signboard, which bore the 'counterfeit' of William Frederick.[94] A few months earlier Cornelis Haubois had remarked in the States-General that Holland appeared 'to hate and suspect everything that was Nassau'. According to John Thurloe such an attitude was understandable, since the stadholder of Friesland and Groningen stood out openly as 'the head of this faction of the House of Orange'.[95] In Gelderland Hendrik van der Capellen recorded in 1652 that rumours of corruption among Orange's clienteles were being spread 'by several gentlemen who were among those who were in Loevestein'. 'The hatred that some have toward those who enjoyed the prince's esteem', he added, was palpable in the States' debating chamber.[96]

It is obvious that the changed political circumstances after 1650 led to a hardening of political attitudes and more ideologically defined factions and clienteles. A similar process had taken place during the quarrels over the Arminian controversy in 1617–19. Even so, these trends did not represent the formation of genuine party programmes by either Orangists or republicans. In recent decades historians have pointed out that in general it is very difficult to measure the importance of political and confessional ideals in the local political practice of the Dutch Republic. Such ideological considerations may have had influence on the conduct of some regents, but a large part of the political elite could not identify with either extreme: Goethals's missionary zeal or the exaggerated sensitivities of the Amsterdam burgomasters. These broad moderate groups attached far more importance to political flexibility than to ideological hair-splitting. In Utrecht Johan van Reede van Renswoude managed to combine his pledged 'services to the House of Orange' with an amicable cooperation with De Witt.[97] Hendrik Thibaut, the former Orange broker in Zeeland, returned to politics in 1662 without making too much of an issue of his previous loyalties.[98]

These regents may have had preferences on principle for or against Orange or the stadholdership, but it is unlikely that they let them tip the balance. The decisive frame of reference for the men who ruled the Republic was always local or at best provincial.[99] This made perfect sense, for these civic regents had family businesses to run and local power bases to secure for the next generation. As regents it was their duty, furthermore, to maintain order and calm – a responsibility that was hard to reconcile with public discussions of the best form of government. And for anyone who was still uncertain of the future of the Republic it made very good sense to stay on good terms with the various centres of power. The so-called Orangist party was therefore nothing like so unanimous or so centrally organised as some contemporary analysts such as John Thurloe suggested. William Frederick himself was forced to admit that the loyalties the House of Orange had built up before 1650 had not proved sufficiently durable or ideologically rooted for him to appeal to them with any success in the unfamiliar circumstances of the 1650s.

Probably, therefore, the considerations that underlay patronage and faction did not change essentially after 1650, although the way in which those involved wrote about them certainly did. As power fell into new hands the discourse used to speak of clienteles was transformed. William Frederick's clients, for example, more frequently justified their conduct by invoking the interests of the Reformed Church, the House of Orange and the Union of the seven provinces. They knew too well that this was exactly what their patron expected of them in these times. William Frederick's growing identification with pietist-Reformed agendas and his hopes of political success in the stadholderless provinces led many clients to adjust their vocabulary to new preoccupations of their patrons.

Notes

1 *Gloria Parendi*, 738.
2 KHA, WF, VIII, 3-IV (day to day notes, n.d.).
3 Cf. Groen, *Archives*, V, esp. 25; Worp, *Briefwisseling*, V, 61–4 and 23–27 ff.
4 *Gloria Parendi*, 738.
5 *Nicholas Papers*, II, 24, cited from Geyl, *Orange and Stuart*, 98.
6 *Gloria Parendi*, 738–9.
7 Groen, *Archives*, V, 12–13 and 25; Worp, *Briefwisseling*, V, 60–3.
8 *Gloria Parendi*, 741. Cf. his other diary notes for January and February 1651. William Frederick read the bible himself, but probably also had it read to him. In May 1651 the diary mentions that he 'had no time to have the bible read'; *Gloria Parendi*, 748.
9 KHA, WF, VIII, 3-I (note of 16 July 1651); Tresoar, SA, 95 (religious notes of William Frederick, 1653–54).
10 See chapter 5.
11 BOX, Clarendon MS 43, fol. 137r–v (William Frederick to Charles Stuart, 5 June 1652, n.p); 44, fols 37r–40r (William Frederick to Charles Stuart, 9–19 November 1652, from Leeuwarden). William Frederick's letters remained unanswered at the instigation of Mary and Louis of Nassau-Beverweert. The latter probably found the family quarrel to his advantage. Cf. Geyl, *Orange and Stuart*, 97–9.
12 Kleijn, *De stadhouders*, 66.
13 BL, Additional MS 21527, fols 60r–61r (William Frederick to the States of Zeeland, 17–27

December 1650, from Leeuwarden). Cf. RDO, 21 (William Frederick to Floris Borre van Amerongen, 8–18 November 1650, from The Hague).

14 KHA,WF,VII, B-III/1a (Reinier Casembroot to William Frederick, n.d., December 1650); UA, Amerongen, 2748 (Reinout van Tuyll van Serooskercken to Johan van Reede van Renswoude, 29 November 1650, from The Hague). Cf. UA, SvU, 232–24 (resolutions of 14 November and 12 December 1650). Van Nierop, *The Nobility of Holland*, 77.

15 UA, SvU, 232–24 (resolution of 27 November 1650). In the corridors John Maurice had said that he 'goes over the head of Count William or anyone else, as being the eldest of the family'; UA, Amerongen, 2748 (Reinout van Tuyll van Serooskercken to Johan van Reede van Renswoude, 29 November 1650, from The Hague). Cf. *Grondigh bericht*, 16–17.

16 Cf. NA, Aitzema, 95 (final resolution on the guardianship; notarised statements of the elector, 1651).

17 KHA, WF, VI, 14 (William Frederick to Johan de Brune, n.d., 1655; Rucquin van Frentz to William Frederick, 3 November 1655, from Arnhem); VIII, 3-I (Note of William Frederick, 7–17 November 1655); Tresoar, Eysinga, 323–02 (William Frederick to Vegelin, 13–23 August, from Turnhout); KHA, WF, VI, 14 (William Frederick to Anthony Pieterson, 23 August 1658, from Turnhout). See also UA, Huydekoper, 29 (William Frederick to Johan Huydekoper, 13–23 August 1658, from Turnhout); UA, SvU, 278–4 (John Maurice to the States of Utrecht, 25 February 1657, from Cleves); Fruin, *Brieven aan De Witt*, I, 266–7.

18 BOX, Clarendon MS 46, fols 128r–129v (Dirck van Ruijven to Edward Hyde, 7 August 1653, from The Hague).

19 Appointments in the domains were the occasion of numerous conflicts between the two princesses. Veeze, *De raad van de prinsen*, esp. 27–35. Cf. also the complaints that Orange clients made to each party about the other. BOX, Rawlinson MS 115; Clarendon MSS 43–47; KHA, WF, VII, C-203 (correspondence between William Frederick and Johan Mauregnault, from Middelburg, 1651–64).

20 KHA, WF, VII A-IX/3 (Elizabeth Stuart to William Frederick, 6–16 February 1651, from The Hague).

21 Tresoar, SA, 65 (letters of recommendation from Charles II to William Frederick, 1650–62).

22 Worp, *Briefwisseling*, V, 122, 155, 196–7 and 200.

23 KHA, WF, VII, A-II/23 (Amalia to William Frederick, 15 September 1656, from The Hague); VII, B-III (deed appointing Jan Martijn, 16 August 1656).

24 'She would not have been willing to give her daughter to count William, but she gave the same to the States'. Full details of the marriage in Kooijmans, *Liefde in opdracht*, especially 166–74 and 198–206.

25 The first letters are dated 5–15 and 7–17 November 1650. GA, Farmsum, 1019; Tresoar, SA, 37, 1-C; DA, FSAD, 323, folder 1650.

26 Eelco van Glinstra was probably one of the deputation; at any rate he accompanied Haubois and Aylva to Drenthe a few weeks later. Tresoar, SA, 37, 1E; DA, OSA, 6/6003, fols 299–301. Aitzema mentions others who were involved: NA, Aitzema, 10 (letterbook, 9 December 1650). Cf. Israel, *The Dutch Republic*, 705.

27 Tresoar, Eysinga, 485 (1650).

28 GA, Farmsum, 1019 (Osebrand Jan Rengers to William Frederick, 18–28 November 1650 and n.d.). On him: De Boer, 'Een Ommelander jonker', esp. 48–9; Feenstra, *De bloeitijd en het verval*, 289–90.

29 Tresoar, SA, 37, 1-D (Joachim Andreae to William Frederick, n.d.). See also GA, Farmsum, 1019 (William Frederick to 'my lords', 17–27 November 1650, from The Hague); Tresoar, SA, 37, 1-C (William Frederick to Onno Tamminga, 8–18 November 1650, from The Hague); 1-L (William Frederick to Johan Sohn, 1 December 1650).

30 Tresoar, SA, 37 1-C (William Frederick to Onno Tamminga, 8–18 November 1650, from The Hague). GA, Farmsum, 1019 (William Frederick to 'my lords', 17–27 November 1650, from The Hague).

31 GA, Farmsum, 1019 (William Frederick to 'my lords', 7–17 November 1650, from The Hague).

William Frederick specifically asked the gentlemen to keep this secret. For other favours and presents, e.g. in the form of silverware, see also Tresoar, Eysinga, 485 (autobiography of Vegelin, 1650). For a fuller discussion of gifts see chapter 7.

32 Waterbolk, 'Staatkundige ontwikkelingen', 242–3; Tonckens, 'Het proces-Schulenborgh', 72–3.

33 DA, FSAD, 323, folder 1650 (Wiedenfelt to Vegelin, 5–15 December 1650, from Assen); KHA, WF, VII, C-153 (Anthony van Haersolte to William Frederick, 1 December 1650, n.p.).

34 DA, OSA, 6/6003, fols 299–303; DA, FSAD, 323, folder 1650 (William Frederick to Johan Struuck, 1–11 December 1650, from Leeuwarden; Rutger van den Boetzelaer to William Frederick, 6–16 December 1650, from Assen; deed of William Frederick, 28 November – 8 December 1650, at Leeuwarden).

35 DA, FSAD, 323 folder 1650 (William Frederick to Joost van Welvelde, 5–15 November 1650, from The Hague; Wiedenfelt to Vegelin, 5–15 December 1650, from Assen; Johan Struuck to William Frederick, 30 November – 10 December 1650, from Assen); KHA, WF, VII, C-153 (Anthony van Haersolte to William Frederick, 1 December 1650).

36 Probably anti-Holland feeling again worked in his favour. The Drenthe agent in The Hague, Marten van Persijn, was kept wholly in the dark about the appointment: DA, OSA, 71 (Marten van Persijn to the States, 14–24 December 1650, from The Hague); for Persijn's connections with De Witt: Fruin, *Brieven aan De Witt*, I, 60, 283 and 288. Cf. also DA, FSAD, 323, folder 1650 (Johan Struuck to Pibo van Doma, 30 November 1650, from Assen); Heringa, *Geschiedenis van Drenthe*, 393, note 74; Smit, 'Jacob Schickhart', 213.

37 Tresoar, SA, 301; KHA, WF, VI, 4.

38 KHA, WF, VI, 4.

39 GA, Feith, 1651–8 (William Frederick to Osebrand Jan Rengers, n.d. 1651); Tonckens, 'Het proces-Schulenborgh', 73.

40 Pauw, *Strubbelingen*, 40–2.

41 GA, Feith, 1652–20 (William Frederick to the burgomasters and council of Groningen, 24 March 1652, from Leeuwarden).

42 LAD, Oranienbaum, A7b, 107, fols 16r–17v (William Frederick to the States of Friesland, 22 May 1654, from Groningen).

43 NA, Aitzema, 99 (documents on Groningen, 1655).

44 De Boer, 'Een Ommelander jonker', 53ff.; Israel, *The Dutch Republic*, 734–5; Tonckens, 'Het proces-Schulenborgh', 76–9; Waterbolk, 'Staatkundige ontwikkelingen', 250–5; Tresoar, SA, 302 (copy of the resolution of the States of Groningen, 13 March 1663).

45 Tonckens, 'Het proces-Schulenborgh', 88–90.

46 Tresoar, SA, 305 (notes of William Frederick, 1661).

47 See chapter 3 for examples.

48 GA, Farmsum, 1019 (contract between Rengers and William Frederick, 19–29 February 1660). The contract resembled the so-called contracts of correspondence. Cf. also GA Groningen, Ommelander archief, 877 and 1079 (letters of William Frederick, 1653–57).

49 De Boer, 'Een Ommelander jonker', 53–63.

50 Heringa, *Geschiedenis van Drenthe*, 401ff; Fockema Andreae, *De Nederlandse staat*, 71–3; Fruin and Colenbrander, *Staatsinstellingen*, 257–9; Smit, *Bestuursinstellingen*, 15.

51 KHA, WF, VI, 4 (instructions of William Frederick, 1651). Cf. Bergsma, *'Zij preekten voor doven'*, 21–31; Smit, *Bestuursinstellingen*, 71–4.

52 E.g. DA, OSA, 110 (Rutger van den Boetzelaer to Johan Struuck, 16 March 1651, from Batinge); DA, FSAD, 323 folder 1651 (Delegated States to William Frederick, 19 March 1651, from Assen); 324 (Jonkheer van Echten to William Frederick, 16 February 1655, n.p.; William Frederick to Rutger van den Boetzelaer, 17 February 1655, from Groningen).

53 Heringa, *Geschiedenis van Drenthe*, 394.

54 Israel, *The Dutch Republic*, 704–5. In the meantime the German emperor had raised William Frederick to the rank of prince of the Empire. This elevation cost William Frederick a large sum of money. Visser, 'De Friese stadhouders', 75.

55 Presumably gifts or other services were promised in the hope of widening William Frederick's circle of supporters. KHA, WF, VII, C-153 (Anthony van Haersolte to William Frederick, 1 December 1650, n.p.); KHA, WF, VII, B-III/1a (William Frederick to Reinier Casembroot, n.d.; report of Reinier Casembroot, December 1650, from Utrecht; letters of William Frederick to various States, November and December 1650). In Utrecht William Frederick hoped to find an entrée thanks to his land commandership of the Teutonic Order, which was based in the town. See RDO, 21 (William Frederick to Floris Borre van Amerongen, 8–18 November 1650, from The Hague).

56 Tresoar, SA, 37, 2 to 4 (correspondence of William Frederick with regents in Utrecht, Overijssel and Gelderland, 1650); KHA, WF, VII, B-I/2a (William Frederick to Johan de Knuyt, 15–25 December 1650, from Leeuwarden); VII, B-III/1a (documents of William Frederick on his solicitations in 1650).

57 See Tresoar, SA, 37 (correspondence of William Frederick with regents in Utrecht, Overijssel and Gelderland, 1650); KHA, WF, VII, B-III/1a (documents of William Frederick on his solicitations, 1650).

58 Israel, *The Dutch Republic*, 713–38.

59 Examples: KHA, WF, VII, C-114 (Hendrik van der Capellen to William Frederick, 3–13 November 1652, n.p.); C-171 (correspondence of William Frederick with Pieter de Huybert at Middelburg, 1652–64); C-203 (correspondence of William Frederick with Johan de Mauregnault at Veere and Middelburg, 1651–64); C-232 (Johan van Reede to William Frederick, April 1652, from The Hague); C-262 (correspondence of William Frederick with Johan van Wevelinchoven at Leiden, 1666)). Instructions to deputies on offices in KHA, F, VII, B-III/2 (correspondence of William Frederick with Johan Aylva, 1651–59).

60 Tresoar, SA, 37, 1652 (Johan Goethals to William Frederick, 7 and 14 August 1652, from Delft); KHA, WF, VII, C-147 (Johan Goethals to William Frederick, 11 July 1652, from Delft); Israel, *The Dutch Republic*, 717–18.

61 ING, Notulen Schot, 2 October 1652; NA, Johan de Witt, 2766 (documents on the mission to Zeeland, 1652). Cf. Rowen, *John de Witt*, 83–7. Israel, *The Dutch Republic*, 718–20.

62 Bussemaker, *Geschiedenis van Overijssel*, I, 68–75; Israel, *The Dutch Republic*, 728–34; Streng, *Stemme in staat*, 345–6.

63 Tresoar, SA, 36 (documents on Overijssel, 1654–57); Slicher van Bath, *Geschiedenis van Overijssel*, 127–8.

64 Kooijmans, *Liefde in opdracht*, 216–31; Panhuysen, *De ware vrijheid*, 202–10; Rowen, *John de Witt*, 356–79; other terms of the Harmony in Van Sypesteyn, *Geschiedkundige bijdragen*, 103ff.

65 The episode about the Harmony and William Frederick's dealings in the 1650s are discussed more extensively in the Dutch version: *Creaturen van de macht*, 189–95.

66 KHA, WF, VIII, 3-I (notes of William Frederick, 21 September – 1 October 1655); VII, 3-IV (scattered notes and papers of William Frederick, *c.* 1660–61).

67 Aitzema, *Saken van Staet en oorlogh*, VI, 454; Ten Raa and De Bas, *Het Staatsche leger*, V, 201 and 205. Cf. Kooijmans, *Liefde in opdracht*, 270.

68 Geyl and Rowen passed substantially the same verdict. Cf. Kooijmans, *Liefde in opdracht*, 271–3; Rogier, 'Oranje en de Nederlandse staat', 271–92; Spanninga, 'Ick laet niet met mij gecken', 55–6.

69 Cf. Perlot, *De Staten van Utrecht*, 36–7.

70 Rowen, *John de Witt*, 154–69; Panhuysen, *De ware vrijheid*, 166–71; Streng, 'Le métier du noble', 83. See also Knevel, *Het Haagse bureau*, 61–71.

71 Cited in De Bruin, *Geheimhouding en verraad*, 377. Cf. Knevel, *Het Haagse bureau*, 147.

72 BOX, Rawlinson MS A13 (Intelligence, 27 April 1654).

73 See chapter 2. Cf. Tresoar, SA, 69 (documents on the deputies to the States-General, 1655); 240 (documents on the deputies to the States-General, 1646); *Gloria Parendi*, 206, 209, 210, 211, 217 and 218.

74 *Gloria Parendi*, 744; Fruin, *Brieven van de Witt*, I, 187.

75 Cf. KHA, WF, VII, B-III/2 (Johan van Aylva); B-III/3 (Horatius Knijf); C-64 (Joachim Andreae);

C-97 (Epo van Bootsma); C-144 (Epeus van Glinstra); C-156 (Willem van Haren); C-157 (Haring van Harinxma); C-158 (Cornelis Haubois); C-237 (Carel Roorda); C-256 (Johan Veltdriel). See also Vries, 'Friese bureaucratie', 11–29; Slothouwer, 'Een provinciale klerk'.

76 *Gloria Parendi*, 521. On 8 July 1648 William Frederick wrote 'I spoke to Messrs Haubois and Jeltinga, who made me a report on everything that was debated in the assembly of their High Mightinesses, and Haubois was to write to me what happened there'. *Gloria Parendi*, 538.

77 KHA, WF, VII, C-64 (Joachim Andreae to William Frederick, 10–20 February 1650, from The Hague).

78 KHA, WF, VII, B-III/2 (Johan van Aylva to William Frederick, 11–21 August 1652, from The Hague); *Gloria Parendi*, 233. Other examples: KHA, WF, VII, C-158 (William Frederick to Cornelis Haubois, 17 July 1654, from Turnhout); C-64 (Joachim Andreae to William Frederick, 18–28 March 1652, from The Hague); C-256 (Johan Veltdriel to William Frederick, 5 August 1645, from The Hague); C-266 (Hans van Wijckel to William Frederick, 2–12 April 1652, from The Hague).

79 KHA, WF, VII, B-III/2 (William Frederick to Johan van Aylva, 20–30 January, 17–27 February and 9–19 March 1654, n.p.). It is not surprising that it cost William Frederick much more effort to influence the voting behaviour of the Groningers. Their correspondence with the stadholder is less voluminous than that of their Friesian colleagues. Perhaps the lower priority that the Groningers gave to Generality affairs played some part in this; they quite often left their seats in the States-General vacant.

80 Cf. *Gloria Parendi*, 521 and 596.

81 KHA, WF, VII, C-64 (Joachim Andreae to William Frederick, 2–12 May 1649, 20–30 March 1650, 2 March and 17 May 1651, from The Hague).

82 See De Bruin, *Geheimhouding en verraad*, 134–50; Van Deursen, 'Staatsinstellingen', 352–3; Schöffer, 'Naar consolidatie en behoud', 64–98.

83 KHA, WF, VII, C-158 (Cornelis Haubois to William Frederick, 30 April 1652, from The Hague).

84 KHA, WF, VII, B-III/2 (William Frederick to Johan van Aylva, 1–11 March 1655, n.p.).

85 Only once, during the Great Assembly of 1651, did Leeuwarden give its official blessing to these ad hoc discussions. Tresoar, SvF, 58 (resolutions 19 April 1651).

86 KHA, WF, VIII, 3-IV (notes of William Frederick, n.d.); KHA, WF, VII, B-III/2 (Johan van Aylva to William Frederick, 7 August 1652, from The Hague).

87 KHA, WF, VII, C-170 (documents of Humalda); C-257 (documents of Vierssen); VIII, 3-IV (documents of Jongestal); LAD, Oranienbaum, A7b, 98 (documents of Jongestal); BOX, Rawlinson MSS, A.13 (documents of Jongestal). Schutte, *Repertorium*, 97–8, 204 and 241. Cf. Roorda, 'Le Secret du prince', 172–89.

88 Israel, *The Dutch Republic*, 748ff; Price, *Holland and the Dutch Republic*, 57–69.

89 KHA, WF, VII, B-III/2 (William Frederick to Johan van Aylva, 25 August 1652, n.p.). In this connection cf. also William Frederick's earlier references to the letter of Lipsius of 1592, which had described the weaknesses of a state ruled by merchants. *Gloria Parendi*, 570 and 683. The letter itself is in Bor, *Oorsprongk*, IV, 60–7.

90 Cited in Kooijmans, *Liefde in opdracht*, 173.

91 Rowen, *John de Witt*, 88.

92 BOX, Rawlinson MS A 17 (Intelligence, 21 December 1654). Cf. also Uit den Bogaart, *De gereformeerden en Oranje*, 117.

93 Tresoar, SA, 37, 1652 (Johan Goethals to William Frederick, 7 August 1652, from Delft). Other letters from him and Maximiliaan Teellinck: KHA, WF, VII, C-146; Tresoar, SA, 37, 1652. Cf. Israel, *The Dutch Republic*, 718; Uit den Bogaart, *De gereformeerden en Oranje*, 205–15; De Jongste, 'Politieke elite', 165–80. On the pamphlets that appeared in these years see Geyl, 'Het stadhouderschap in de partij-literatuur'; Van de Klashorst, 'Metten schijn van monarchie getempert'; Kossmann, *Political Thought*; Velema, 'That a Republic', 9–19.

94 Tresoar, SA, 367, I (Onias Geldrop to William Frederick, 27 August 1654, from Amsterdam).

95 Aitzema, *Saken van Staet en oorlogh*, III, 815. Thurloe, *A Collection*, II, 537. Cf. Spanninga, 'Ick laet niet met mij gecken', 63.
96 RAG, Van der Capellen, 89 (Hendrik van der Capellen to Alexander van der Capellen, 31 January – 10 February 1652, from The Hague).
97 Cf. Tresoar, SA, 36 (Johan van Reede to William Frederick, 14–24 October 1654, from The Hague); Rowen, *John de Witt*, 156, 361, 461, 689.
98 Van der Bijl, *Idee en interest*, 18–21. Other examples in Groenveld, *Evidente factiën*.
99 Cf. Price, *Holland and the Dutch Republic*, 57–69, 154–71; Uit den Bogaart, *De gereformeerden en Oranje*; Groenveld *Evidente factiën*, 53–64; Stern, 'The Rhetoric', 202–24.

7

The limits of power

Alle van Burum, burgomaster of Leeuwarden, was a regent with an instinct for survival. During his long career he faced almost every form of opposition: he had been attacked in petitions and pamphlets, and legal proceedings had been brought against him, but Van Burum survived them all.[1] The secret agreement he signed on 5 February 1658 throws some light on the background to this remarkable career. The burgomaster declared that he felt 'obliged' for the help and protection that 'his princely grace' had always offered him behind the scenes. Van Burum went on to promise his protector that he would 'be true in all things'. Specifically, he undertook to 'put all the votes that I have or can get under my direction, at the disposition of His Princely Grace'.[2]

Van Burum's agreement is part of a collection of contracts that at least ten prominent Friesian regents signed in the years 1657 to 1663.[3] In form they resembled the so-called 'contracts of correspondence', which the political elites in the Dutch Republic often signed with one another to regulate the practice by which local offices were shared between them. These contracts became more frequent from the end of the seventeenth century as a means of consolidating the existing distribution of power between urban and provincial factions.[4] William Frederick's variants, however, were significantly different from the typical model. The humble language used by the signers makes it clear that there was no question of an agreement between equals. In most of them William Frederick promised the other parties one or more offices, in return for which they undertook to be 'loyal to the stadholder in all things', to be 'regulated' by 'his wise recommendations and advices', or to 'maintain, help and support' him. In a few cases, such as that of Alle van Burum, the services promised were even specified.

Formalised patronage

The stadholder's contracts are in fact among the last snapshots of William Freder-ick's patronage process in Friesland. As such, they do not so much represent the beginning of a new custom as the confirmation of an established practice. The contracts are, however, exceptional as a formalised expression of stadholderly clientage, because other stadholders left nothing like them. To be sure, there is documentary evidence for the instructions that Frederick Henry, William III or William V gave to their clients, but in those cases their aim was always to acquire political influence on the basis of tacit expectations or, at most, informal arrangements. William Frederick's written contracts, in this respect, fall into another category.[5]

The uniqueness of the Friesian contracts from the 1650s and 1660s raises the question of what motive could have induced William Frederick to put his existing patronage contacts on such a quasi-formal basis? The stadholder never explained his intentions in so many words, but some explanations can be suggested. In the first place it is noticeable that most of these contracts date from the years when William Frederick was trying to establish his son's claim to succeed him in office. This son, Henry Casimir II, was born at The Hague in January 1657, but his youth was no obstacle to William Frederick's efforts to secure an act of reversion that would guarantee his succession as stadholder. In 1659, in fact, William Frederick got his way in Friesland, and two years later in Groningen and Drenthe. Clearly his object was to prevent the need for a repeti-tion of his own arduous campaign for the stadholdership in 1640. Against this backdrop, it is not surprising that the Friesian stadholder also wanted to pass his informal authority on to his son with as little fuss as possible. He may have believed that confirming his existing patronage relationships in writing was the best way to achieve this. Several of the contracts did in fact require an explicit promise of continued loyalty to 'our beloved son prince Henry Casimir' or his guardian during his minority.

The stadholder also had a more immediate reason to consolidate his Friesian networks. As we saw, William Frederick's grip on politics in the province was regularly relaxed during his lengthy absences, for it was difficult to control his local clients and brokers while he was away in The Hague. The stadholder still faced this logistical problem in the last years of his life, chiefly because he spent many summers in the 1650s and 1660s at Amalia's castle in Turnhout. The contracts therefore met his requirement for a way of controlling his clients' conduct more closely during his absences. These were also the years when William Frederick was in most need of his Friesian network to reinforce his position in the other provinces of the Republic. The contracts with his clients were thus both a product of the patronage he had built up earlier and a response to the new political conditions, which made an adjustment of that patronage necessary.

This impression of adjustment and change in the outward forms of William Frederick's dealings with his clients is confirmed by the variations in the contracts themselves. They fell into three broad categories. The first and most unequal, which exacted the greatest loyalty, included those that the stadholder made with his clients in the towns of Friesland. Such men as Cornelis Haubois of Sneek or Sjoerd Potter of Dokkum simply promised to 'regulate' their conduct by William Frederick's recommendations, but the stadholder did not commit himself to any specific obligations in return.[6] The second category comprised the contracts with the country gentlemen who served as *grietmannen*, and in these the relationship was more explicitly reciprocal. Oeno van Grovestins and Douwe van Aylva promised in 1663 'to maintain, help and assist our lord and stadholder, ... to avert and avoid damage and detriment to him on all occasions', and after the stadholder's death 'to help maintain the princess'. In return William Frederick promised 'to maintain and help advance Mr Douwe van Aylva and the children and friends of the same in the quarter of Oostergo and to maintain and help advance Mr Oeno van Grovestin and the children and friends of the same in the quarter of Westergo'.[7]

Finally there was a third type, exemplified by William Frederick's agreement with the Groningen *jonker* Osebrand Jan Rengers. This illustrated the greater bargaining power of the Groningen elite in their dealings with the stadholder. Though Rengers promised 'always to remain loyal to His Princely Grace and Her Princely Grace and the young prince', William Frederick in return had to thank Rengers profusely for 'obtaining the stadholdership of the province of the city and the Ommelanden in the year 1650', and for his help in obtaining the reversion 'for our beloved son prince Henry Casimir'. The stadholder assured the *jonker* of his backing in the near future, and promised him 'the first company of horse that we shall have to dispose of'.[8]

The subtle distinction in tone and in the degree of reciprocal service expected reflects the differences between William Frederick's various patronage networks in Friesland and Groningen. It also forces us to approach clientage as a permanent process, in which mutual dependence and loyalty could fluctuate over the years. As William Frederick's patronage relationships took many different forms at different times and in different social settings, they cannot be understood in terms of static definitions and clear-cut figures. Nor can the contractual form that William Frederick gave to the dealings with some of his clients be distinguished from more common, unwritten forms of clientage. These written agreements merely formalised existing practices and codes, and did not mark a transition to a new and fundamentally different social nexus.

Corrupted patronage

The processes described above did not mean that the possibilties of the patronage open to William Frederick and other stadholders were unlimited. Indeed, the scope and effectiveness of clientage in the republican body politic were always subject to innumerable restrictions. The previous chapters have already dealt with the practical obstacles that could restrain the exercise of patronage: the limits on William Frederick's official powers, the political instability in some regions or logistical problems between Friesland and The Hague. Yet William Frederick's ability to manage his affairs was also constrained by certain moral codes and scruples. His contracts say little or nothing about the social accept- ability of certain patronage customs, but this silence itself compels the question as to what possible forms of mutual service were considered unacceptable in the United Provinces, and why. In other words, when did tolerable clientage practices become objectionable 'corruption' in seventeenth-century eyes? A general answer to this question was given in local, provincial and national legis- lation, but these laws do not appear to have always been enforced in practice.[9] William Frederick's papers nevertheless reveal him wrestling with such questions in his role as patron. His correspondence in particular allows us to examine his ideas and social norms in this respect, and to test them against those of others.

Clientelistic practices as such were not an unusual or disreputable aspect of political culture in the seventeenth century. Social inequality and political exclusion were even enshrined in the laws of most early modern states, including the Dutch Republic. In the latter, the habit of leaving the recruitment of certain government posts to the personal preferences of the stadholder continued an old tradition of Burgundian and Habsburg times, which illustrates that the United Provinces were republican in name but had a constitutional framework based on a monarchical past. It was not just the concern for continuity and tradition, however, that legitimised the stadholder's ambiguous position. His 'monarchical' right of appointment in the republican system was also regularly justified from the need for 'order and stability', a ideal that preoccupied many in the decentral- ised Republic. The stadholder's prerogatives should prevent the public adminis- tration being paralysed by quarrels whenever a vacant post had to be filled.[10]

Both these concerns for historical continuity and political harmony can also be traced in William Frederick's reading of his role as patron. As stadholder he saw no conflict between the informal loyalty he exacted from the Friesian regents and his formal position as their servant; on the contrary, as his arguments discussed in chapter 2 made clear, he believed that the public interest was best served if he played a guiding role. To William Frederick's mind the glorious past of his 'forefathers' was proof that the duty of 'their descendants, succeeding them in their charges' must be to guarantee political harmony and religious uniformity in the government.[11] 'They see very well now that I seek only quiet in the country and not my own honour or authority', he remarked with satisfaction in September 1648, after 'all praise' had been lavished on him for bringing 'peace' and 'unity' to the province.[12]

Conversely, it followed from this reasoning that clientelistic practices that worked against 'calm and harmony' were unacceptable. William Frederick was therefore particularly sensitive to charges that his clients were sabotaging unity in government or the established political order. One who was accused of this was the burgomaster of Sneek, Cornelis Haubois, who had exploited years of the stadholder's protection to make himself into a local potentate. The town's administration became so disorderly in the 1640s that the regents of Sneek complained to William Frederick. They voiced their grievance against Haubois by complaining that he was abusing his influence at court to set himself up as 'stadholder of Sneek'. In other words Haubois did not know his place and was misusing the protection of his patron to amass greater authority than local customs prescribed. William Frederick was receptive to such objections. In November 1647 he reminded himself that 'I must live cautiously, do nothing that is not well premeditated and considered, and that is in the slightest degree against the privileges and laws, so that I do not give cause for complaint here'. He therefore publicly rapped his broker in Sneek over the knuckles and passed him over for a seat in the Delegated States in 1645. Vegelin wrote that the stadholder was not only demonstrating that he 'observed equality between the towns', but also that as the natural patron he 'would not let himself be governed'.[13]

This argument presents some parallels with Robert Harding's analysis of early modern perceptions of corruption. Harding claimed that in seventeenth-century France the charge of 'corruption' was generally linked to the abuse of patronage. Contemporaries condemned clientelistic practices as corrupt or abusive when they violated existing power relationships or weakened the unity of an administration. It was not patronage as such but its use for improper purposes that they deplored. Harding cites the example of French nobles who stigmatised royal clientage as corrupt, because it forced the *noblesse d'épée* to cede its natural God-given authority to a new *noblesse de robe*.[14] For these nobles the severity of this threat to the natural order of society was the criterion by which they distinguished between honourable patronage and its corrupt abuse.

Although feudal privileges were at stake in the French case and not in the United Provinces, William Frederick did face similar problems. As Haubois's example illustrated, the stadholder's patronage could also conflict with existing local customs and be perceived as a dangerous novelty. 'Bruinsma attacked me very bitterly', William Frederick wrote in February 1648, 'and said "How this bald count torments us. He is our servant, we made him great and now he wants to rule everything"'. Pieter Walta shared this view, criticising 'Our stadholder, who wants to make himself sovereign and rule everything as he sees fit'.[15] Several Friesian noblemen objected to William Frederick's having 'so much credit' in the province, while his predecessors 'had not had such credit'.[16] They also deplored the way in which he had acquired such novel authority: 'Walta said I left my friends once I had used them as I liked, and then I took up others, and used them as long as I could'. These remarks made little impression on the stadholder, who soberly observed that 'He is vexed that he is not the stadholder and does not have the authority that I have'.[17]

In this connection, however, the possible opportunistic motives that provoked Bruinsma and Walta to make their remarks are less important than the shared moral frame of reference from which both men criticised patronage practices. Both Bruinsma and Walta voiced their frustration by complaining that William Frederick's patronage was disturbing the traditional balance of power in Friesland. It was not the unwritten norm as such on which they differed from the stadholder, but the degree to which he was overstepping it.

Corrupted gifts

The subtle line between good and bad patronage or between the acceptable or objectionable management of one's dealings did not have to be drawn only when appointments were being made. It was equally subtle and no less essential when gifts were exchanged. Although William Frederick's process of clientage was based chiefly on appointment to offices and mediation on behalf of office-seekers, these activities were supplemented by gifts and presents, which often marked specific annual occasions. The count regularly received gifts of game and fruit in the hunting or harvest seasons, and Hessel van Aylva typically wished William Frederick a happy new year in 1658 by sending him three roe deer as 'a small present from his servant'. When Albertine gave birth to a daughter in the summer of 1664, the count's court was inundated with gifts of fresh fruit and jam.[18]

Gifts were an obvious and sometimes even an institutionalised part of early modern social relationships.[19] Consequently their status was as ambiguous as the offices that were William Frederick's to dispose of. Although gifts were always ostensibly given with no expectation of return, that was in fact usually their implicit message. They were therefore sometimes politely declined: the pensionary Johan de Witt was known for his consistent refusal of gifts or presents, a habit which has earned him a reputation among historians as an incorruptible regent who rejected every form of corruption on principle.[20] Yet it is doubtful that De Witt really objected to the exchange of services and gifts as such, and much more likely that he found the consequences of accepting them personally inconvenient. After all, one who accepted a gift admitted to feeling 'obliged', and thus prepared to render a service in return in the future. As pensionary of Holland, who wished to stay on good terms with all parties and not commit himself, it made very good sense not to become 'obliged' if there was no good reason for it.

William Frederick too was well aware of the implications of accepting gifts, and kept a very sharp eye on when and how they were offered. Natalie Davis has described how the form and timing of gift-giving influenced contemporaries' perceptions and expectations.[21] The stadholder regarded excessively lavish gifts given in thanks for specific offices and favours as unseemly and even dishonourable. Presents of money in return for favours were particularly liable to be stigmatised as corrupt. Alle van Burum told the stadholder that Cornelis Haubois 'had a bad name ... for corruption', because he had been willing to buy his office for cash. Such scandals were not exceptional. Hessel van Sminia warned William Frederick against his colleague Albert Loo, another who 'had a bad reputation, and how corruptible he was, and had received 5,000 from Aylva, Swartzenburg and Potter'.[22] Luuc Kooijmans mentions a similar case in his study of the Amsterdam burgomaster Johan Huydekoper, who was insulted when an acquaintance promised him money if he would help him to an office. 'I must acknowledge', the burgomaster wrote, 'that a worse or more scandalous thing has never happened to me ... that against my honour and my oath I should be compelled to seek my advantage by selling considerable offices, and consequently tarnish my good name and fame by such foul and unlawful gain.'[23]

In theory, here too the norms upheld by Dutch office-holders appear to coincide up to a point with those of their French counterparts. Sharon Kettering has pointed out that gifts or presents as a form of requital of service were acceptable among the French elite only if they grew out of an existing long-term relationship; but if a gift was a one-off present given with a clearly specified service in view, it became dishonourable and therefore corrupt.[24] Indeed, when he received presents William Frederick was repeatedly assured that they were exclusively 'for the continuance' of good relations.[25] There was an essential distinction in perception between gifts given in the hope of opening a relationship, and continuing periodical presents.

In practice, of course, the distinction was sometimes so subtle that it could hardly be detected. In which class were the gifts that William Frederick distributed during the election for stadholder of Groningen in 1640? 'The expenses among the aforesaid householders shall be paid by His Grace', we read in a list of names of rural electors whose support he canvassed.[26] When there was another election for stadholder ten years later, William Frederick considered it essential to tempt the Groningen elite with more substantial gifts. As we saw, the stadholder frankly told some of the freeholders that he would 'pay them the sum of twenty thousand guilders if the stadholdership of the Ommelanden is conferred upon me'. He justified this remarkably blatant offer as a necessary evil, 'because I know very well that the freeholders cannot be led except by some means'.[27]

William Frederick probably realised that this excuse would not convince everyone, and so he emphasised to the gentlemen of the Ommelanden that his gifts were to be kept a strict secret. The 'means' were also offered in kind, probably for the sake of discretion. It is not impossible that silver-gilt articles had become fairly customary gifts in Groningen circles, for Lieuwe van Aitzema refers to very similar presents in Frederick Henry's case, ten years earlier.[28] This similarity in the form and timing of the gift shows how hard it can be to put bribes, gifts and financial compensation into separate pigeon-holes in an early modern context.

The ambiguous status of gifts was revealed in a similar but less expensive undertaking in Groningen eleven years later. In 1661 Vegelin was ordered to distribute all kinds of 'honours' in the Ommelanden, in the hope of hastening a promise of an act of reversion for Henry Casimir II.[29] The secretary entertained the Groningen notables in several taverns, treating them to barrels of wine and other delicacies, which once again the stadholder urged him 'to keep secret for good reasons'.[30] These precautions support Kettering's theory that gifts or services offered to effect a specific purpose could be regarded as questionable. The same pressure for secrecy was evident in William Frederick's contracts, in which the parties agreed 'to keep this secret for all time'.[31] The degree of secrecy that the stadholder judged appropriate for certain forms of management of his relations can therefore be used as an index of what he considered justifiable in each case.

Public and private patronage

Existing studies of gift-giving in early modern Europe have naturally paid little attention to the specific problem that faced William Frederick and other stadholders in the Dutch republican system: the differences between their public and private patronage roles, discussed in previous chapters. For it was not just the different selection criteria that the patron applied in recruiting his clients that marked the difference between his two positions; the social norms by which patronage was judged contrasted as well. In his capacity as stadholder William Frederick's practices as patron were circumscribed by the official guidelines that limited his authority; but these restrictions did not apply to him as a private patron in his own household and domains. In other words, because their defining conditions were so dissimilar, William Frederick could permit himself to operate in different ways in the two circuits.

That meant that certain forms of clientage were more or less acceptable depending on the institutional sphere in which they were practised. In any case, William Frederick himself felt bound by one set of norms in his role as a high nobleman, and by another in his capacity as stadholder. His election campaigns in Groningen revealed that gifts of luxury goods such as silverware were regarded as inappropriate for his relations in the republican government, but they were frequently exchanged in court circles. He openly received diamond rings from courtiers and relatives such as William II and Charles II, and gave presents of expensive jewellery and paintings at the Orange court.[32] At his wedding feast the guests were presented with precious stones, pearls and jewels, while the count's personnel received silver. Presumably the meaning attached to these gifts was very different from that to the silver ewers with which the Groningen regents had been rewarded. That does not mean that wedding gifts were given with no expectation at all of mutual service, but perhaps that such reciprocity in private court circles was not felt to impinge on the public, republican domain in the United Provinces.[33]

The regular exchange of costly presents was such an accepted social obligation and an unwritten condition of employment at court that William Frederick's courtiers openly claimed them as their due, possibly as a form of reimbursement of their expenses. In 1657, for example, the secretary Vegelin calculated that the count was still in his debt, after meticulously listing the gifts with which William Frederick had rewarded the services of other men in his confidence: 'Baron Hohenfeld was honoured with the best horses from the prince's stable for his trouble; Mr Tap's services were acknowledged by an honour of 100 RR, and although I have travelled more than a thousand miles in this work over ten years, I am still waiting for my recompense'.[34] It was not the practice of giving gifts, as such, that Vegelin deplored, but the selective way in which his lord handed them out at court. While making claims to regular gifts and presents was certainly unusual and objectionable in public, administrative circles, as a private nobleman William Frederick could not afford to deny them.

The distinction between public and private patronage, so clearly revealed in the different patronage norms that William Frederick applied in his various roles, is further reflected in the support that he was willing to give in legal proceedings before the Court of Friesland. As stadholder he could exert a far-reaching influence on the composition of this body, the highest court in the province.[35] The councillors who sat in it on behalf of the Friesian towns were always appointed on his recommendation, and occasionally those from the other quarters as well.[36] For this reason William Frederick regularly referred in his diaries to councillors whom he had 'made', a term evidently endorsed by the councillors themselves. 'Ockinga thanked me that he had become a councillor', the stadholder noted in his diary in 1645, while in the following year Henningh Andreae admitted that he had 'become a councillor' thanks to William Frederick's mediation.[37]

The lines of communication between the Friesian Court of justice and the stadholder were therefore short, and it was not uncommon for him to receive requests from people to send a 'recommendation' to the councillors, so that their cases could be dealt with 'as quickly as possible' or even 'favourably'.[38] But William Frederick's use of his influence with the Court was remarkably selective. Hommo Camstra was indignant when his request was turned down in 1647, as the stadholder recorded: 'Hommo Camstra told me he would no longer eat with me, I had left him in the lurch; he is angry with me for losing his case'.[39] Yet William Frederick's refusal did not necessarily mean that he objected to meddling in civil or criminal cases on principle; on the contrary, his private courtiers often successfully appealed to their patron for support. The count was happy to approach the councillors of the Court informally on behalf of his financial adviser Reinier Casembroot, to recommend that 'his pending matter might be brought to the desired conclusion'. His groom Jan Michels could also count on his lord during his trial. The councillors Joachim Andreae and Matthias Vierssen received instructions in 1642 to decide the Michels case with 'mature consideration' but above all 'as quickly and favourably' as they could. William Frederick justified his request by referring to the 'long years of service' that Michels had given 'Our House'. Not long afterward Andreae was able to tell the stadholder that his request had been honoured.[40]

William Frederick's services were selective but not random or arbitrary. Since the conditions on which his patronage was based varied, his responsibilities to his clients were bound to vary also. On the whole his court clientele could make larger and more frequent claims to social protection or special incomes than their colleagues in the public administration. It was not the type of judicial institution or the nature of the case before it that decided when William Frederick was willing to give the protection sought, but rather the role that he considered appropriate in his two patronage spheres. As the conduct of Andreae illustrates, the distinction William Frederick drew between his various capacities as patron was also recognised by his clients as well as by others in the Friesian administration.

Succession

In the late 1650s and early 1660s William Frederick's life as a patron came to be dominated by his concern about his successor. From 1657 he began to take steps to secure for Henry Casimir II the powers that he had acquired and that he himself regarded as a legacy from his ancestors. As a count it was not necessary to formalise the takeover, as his household clientele was regarded as a kind of hereditary asset that would pass to him without any complications. On his deathbed William Frederick would make this expectation of continuity explicit to some of his courtiers. 'Vegelin shall stay with my wife and children', he simply wrote in one of his last notes.[41]

A clientele takeover in the republican sphere, on the other hand, required more preparation. Acts of reversion were necessary to guarantee that Henry Casimir would be granted the three stadholderships. Similarly, contracts with the Friesian and Groningen elite would safeguard William Frederick's informal network in the future. A few of these agreements stipulated that if Henry Casimir succeeded as a minor, the client was to owe loyalty to his guardian Albertine Agnes.[42] This was a remarkable stipulation, since the guardianship was really a matter of purely family arrangements. It was a consequence of the marriage agreement, and as such referred only to Henry Casimir's position as count and not to the stadholderships. The acts of reversion and William Frederick's contracts gave this originally private relationship thus a new, public relevance. In other words, William Frederick appears to have hoped that Albertine's private guardianship would develop into a public regency. Nine of the Friesian towns had already anticipated this eventuality in 1659 by promising to entrust her with the appointment of their magistrates, if Henry Casimir II had not reached the age of seventeen when William Frederick died.[43]

The relevant documents are among the few in which the wife whom William Frederick had married in 1652 appears in the foreground.[44] In his biography Luuc Kooijmans has pointed out that the couple lived largely separate lives. When William Frederick left for Friesland, Albertine very often preferred to remain in The Hague or Turnhout, in itself not an uncommon habit in high noble circles. Even when the count of Nassau-Dietz and the princess of Orange-Nassau were staying at the same court residence, Albertine had her own quarters and her personal household.[45] Its precise composition and background are not well known, but according to the marriage contract it was to consist of twenty-two persons, many of them drawn from the Orange entourage in The Hague.[46] William Frederick's own personnel were sharply distinguished from his wife's household, and his court therefore kept its very masculine character even after his marriage, a character reinforced by the presence of numerous military officers.

More remarkably, William Frederick's diary notes give the impression that Albertine herself was responsible for the separation between the two courts as well. His descriptions of their marital relations suggest that the princess of Orange considered herself too well-born to be incorporated into her husband's household and his Friesian networks.[47] William Frederick's analysis should be treated with some reserve, because his relations with women at court in general were not uncomplicated.[48] The difficulty was that, as a count, William

Frederick was of significantly lower social status than his wife, who had been born a princess. The full implications of this tension between sexual inequality and aristocratic hierarchy cannot be traced from William Frederick's fragmentary descriptions. At the most, we can try to place Albertine's position and her remarkable appearance in William Frederick's contracts in a wider perspective.

Historians have pointed out that noblewomen at early modern courts generally enjoyed relative independence, thanks to their exalted birth and the financial resources they could inherit.[49] Natalie Davis has therefore argued that a princely environment probably gave women a stronger position than did a republican one, in which no formal position at all was allowed them. Albertine's freedom of action at court and her virtual absence from the public or republican sphere of William Frederick's stadholdership may lend some support to this hypothesis. Public and private spheres, as discussed in this study, more or less coincide with Davis's distinction between republican and princely environments, which in the United Provinces to some extent coexisted because of the ambiguous status of the stadholdership. In that respect William Frederick's contracts were indeed a way of enabling Albertine to extend her authority from the private sphere of the guardianship into the public sphere of a regency. The princess's own behaviour suggests the same motives. After William Frederick's death Albertine not only took over his household duties but also continued his correspondence with the Friesian regents without a break.[50] Although the States of Friesland never formally recognised her as regent, William Frederick's precautions allowed his widow to take over his public clientele and play a role in the republican state system. In so doing, she became the first woman in the Dutch Republic to be unofficial acting stadholder.[51]

An accidental death

By 1663 William Frederick had completed his formal preparations for a successful transfer of his powers to the 6-year-old Henry Casimir, but his son's future as the new patron was not yet guaranteed. William Frederick's own experience had taught him how much patronage was a question of trust, which could never be taken for granted. He therefore drew up brief instructions to guide his son in his future role. At the head of one such note he wrote, 'I hope my son Henry Casimir will follow these to become a good lord, prince and governor'.[52] William Frederick underlined the importance of the aristocratic norms he himself had learned from his own father, and added some practical hints drawn from his experience. As a patron Henry must appear self-assured above all; and to achieve this he needed to cultivate habits of courtesy and self-control, but also physical exercise and early rising. To keep an account of his conduct and to watch over his social contacts, the father ended by advising his son 'to write down every-thing that happens daily'.[53] In effect William Frederick sketched an idealised self-portrait.

Although the count had been anticipating his succession for some time, his death when it came was rather unexpected. On Friday 24 October 1664 William Frederick was seriously wounded while inspecting one of his guns. 'It would not fire', he wrote a day or two later, 'so I looked at it, and it went off'.[54] His jaw shattered, his palate split, and bleeding from several internal injuries, William Frederick was laid in his bed and attended by three physicians and two surgeons. He lived another seven days. Because it was almost impossible for him to eat or speak, he communicated with his family, his personnel and the regents by written notes. On 3 October he had a final statement drawn up, which in many ways resembled the one his brother had made on his deathbed twenty-four years earlier. It was addressed to the same recipients: the States of Friesland. William Frederick thanked the States for 'all the inclination, honour and friend-ship' they had shown him, and expressed the hope that they would 'continue the same to my little son in particular'.[55] The 7-year-old Henry and his sisters were summoned to the deathbed that same day, where their father gave all three a ring and his blessing. 'About a quarter of an hour before his death', Agatha Tjaerda van Starckenborgh wrote later, 'a light like a fiery arrow came down from heaven before his Court'. The phenomenon sent by God 'passed over his Court' and then vanished as suddenly as it had appeared.[56] 'Softly, as in a slumber' the count then died 'in the bliss of the Lord'.[57]

Notes

1 Boomsma, 'Een werck van factie en staetsucht', 7–30; Spanninga, 'Ick laet niet met mij gecken', 141–4.
2 KHA, WF, VI, 5 (deed of Alle van Burum, 5 February 1658, at Leeuwarden).
3 These and the following contracts are all in KHA, WF, VI, 5.
4 Price, *Holland and the Dutch Republic*, 25–6. Cf. the remarks of Fockema Andreae, *De Neder-landse staat*, 10.
5 Israel, 'Frederick Henry', 1–27; Groenveld, 'Frederik Hendrik', 18–33; Roorda, 'Le Secret du prince', 172–211; Gabriels, *De heren als dienaren*. Jonathan Israel also refers to a contract between William III and Henry Casimir II on the distribution of army commissions, Israel, *The Dutch Republic*, 837.
6 KHA, WF, VI, 5 (for example the contracts with Cornelis Haubois, Sjoerd Potter and Junius Alema, 8 February 1657, and with Ewout Steinsma, 1 June 1658).
7 KHA, WF, VI, 5 (contract with Douwe van Aylva and Oeno van Grovestins, 8 May 1663).
8 The contract with Rengers is in GA, Farmsum, 1019 (deed of 19–29 December 1660 and correspondence of William Frederick with Rengers, 7–17 April 1660 and 21–31 January 1661).
9 For the legal definition of corruption in the Republic and the defective observance of the norm see De Bruin, *Geheimhouding en verraad*, 373–86; Dekker, 'Corruptie en ambtelijke ethiek'; Egmond, 'Strafzaken', 63–75; idem, 'Recht en krom'; Hartog, *Onrechtmatige overheidsdaden*; Huiskamp, 'Tussen centrum en periferie', 27–58; Knevel, *Het Haagse bureau*, 145–68; Wagenaar and Van der Meij, 'Een schout in de fout?'.

Epilogue

William Frederick was 51 when he died, not unusually young or old given his family background. His father and brother had died at 58 and 28 respectively. All three met an unnatural death. William Frederick himself would certainly not have failed to remark on this similarity, for he had always been keenly aware of historical parallels. One so eager to follow in the footsteps of his 'forefathers' would be apt to see his own experiences as a reflection of those of his predecessors. The instructions that he left for his son also illustrated this feeling for tradition and dynastic continuity.

It followed from his deep sense of his family history that William Frederick also interpreted his patronage networks and customs as a natural continuation, or at least a logical consequence, of the efforts of his predecessors. As a patron in his own household and as a client of the prince of Orange he had always tried to present himself as a chain in a long family tradition.

Yet the way in which these patronage roles developed in the course of his career suggests that William Frederick's conduct was in fact a very personal response to the challenges he faced in his life. This book has argued that clientage was not a matter of fixed relationships, but a process of continual adaptation to change and to different social environments. In his diaries and letters William Frederick tried to make sense of these developments and experiences by comparing them with historical or scriptural examples. Probably his motive was not to conceal his own choices or ambitions, but to explain and legitimise his patronage practices within that aristocratic frame of reference. The discourse of continuity and predicated roles in which William Frederick expressed himself was therefore no mere rhetorical façade, but a conscious attempt to invest the great changes and personal efforts in his life with a religious significance, and to explain where they fitted in the history of his family.

The changes that William Frederick had to cope with in his lifetime were radical indeed. Both in his family and in the Dutch Republic the balance of power shifted drastically in barely twenty-four years. When he took office as stadholder in 1640, the Republic was still at war with Spain, and Frederick Henry was indisputably the Boss in the House of Orange. When William Frederick died in 1664 the future of that House had become highly uncertain, while England had replaced Spain as the common enemy. William Frederick's patronage bore the scars of all these social and political transformations. This book has described how he reacted to them, and how they shaped the roles he chose to assume as patron in Friesland and client in The Hague.

The tale of William Frederick does not just illustrate the ways in which a high nobleman in the Dutch Republic negotiated the consequences of patronage in his life. The exceptional sources he left also make it possible to reconsider some assumptions that have often coloured modern research into early modern clientage. Basing themselves on paradigms from the social sciences, historians have long tended to describe clientage as a rather static and single phenomenon that could best be analysed in clear-cut tables and graphs. The case of William Frederick has made it clear, however, that patronage was a continuous process and not a particular 'status' that could be 'achieved'. Moreover, his example demonstrates that clientage was in fact a characteristic of countless social relations, rather than a distinct category of social relationship in itself. Clientelistic qualities shaped and guided many of William Frederick's professional relations, friendships and family contacts. In all those cases, the degree of dependence, reciprocity and intensity could differ and develop.

The more aware of this variety in forms of patronage we become, the more important it is to recognise that many individuals united in themselves not one but many, sometimes competing, patronage identities. In his career William Frederick consciously developed different roles as a patron in the republican government and in his princely household. A similar reorientation could be observed as soon as he exchanged Leeuwarden for The Hague and adopted a role of client at the court of his relatives, the princes of Orange. Because the conditions for patronage diverged in these distinctive social settings, William Frederick was continually obliged to redefine his patronage positions.

These transformations of roles and identities not only reveal the complexity of clientage as a process, but also the public and private spheres that left their mark on it. In the Dutch Republic, unlike many early modern monarchies, sovereignty of the state and the headship of a princely household did not coincide in one and the same person. The case of William Frederick shows that the republican state thus created two different institutional spheres, in which patronage had different functions and characteristics. While the possibilities open to the patron as stadholder in the republican or public sphere were limited by his formal authority and the rules by which he was bound, no such public regulations restricted his patronage as nobleman in the domestic or private sphere. It is possible that William Frederick may have taken a very personal view of these distinct spheres and appropriate patronage roles, one which cannot be called representative. Even if that were true, his case allows us some insight into the forms that clientage could take in the Dutch Republic, and on the circumstances that shaped the development of patronage identities in Dutch society.

Bibliography

Manuscript sources

The Netherlands

Koninklijk Huisarchief (The Hague)
Archief Willem II
Archief Willem III
Archief Ernst Casimir
Archief Willem Frederik

Nationaal Archief (The Hague)
Staten-Generaal
Hof van Holland
Archief van de raadpensionaris
Nassause domeinraad
Archief Johan de Witt
Archief Van Aitzema
Collectie aanwinsten

Tresoar (Leeuwarden)
Staten van Friesland
Stadhouderlijk archief
Archief Eysinga-Vegelin van Claerbergen
Archief Thoe Schwartzenberg en Hohenlansberg

Rijksarchief Gelderland (Arnhem)
Archief van der Capellen

Groninger Archieven (Groningen)
Ommelander archief
Archief Borg Farmsum
Register Feith

Historisch Centrum Overijssel (Zwolle)
Archief Haersolte

Utrechts Archief (Utrecht)
Staten van Utrecht
Stadsarchief Utrecht
Archief Des Tombes
Archief Huis Amerongen
Archief Hardenbroek
Archief Huydekoper

Drents Archief (Assen)
Oude Staten archief
Fries stadhouderlijk archief betreffende Drenthe

Archiefdienst Kennemerland (Haarlem)
Stadsarchief Haarlem

Archiefdienst West-Friese Gemeenten (Hoorn)
Oud archief Medemblik

Gemeentearchief Amsterdam (Amsterdam)
Burgemeesters- en vroedschapsarchief

Stadsarchief Dordrecht (Dordrecht)
Stadsarchief oudraad

Archief van de Ridderlijke Duitsche orde (Teutonic order), Balije Utrecht (Utrecht)
Collectie brieven

Instituut voor Nederlandse Geschiedenis (The Hague)
Notulen Sijbrand Claesz. Schot 1640–1652

Universiteitsbibliotheek Leiden (Leiden)
Collectie Handschriften

United Kingdom

British Library (London)
Egerton Manuscripts
Autographs of the House of Orange (Add. 21527)

Bodleian Library (Oxford)
Rawlinson Manuscripts
Clarendon Manuscripts

Germany

Landesarchiv Anhalt-Dessau (Oranienbaum)
Abteilung Oranienbaum

Printed sources and literature

Printed sources

Bontemantel, Hans, *De regeeringe van Amsterdam soo in 't civiel als crimineel en militaire (1653–1672)*, ed. G.W. Kernkamp (2 vols: Amsterdam, 1897).

Borkowski, H. (ed.), *Les mémoires du Burgrave et comte Frédéric de Dohna* (Königsberg, 1898).

Capellen, R.J. van der (ed.), *Gedenkschriften van jonkheer Alexander van der Capellen* ... (2 vols: Utrecht, 1787–88).

Drossaers, S.W.A. and Th.H. Lunsingh Scheurleer (eds), *Inventarissen van de inboedels in de verblijven van de Oranjes 1567–1795* (2 vols: The Hague, 1974).

Fruin, R. and G.W. Kernkamp (eds), *Brieven van / aan Johan de Witt* (6 vols: Amsterdam, 1906–1922).

Groen van Prinsterer, G. (ed.), *Archives ou correspondance inédite de la maison d'Orange-Nassau. 2ᵉ serie* (vols 4 and 5: Utrecht, 1859 and 1861).

Grondigh bericht, Nopende den Interest van desen Staet, vermidts de doodt van Sijn Hoogheyt ... (Knuttel Catalogue, 7009).

Kernkamp, G.W. (ed.), 'Memorie van Nanning Keyser betreffende de gebeurtenissen van het jaar 1650', *BMHG*, 18 (1897), 342–406.

Kluiver, J.H. (ed.), 'Brieven van de Middelburgse regent Hendrick Thibaut aan stadhouder Willem II en diens secretaris Johan Heilersich (1648–1650)', in: *Nederlandse historische bronnen* (vol. 10: The Hague, 1992), 33–97.

Knuttel, W.P.C. (ed.), *Acta der particuliere synoden van Zuid-Holland, 1621–1700* (vol. 3: The Hague, 1910).

Krämer, F.J.L. (ed.), 'Journalen van den Stadhouder Willem den Tweede, uit de jaren 1641–1650', *BMHG*, 27 (1906), 413–535.

Polyander van Kerkhoven, J. van (Heer van Heenvliet), 'Journaal van Johan van Kerckhoven, heer van Heenvliet, hofmeester van de princes-royaal, over de ziekte en den dood van prins Willem II en de kwestien omtrent de voogdij van den jonggeboren prins', *Kroniek van het Historisch Genootschap*, 25 (1869), 541–647.

Schoon, F., 'Het vermoeden van vergiftiging van prins Willem II gelogenstraft', *Kronijk van het Historisch Genootschap*, 5 (1849), 7–15.

Sohnius, J., 'Brieven betreffende de zaak van Sohnius', *Kronijk van het Historisch Genootschap*, 24 (1868), 128–32.

Thoe Schwartzenberg en Hohenlansberg, G.F. (ed.), *Groot Placcaat- en Charterboek van Vriesland* ... (vol. 5: Leeuwarden 1768–95).

Thurloe, J. (ed.), *A Collection of the State Papers of John Thurloe, Secretary, First, to the Council of State and Afterwards to the Two Protectors, Oliver and Richard Cromwell* (vol. 1: London, 1742).

Verdragh, Ghemaeckt tusschen sijne Hoogheyt aen d'eene zyde: ende de Heeren Burgermeesteren ... (Knuttel Catalogue, 6699).

Visser, J. (ed.), *Gloria Parendi. Dagboeken van Willem Frederik, stadhouder van Friesland, Groningen en Drenthe 1643–1649, 1651–1654* (The Hague, 1995).

Warner, G.F. (ed.), *The Nicholas Papers. Correspondence of Sir Edward Nicholas, Secretary of State* (4 vols, London, 1886–1920).

Witt, J. de, *Resolutien van de Heeren Staten van Hollandt ende West-Vriesland van consideratie, ende oock voor de toekomende tijden dienende ... beginnende met den tweeden Augusti 1653. ende eyndigende met den negenthienden december 1668* (Utrecht, 1706).

Worp, J.A. (ed.), *De briefwisseling van Constantijn Huygens (1608–1687)* (vols 3, 4 and 5: The Hague, 1914, 1915 and 1916).

Literature

Aa, A.J. van der (ed.), *Biographisch woordenboek der Nederlanden* (21 vols: Haarlem, 1852–78).

Adamson, J. 'The Aristocracy and their Mental World', in: J. Morrill (ed.), *The Oxford Illustrated History of Tudor and Stuart Britain* (Oxford, 1996), 173–90.

——, 'The Making of the Ancien-Régime Court 1500–1700', in: J. Adamson (ed.), *The Princely Courts of Europe. Ritual, Politics, and Culture under the Ancien Régime 1500–1750* (London, 2000), 7–42.

Aitzema, L. van, *Herstelde leeuw, of discours, over 't gepasseerde in de Vereenigde Nederlanden, in 't jaer 1650 ende 1651* (Utrecht, 1652).

——, *Saken van Staet en oorlogh, in, ende omtrent de vereenigde Nederlanden* (6 vols: The Hague, 1669–72).

Ariès, Ph., G. Duby and R. Chartier (eds), *A History of Private Life. III: Passions of the Renaissance* (trans.: Cambridge, MA, 1989).

Asch, R.G., 'Introduction', in: R.G. Asch and A.M. Birke (eds), *Princes, Patronage and the Nobility. The Court at the Beginning of the Modern Age, c.1450–1650* (Oxford, 1991), 1–40.

——, and A.M. Birke (eds), *Princes, Patronage and the Nobility. The Court at the Beginning of the Modern Age, c.1450–1650* (Oxford, 1991).

——, 'Corruption and Punishment? The Rise and Fall of Matthäus Enzlin (1556–1613), Lawyer and Favourite', in: J.H. Elliott and L.W.B. Brockliss (eds), *The World of the Favourite* (New Haven and London, 1999), 96–111.

Aylmer, G.E., *The Crown's Servants. Government and Civil Service under Charles II, 1660–1685* (Oxford, 2002).

Aymard, M., 'Friends and Neighbours', in: R. Chartier (ed.), *Passions of the Renaissance* (vol. 3: Cambridge, MA, 1987).

Baggerman, A., 'Autobiography and Family Memory in the Nineteenth Century', in: R. Dekker (ed.), *Egodocuments and History. Autobiographical Writing in its Social Context since the Middle Ages* (Hilversum, 2002), 161–74.

Baron, S.A., 'The Guises of Dissemination in Early Seventeenth-Century England. News in Manuscript and Print', in: B. Dooley and S.A. Baron (eds), *The Politics of Information in Early Modern Europe* (London and New York, 2001), 41–56.

Beaufort, W.H. de, 'De aanslag van Willem II op Amsterdam', in: W.H. de Beaufort, *Geschiedkundige opstellen* (vol. 1: Amsterdam, 1893), 66–101.

——, 'De dood van den stadhouder Willem II', in: W.H. de Beaufort, *Geschiedkundige opstellen* (vol. 1: Amsterdam, 1893), 102–14.

Béguin, K., *Les princes de Condé. Rebelles, courtisans et mécènes dans la France du grand siècle* (Paris, 1999).

Benedict, P., 'Introduction', in: P. Benedict et al. (eds), *Reformation, Revolt and Civil War in France and the Netherlands 1555–1585* (Amsterdam, 1999), 1–21.

——, *Christ's Churches Purely Reformed. A Social History of Calvinism* (New Haven and London, 2002).

Bergsma, J., *J. van Vondels hekeldichten* (Zutphen, 1920).

Bergsma, W., 'Willem Lodewijk en het Leeuwarder hofleven', *It Beaken*, 60 (1998), 191–256.

——, 'De godsdienstige verhoudingen tijdens de Vrede van Munster', in: J. Dane (ed.), *1648. Vrede van Munster. Feit en verbeelding* (Zwolle, 1998), 83–108.

——, 'Kerk en staat in Friesland na 1580', in: J. Frieswijk et al. (eds), *Fryslân, staat en macht 1450–1650* (Hilversum, 1998), 158–72.

——, *Tussen Gideonsbende en publieke kerk. Een studie over het gereformeerd protestantisme in Friesland, 1580–1650* (Hilversum, 1999).

——, *'Zij preekten voor doven'. De reformatie in Drenthe* (Assen, 2002).

——, 'Een geleerde en zijn tuin. Over de vriendschap tussen Lubbertus en Vulcanius', *De zeventiende eeuw,* 20 (2004), 96–121.

Berkvens-Stevelinck, C., J.I. Israel and G.H.M. Posthumus Meyes (eds), *The Emergence of Tolerance in the Dutch Republic* (Leiden, New York and Cologne, 1997).

Bijl, M. van der, *Idee en interest. Voorgeschiedenis, verloop en achtergronden van de politieke twisten in Zeeland en vooral in Middelburg tussen 1702–1715* (Groningen, 1981).

Bijlsma, R., *Rotterdams welvaren 1550–1650* (The Hague, 1918).

Blaak, J., 'Autobiographical Reading and Writing: the Diary of David Beck (1624)', in: R. Dekker (ed.), *Egodocuments and History. Autobiographical Writing in its Social Context since the Middle Ages* (Hilversum, 2002), 61–88.

——, *Geletterde levens. Dagelijks lezen en schrijven in de vroegmoderne tijd in Nederland 1624–1777* (Hilversum, 2004).

Blockmans, W., 'Patronage, Brokerage and Corruption as Symptoms of Incipient State Formation in the Burgundian-Habsburg Netherlands', in: A. Mączak (ed.), *Klientelsysteme im Europa der frühen Neuzeit* (Munich, 1988), 117–26.

Blok, A., 'Variations in Patronage', *Sociologische Gids* 16 (1969), 365–78.

——, *Wittgenstein en Elias. Een methodische richtlijn voor de antropologie* (Amsterdam, 1976).

——, *The Mafia of a Sicilian Village, 1860–1960. A Study of Violent Peasant Entrepreneurs* (Prospect Heights, 1988).

Boer, M.G. de, *De woelingen in stad en lande in het midden der zeventiende eeuw* (Groningen, 1893).

——, 'Een ommelander jonker in de zeventiende eeuw', *TvG*, 39 (1924), 44–72.

Bogaart, M.Th. uit den, *De gereformeerden en Oranje tijdens het eerste stadhouderloze tijdperk* (Groningen, 1954).

Boissevain, J., 'Patrons as Brokers', *Sociologische Gids,* 16 (1969), 379–86.

——, *Friends of Friends. Networks, Manipulators and Coalitions* (Oxford, 1974).

Boomsma, C., 'Een werck van factie en staetsucht. Factiestrijd in Leeuwarden tussen 1644 en 1647', *Leeuwarder historische reeks,* 5 (1995), 7–38.

Bor, P.C., *Oorsprongk, begin, en vervolgh der Nederlandsche oorlogen, beroerten, en borgerlyke oneenigheden* … (4 vols, Amsterdam, 1679–84).

Bosch, A.G., 'Soo staen de Raden provinciaal als perplex ... Hof van Friesland en provinciaal bestuur. Een verkenning', in: D.P. de Vries and P. Nieuwland (eds), *500 jaar Hof van Friesland. Bijdragen aan het herdenkingssymposium, gehouden te Leeuwarden 24 september 1999* (Hilversum and Leeuwarden, 2000), 41–58.

Braddick, M.J. and J. Walter, 'Introduction', in: M.J. Braddick (ed.), *Negotiating Power in Early Modern Society. Order, Hierarchy and Subordination in Britain and Ireland* (Cambridge, 2001), 1–42.

Breuker, Ph., *It wurk fan Gysbert Japix* (2 vols: Leeuwarden, 1989).

——, *Friese cultuur in de jonge Republiek* (Leiden, 1991).

——, 'Court Culture in seventeenth-century Friesland', *Dutch Crossing*, 18 (1994), 61–83.

——, 'Over de Nadere Reformatie in Friesland', *Documentatieblad Nadere Reformatie*, 25 (2001), 19–38.

——, 'Nogmaals over de positie van de gereformeerde kerk in Friesland rond het midden van de zeventiende eeuw', *Documentatieblad Nadere Reformatie*, 25 (2001), 39–42.

Bruggeman, M., 'Het hof van Maria Louise van Hessen-Kassel (1711–1731)', *It Beaken*, 60 (1998), 293–304.

——, *Nassau en de macht van Oranje. De strijd van de Friese Nassaus voor de erkenning van hun rechten, 1702–1747* (Amsterdam, 2005).

Bruin, G. de, *Geheimhouding en verraad. De geheimhouding van staatszaken ten tijde van de Republiek (1600–1750)* (The Hague, 1991).

——, 'Het politieke bestel van de Republiek: een anomalie in het vroegmodern Europa?', *BMGN*, 114 (1999), 16–38.

Burke, P., *Venice and Amsterdam. A Study of seventeenth-century Elites* (Cambridge, 1994).

——, 'Representations of the Self from Petrarch to Descartes, in: R. Porter (ed.), *Rewriting the Self. Histories from the Renaissance to the Present* (New York and London, 1997), 17–28.

——, and R. Porter, *The Social History of Language* (Cambridge, 1987).

Busken Huet, C., *Het land van Rembrandt* (reprint: Amsterdam, 1987 [1884]).

Bussemaker, C.H.Th., *Geschiedenis van Overijssel gedurende het eerste stadhouderlooze tijdperk* (2 vols: The Hague, 1888–89).

Dam, J.M. van, 'Stadhouderlijke verblijven buiten Friesland', in: J.J. Huizinga (ed.), *Van Leeuwarden naar Den Haag. Rond de verplaatsing van het stadhouderlijk hof in 1747* (Leeuwarden, 1997), 85–96.

Davis, N.Z., 'Women in Politics', in: N.Z. Davis and A. Farge (eds), *A History of Women in the West. Renaissance and Enlightenment Paradoxes* (Cambridge, MA, 1993), 167–83.

——, *Women on the Margins. Three Seventeenth-century Lives* (Cambridge, MA, 1995).

——, *The Gift in sixteenth-century France* (Oxford, 2000).

Daydell, J. (ed.), *Women and Politics in Early Modern England, 1450–1700* (Aldershot, 2004).

Dayton, C.H., 'Rethinking Agency, Recovering Voices', *American Historical Review*, 109 (2004), 827–43.

Dekker, R.M., 'Corruptie en ambtelijke ethiek in historisch perspectief', *De Gids*, 194 (1986), 116–21.

——— (ed.), *Egodocuments and History. Autobiographical Writing in its Social Context since the Middle Ages* (Hilversum, 2002).

Delen, M.A., *Het hof van Willem van Oranje* (Amsterdam, 2002).

Deursen, A.Th. van, 'De raadpensionaris Jacob Cats', *TvG*, 92 (1979), 149–61.

———, 'Staatsinstellingen in de Noordelijke Nederlanden 1579–1780', in: D.P. Blok et al. (eds), *NAGN* (vol. 5: Haarlem, 1981), 350–87.

———, *Plain Lives in a Golden Age. Popular Culture, Religion and Society in seventeenth-century Holland* (Cambridge, 1991).

———, *Een dorp in de polder. Graft in de zeventiende eeuw* (Amsterdam, 1995).

———, *Maurits van Nassau. De winnaar die faalde* (Amsterdam, 2000).

Dewald, J., *Aristocratic Experience and the Origins of Modern Culture. France, 1570–1715* (Berkeley, 1993).

Diepen, H.J.J.M. van, 'Een historisch plekje', *Jaarboek Die Haghe* (1941), 66–122.

———, 'Het Hof van Friesland', *Jaarboek Die Haghe* (1942), 52–81.

Dooley, B., and S.A. Baron (eds), *The Politics of Information in Early Modern Europe* (London and New York, 2001).

Dorren, G., *Eenheid en verscheidenheid. De burgers van Haarlem in de Gouden Eeuw* (Amsterdam, 2001).

Droste, H., 'Patronage in der frühen Neuzeit. Institutionen und Kulturform', *Zeitschrift für Historische Forschung*, 30 (2003), 555–90.

Duindam, J., 'Versailles als dwaallicht. Hoven, vorsten en stadhouders', *It Beaken*, 60 (1998), 177–90.

———, *Vienna and Versailles. The Courts of Europe's Dynastic Rivals, 1550–1780* (Cambridge, 2003).

Dumolyn, J., 'Investeren in sociaal kapitaal. Netwerken en sociale transacties van Bourgondische ambtenaren', *TvSG*, 28 (2002), 417–38.

Durand, Y., 'Clientèles et fidélités dans le temps et l'espace', in: Y. Durand (ed.), *Hommage à Rouland Mousnier. Clientèles et fidélités en Europe à l' époque moderne* (Paris, 1981), 3–24.

Edelmayer, F., *Söldner und Pensionäre. Das Netzwerk Philipps II. im Heiligen Römischen Reich* (Vienna and Munich, 2002).

Egmond, F., 'De aansprakelijkheid van God: "gewone" Nederlanders en bijzondere natuurverschijnselen in de zestiende eeuw', in: F. Egmond and M. Gijswijt-Hofstra (eds), *Of bidden helpt? Tegenslag en cultuur in Europa, circa 1500–2000* (Amsterdam, 1997), 11–28.

———, 'Strafzaken in hoogste instantie. Rechtsbescherming, corruptie en ongelijkheid in de vroeg-moderne Nederlanden', in: R. Huijbrecht (ed.), *Handelingen van het tweede hof van Holland symposium gehouden op 14 november 1997 in de trêveszaal te Den Haag* (The Hague, 1998), 63–75.

———, 'Recht en krom. Corruptie, ongelijkheid en rechtsbescherming in de vroegmoderne Nederlanden', *BMGN*, 116 (2001), 1–33.

Eisenstadt, S.N. and L. Roniger, *Patrons, Clients and Friends. Interpersonal Relations and the Structure of Trust in Society* (Cambridge, 1984).

Ekkart, R.E.O., 'Schilders aan het hof', in: S. Groenveld, J.J. Huizinga and Y.B. Kuiper (eds), *Nassau uit de schaduw van Oranje* (Franeker, 2003), 113–26.

Elias, J.E., *De vroedschap van Amsterdam* (2 vols: Amsterdam, 1903 and 1905).

Elias, N., *Die höfische Gesellschaft. Untersuchungen zur Soziologie des Königtums und der höfischen Aristokratie* (Neuwied, 1969).

Ellemers, J.E., 'Patronage in sociologisch perspectief', *Sociologische Gids*, 16 (1969), 432–40.

Elliot, J.H. and L.W.B. Brockliss (eds), *The World of the Favourite* (New Haven and London, 1999).

Engelbrecht, E.A., *De vroedschap van Rotterdam 1572–1795* (Rotterdam, 1973).

Engels, M.H.H., *Naamlijst van de gedeputeerde Staten van Friesland 1577–1795* (Leeuwarden, 1979).

Eysten, J., *Het leven van prins Willem II (1626–1650)* (Amsterdam, 1916).

Faber, D.E.A. and R.E. de Bruin, 'Tegen de vrede. De Utrechtse ambassadeur Godard van Reede van Nederhorst en de onderhandelingen in Munster', in: J. Dane (ed.), *1648.Vrede van Munster. Feit en verbeelding* (Zwolle, 1998), 107–34.

Faber, J.A., 'De oligarchisering van Friesland in de tweede helft van de 17ᵉ eeuw', *AAG Bijdragen*, 15 (1970), 39–65.

———, *Drie eeuwen Friesland. Economische en sociale ontwikkelingen van 1500 tot 1800* (2 vols: Leeuwarden, 1973).

Feenstra, H., *Bloeitijd en het verval van de Ommelander adel (1600–1800)* (Groningen, 1981).

Flap, H.D., 'Patronage. An Institution in its own Right', in: M. Hechter, K. Opp and R. Wippler (eds), *Social Institutions. Their Emergence, Maintenance and Effects* (New York, 1990), 225–44.

Fockema Andreae, S.J., *De Nederlandse staat onder de Republiek* (Amsterdam, 1961).

———, and G. Bakker, *IJlst 1268–1968* (Bolsward, 1968).

Formsma, W.J. (ed.), *Historie van Groningen. Stad en Land* (Groningen, 1976).

Franken, M.A.M., *Dienaar van Oranje. Andries Schimmelpenninck van der Oije 1705–1776* (Zutphen, 2002).

Frieswijk, J. et al., *Frieslands verleden verkend* (Leeuwarden, 1987).

———, et al. (eds), *Fryslân, staat en macht 1450–1650* (Hilversum and Leeuwarden, 1999).

Frijhoff, W., 'Identiteit en identiteitsbesef. De historicus en de spanning tussen verbeelding, benoeming en herkenning', *BMGN*, 107 (1992), 614–34.

———, *Wegen van Evert Willemsz. Een Hollands weeskind op zoek naar zichzelf 1607–1647* (Nijmegen, 1995).

———, 'Het Haagse hof in nationaal en Europees perspectief', in: M. Keblusek and J. Zijlmans (eds), *Vorstelijk vertoon. Aan het hof van Frederik Hendrik en Amalia* (Zwolle and The Hague, 1997), 10–17.

———, 'Dimensions de la coexistence confessionelle', in: C. Berkvens-Stevelinck, J. Israel and G.H.M. Posthumus Meyes (eds), *The Emergence of Tolerance in the Dutch Republic* (Leiden, New York and Cologne, 1997), 213–37.

———, 'Religious Toleration in the United Provinces: from 'Case' to 'Model', in: R. Hsia and H.F.K. van Nierop (eds), *Calvinism and Religious Toleration in the Dutch Golden Age* (Cambridge, 2002), 27–52.

———, and M. Spies, *Dutch Culture in European Context. 1650. Hard-won Unity* (Basingstoke, 2004).

Fruin, R., 'Over de oorlogsplannen van prins Willem II na zijn aanslag op Amsterdam in 1650', in: R. Fruin, *Verspreide geschriften* (vol. 4: The Hague, 1901), 122–94.

———, and H.T. Colenbrander, *Geschiedenis der staatsinstellingen in Nederland tot den val der Republiek* (The Hague, 1980).

Gaastra, F.S., 'Friesland en de VOC', in: A. Janse and P. Breuker (eds), *Negen Eeuwen Friesland-Holland. Geschiedenis van een haat-liefde verhouding* (Leeuwarden and Zutphen, 1997) 184–96.

Gabriëls, A.J.C.M., *De heren als dienaren en de dienaar als heer. Het stadhouderlijk stelsel in de tweede helft van de 18ᵉ eeuw* (Leiden, 1989).

Gelder, R. van, *Naporra's omweg. Het leven van een VOC-matroos (1731–1793)* (Amsterdam, 2003).

Gellner, E. and J. Waterbury (eds), *Patrons and Clients in Mediterranean Societies* (London, 1977).

Geyl, P., 'Een Engelsch republikein over Willem II's staatsgreep in 1650', *BMHG*, 45 (1924), 77–88.

———, 'Het stadhouderschap in de partij-literatuur onder De Witt', *Mededeelingen der Koninklijke Nederlandsche Akademie van Wetenschappen* (vol. 10: Amsterdam, 1947), 17–84.

———, *Orange and Stuart 1642–1672* (London, 1969).

Gietman, C., 'Het adellijk bewustzijn van Sweder Schele tot Weleveld', *Overijsselse historische bijdragen*, 107 (1992), 83–114.

Ginzburg, C., *The Cheese and the Worms. The Cosmos of a Sixteenth-century Miller* (Baltimore, 1992).

Greengrass, M., 'Noble Affinities in Early Modern France. The case of Henri I de Montmorency, Constable of France', *European History Quarterly*, 16 (1986), 275–312.

———, 'The Functions and Limits of Political Clientelism in France before Cardinal Richelieu', in: N. Bulst, R. Descimon and A. Guerreau (eds), *L'État ou le roi. Les fondations de la modernité monarchique en France (XIVe–XVIIe siècles)* (Paris, 1996), 69–82.

Groenhuis, G., *De predikanten. De sociale positie van de gereformeerde predikanten in de Republiek der Verenigde Nederlanden voor ± 1700* (Groningen, 1977).

Groenveld, S., *De prins voor Amsterdam. Reacties uit pamfletten op de aanslag van 1650* (Bussum, 1967).

———, 'Verdicht verleden. Kanttekeningen bij een zeventiende-eeuws manuscript over Jacoba van Beieren', *Hollandse studiën*, 8 (1975), 275–348.

———, *Verlopend getij. De Nederlandse Republiek en de Engelse burgeroorlog 1640–1646* (Dieren, 1984).

———, 'Een enckel valsch ende lasterlijck verdichtsel. Een derde actie van prins Willem II in juli 1650', in: S. Groenveld et al. (eds), *Bestuurders en geleerden. Opstellen over onderwerpen uit de Nederlandse geschiedenis van de 16ᵉ, 17ᵉ en 18ᵉ eeuw, aangeboden aan prof. dr. J.J. Woltjer bij zijn afscheid als hoogleraar aan de Rijksuniversiteit Leiden* (Amsterdam and Dieren, 1985), 113–25.

———, 'Adriaan Pauw (1585–1653). Een pragmatisch Hollands staatsman', *Spiegel historiael*, 20 (1985), 432–9.

———, 'C'est le pere, qui parle. Patronage bij Constantijn Huygens (1596–1687)', *Jaarboek*

Oranje-Nassau museum (1988), 63–106.

——, 'Een out ende getrouw dienaer, beyde van den staet ende welstant in 't huys van Oragnen. Constantijn Huygens (1596–1687), een hoog Haags ambtenaar', *Holland*, 20 (1988), 3–32.

——, 'Willem II en de Stuarts, 1647–1650', *BMGN*, 103 (1988), 157–81.

——, *Evidente factiën in den Staet. Sociaal-politieke verhoudingen in de 17ᵉ eeuwse Republiek der Verenigde Nederlanden* (Hilversum, 1990).

——, 'Een Schaep in 't Schapelandt. Het Hollandse gezantschap van Gerard Schaep Pietersz naar Engeland, 1650–1651', *Jaarboek Amstelodamum*, 87 (1992), 179–96.

——, *Huisgenoten des geloofs.Was de samenleving in de Republiek der Verenigde Nederlanden verzuild?* (Hilversum, 1995).

——, 'Nassau contra Oranje in de 17ᵉ eeuwse Republiek', *Jaarboek Oranje-Nassau museum* (1997), 11–53.

——, 'Frederik Hendrik en zijn entourage. Een politieke levensschets', in: P. van der Ploeg and Carola Vermeeren (eds), *Vorstelijk verzameld. De kunstcollectie van Frederik Hendrik en Amalia* (Zwolle and The Hague, 1997), 18–33.

——, 'Unie, Religie en Militie. Binnenlandse verhoudingen in de Republiek voor en na de Munsterse vrede', *De zeventiende eeuw*, 13 (1997), 67–87.

——, 'Gemengde gevoelens. De relaties tussen Nassaus en Oranjes als stadhouders en kapiteins-generaal', in: S.Groenveld, J.J. Huizinga and Y.B. Kuiper (eds), *Nassau uit de schaduw van Oranje* (Franeker, 2003), 23–44.

——, J.J. Huizinga and Y.B. Kuiper (eds), *Nassau uit de schaduw van Oranje* (Franeker, 2003).

——, 'König ohne Staat. Friedrich V. und Elizabeth als Exilierte in Den Haag 1621–1632–1661', in: P. Wolf et al. (eds), *Der Winterkönig. Friedrich V. Der letzte Kurfürst aus der Oberen Pfalz* (Augsburg, 2003), 162–87.

Guibal, C.J., *Democratie en oligarchie in Friesland tijdens de Republiek* (Assen, 1934).

Habermas, J., *The Structural Transformation of the Public Sphere. An Inquiry into a Category of Bourgeois Society* (Cambridge, 1989).

Haddad, Elie, 'Noble Clienteles in France in the Sixteenth and Seventeenth Centuries. A Historiographical Approach', *French History*, 20 (2006), 75–109.

Harding, R.R., *Anatomy of a Power Elite. The Provincial Governors of Early Modern France* (New Haven and London, 1978).

——, 'Corruption and the Moral Boundaries of Patronage', in: G. Fitch Lytle and S. Orgel (eds), *Patronage in the Renaissance* (Princeton, 1981), 47–64.

Harris, B.J., 'Women and Politics in Early Stuart England', *Historical Journal*, 33 (1990), 259–81.

Hart, G. 't, *Historische beschrijving der vrije en hoge heerlijkheid van Heenvliet* (n.p., 1949).

Hart, M.C. 't, 'Autonoom maar kwetsbaar. De Middelburgse regenten en de opstand van 1651', *De zeventiende eeuw*, 9 (1993), 51–62.

Hartog, R.H., *Onrechtmatige overheidsdaden in de Republiek der verenigde Nederlanden. Een onderzoek naar de toenmalige rechtspraktijk* (Deventer, 1971).

Heller, T. et al. (eds), *Reconstructing Individualism. Autonomy, Individuality and the Self in Western Thought* (Stanford, 1986).

Heringa, J. et al. (eds), *Geschiedenis van Drenthe* (Meppel, 1985).

Hitters, E., *Patronen van patronage. Mecenaat, protectoraat en markt in de kunstwereld* (Utrecht, 1996).

Hsia, R. and H.F.K. van Nierop (eds), *Calvinism and Religious Toleration in the Dutch Golden Age* (Cambridge, 2002).

Huiskamp, R., 'Tussen centrum en periferie. Giften en corruptie in de vroegmoderne politiek', *Volkskundig bulletin*, 21 (1995), 27–58.

Huizinga, J.H., *Dutch Civilization in the Seventeenth Century, and Other Essays* (London, 1968).

Huizinga, J.J. (ed.), *Van Leeuwarden naar Den Haag. Rond de verplaatsing van het stadhouderlijk hof in 1747* (Leeuwarden, 1997).

Huussen, A.H., *Veroordeeld in Friesland. Criminaliteitsbestrijding in de eeuw der Verlichting* (Leeuwarden, 1994).

Israel, J.I., 'The Holland Towns and the Dutch-Spanish Conflict, 1621–1648', *BMGN*, 94 (1979), 41–69.

——, 'Frederick Henry and the Dutch Political Factions, 1625–1642', *English Historical Review*, 98 (1983), 1–27.

——, *The Dutch Republic. Its Rise, Greatness and Fall 1477–1806* (Oxford, 1998).

——, 'The Courts of the House of Orange c.1580–1795', in: J. Adamson (ed.), *The Princely Courts of Europe. Ritual, Politics, and Culture under the Ancien Régime 1500–1750* (London, 2000), 119–40.

Jansen, D.J., 'Het stadhouderlijk kwartier in de 17ᵉ eeuw', in: R.J. van Pelt and M.E. Spliethoff-Tiethoff (eds), *Het Binnenhof. Van grafelijke residentie tot regeringscentrum* (Dieren, 1984), 57–70.

Janssen, G.H., 'De kunst van het kopiëren. Opdrachten van stadhouder Willem Frederik van Nassau aan Pieter Nason', *Jaarboek Oranje-Nassau museum* (2001), 36–47.

——, 'Dutch Clientelism and News Networks in Public and Private Spheres. The Case of Stadholder William Frederick (1613–1664)', in: J.W. Koopmans (ed.), *News and Politics in Early Modern Europe (1500–1800)* (Leuven, 2005), 151–65.

——, 'Dynastieke transfer in de Republiek. De politieke en religieuze betekenis van de stadhouderlijke begrafenisstoet', *BMGN*, 122 (2007), 208–32.

Japikse, N., 'Cornelis Musch en de corruptie van zijn tijd', *De Gids* (1907), 498–523.

Jenniskens, A.H., *De magistraat van Nijmegen 1618–1648* (Nijmegen, 1973).

Jong, J.J. de, 'Prosopografie, een mogelijkheid', *BMGN*, 111 (1996), 201–15.

Jongste, J.A.F. de, 'Politieke elite en kerkelijke ambtsdragers in enkele Hollandse steden, 1650–1672', in: M. Ebben and P. Wagenaar (eds), *De cirkel doorbroken. Met nieuwe ideeën terug naar de bronnen. Opstellen over de Republiek* (Leiden, 2006), 165–80.

Jorink, E., *Het boeck der natuere. Nederlandse geleerden en de wonderen van Gods schepping, 1575–1715* (Leiden, 2006).

Kalma, J.J., J.J. Spahr van der Hoek and K. de Vries (eds), *Geschiedenis van Friesland* (Drachten, 1968).

Kaplan, B.J., *Calvinists and Libertines. Confession and Community in Utrecht 1578–1620* (Oxford, 1995).

——, 'Fictions of Privacy. House Chapels and the Spatial Accommodation of Religious Dissent in Early Modern Europe', *American Historical Review*, 107 (2002), 1030–64.

——, 'Dutch Religious Tolerance. Celebration and Revision', in: R. Hsia and H.F.K. van Nierop (eds), *Calvinism and Religious Toleration in the Dutch Golden Age* (Cambridge, 2002), 8–26.

Keblusek, M., *Boeken in de hofstad. Haagse boekcultuur in de Gouden Eeuw* (Hilversum, 1997).

——, 'Het Boheemse hof in Den Haag', in: M. Keblusek and J. Zijlmans (eds), *Vorstelijk vertoon. Aan het hof van Frederik Hendrik en Amalia* (Zwolle and The Hague, 1997), 47–57.

——, 'Profiling the Early Modern Agent', in: H. Cools, B. Noldus and M. Keblusek (eds), *Your Humble Servant. Agents in Early Modern Europe* (Hilversum, 2006), 9–16.

——, and J. Zijlmans (eds), *Vorstelijk vertoon. Aan het hof van Frederik Hendrik en Amalia* (Zwolle and The Hague, 1997).

Kernkamp, G.W., *Prins Willem II* (Amsterdam, 1943).

Kettering, S., *Patrons, Brokers, and Clients in Seventeenth-century France* (Oxford, 1986).

——, 'Gift-giving and Patronage in Early Modern France', *French History*, 2 (1988), 131–51.

——, 'The Historical Development of Political Clientelism', *Journal of Interdisciplinary History*, 18 (1988), 419–47.

——, 'Clientage during the French Wars of Religion', *Sixteenth Century Journal*, 20 (1989) 221–39.

——, 'Patronage and Kinship in Early Modern France', *French Historical Studies*, 16 (1989), 408–35.

——, 'The Patronage Power of Early Modern French Noblewomen', *Historical Journal*, 32 (1989), 817–41.

——, 'Friendship and Clientage in Early Modern France', *French History*, 6 (1992), 139–58.

——, 'Patronage in Early Modern France', *French Historical Studies*, 17 (1992), 839–62.

——, 'The Household Service of Early Modern French Noblewomen', *French Historical Studies*, 20 (1997), 55–85.

——, *Patronage in Sixteenth- and Seventeenth-century France* (Aldershot, 2002).

Klashorst, G.O. van de, 'Metten schijn van monarchie getempert. De verdediging van het stadhouderschap in de partijliteratuur, 1650–1686', in: H.W. Blom and I.W. Wildenberg (eds), *Pieter de la Court in zijn tijd. Aspecten van een veelzijdig publicist (1618–1685)* (Amsterdam and Maarssen, 1986), 93–136.

Kleijn, A.A., *De stadhouders van Friesland uit het huis van Nassau* (Nijkerk, 1904).

Kloek, E., 'De vrouw', in: H.M. Beliën, A.Th. van Deursen and G.J. van Setten (eds), *Gestalten van de Gouden Eeuw. Een Hollands groepsportret* (Amsterdam, 1995), 241–80.

Kluiver, J.H., *De souvereine en independente staat Zeeland. De politiek van de provincie Zeeland inzake vredesonderhandelingen met Spanje tijdens de tachtigjarige oorlog tegen de achtergrond van de positie van Zeeland in de Republiek* (Middelburg, 1998).

Knevel, P., *Het Haagse bureau. 17ᵉ-eeuwse ambtenaren tussen staatsbelang en eigenbelang* (Amsterdam, 2001).

Knuttel, W.P.C. (ed.), *Catalogus van de pamfletten-verzameling berustende in de Koninklijke Bibliotheek ... 1649–1667* (Utrecht, 1978 [1889–1910]).

Koenheim, A.J.M. (ed.), *Johan Wolfert van Brederode. Een Hollands edelman tussen Nassau en Oranje* (Zutphen, 1999).

Koenigsberger, H.G., 'Patronage and Bribery during the Reign of Charles V', in: H.G. Koenigsberger (ed.), *Estates and Revolutions. Essays in Early Modern European History* (London, 1971), 166–75.

——, 'Patronage, Clientage and Elites in the Politics of Philip II, Cardinal Granvelle and William of Orange', in: A. Mączak (ed.), *Klientelsysteme im Europa der frühen Neuzeit* (Munich, 1988), 127–48.

Kooijmans, L., *Vriendschap en de kunst van het overleven in de zeventiende en achttiende eeuw* (Amsterdam, 1997).

——, 'Haagse dames en Friese heren. Hofcultuur en de dagboeken van Willem Frederik', *It Beaken*, 60 (1998), 257–68.

——, 'Hoe Willem Frederik stadhouder van Friesland werd', in: J. Frieswijk et al. (eds), *Fryslân, staat en macht 1450–1650* (Hilversum and Leeuwarden, 1999), 205–17.

——, *Liefde in opdracht. Het hofleven van Willem Frederik van Nassau* (Amsterdam, 2000).

Kossmann, E.F., *De boekverkoopers, notarissen en cramers op het Binnenhof* (The Hague, 1932).

Kossmann, E.H., *Political Thought in the Dutch Republic* (Amsterdam, 2000).

Kuiper, Y., 'Hofleven van de Friese Nassaus in de zeventiende en achttiende eeuw. Een verkenning van recent onderzoek', *It Beaken*, 60 (1998), 326–47.

——, 'Profijt, eer en reputatie. Friese adel en politieke cultuur in het tweede kwart van de zeventiende eeuw', in: J. Frieswijk et al. (eds.), *Fryslân, staat en macht 1450–1650* (Hilversum and Leeuwarden, 1999), 173–204.

Landé, C., 'The Dyadic Basis of Clientelism', in: S.W. Schmidt et al. (eds), *Friends, Followers and Factions. A Reader in Political Clientelism* (Berkeley, 1977), xiii–xxxvii.

Lankhorst, O., 'Newspapers in the Netherlands in the Seventeenth Century', in: B. Dooley and S.A. Baron (eds), *The Politics of Information in Early Modern Europe* (London and New York, 2001), 153–4.

Lieburg, F.A. van, *Levens van vromen. Gereformeerd piëtisme in de achttiende eeuw* (Kampen, 1991).

Lind, G., 'Great Friends and Small Friends. Clientelism and the Power Elite', in: W. Reinhard (ed.), *Power Elites and State Building* (Oxford, 1996), 123–48.

Lindler, Th.J.M. (ed.), *Raad van State 450 jaar. Repertorium* (The Hague, 1983).

Lytle, G., 'Friendship and Patronage in Renaissance Europe', in: F.W. Kent and P. Simons (eds), *Patronage, Art, and Society in Renaissance Italy* (Oxford, 1987), 47–61.

—— and S. Orgel (eds), *Patronage in the Renaissance* (Princeton, 1982).

MacHardy, K.J., *War, Religion and Court Patronage in Habsburg Austria. The Social and Cultural Dimensions of Political Interactions, 1521–1622* (Basingstoke, 2003).

Maclean, I., *The Renaissance Notion of Woman. A Study in the Fortunes of Scholasticism and Medical Science in European Intellectual Life* (Cambridge, 1995).

Mączak, A. (ed.), *Klientelsysteme im Europa der frühen Neuzeit* (Munich, 1988).

——, 'From Aristocratic Household to Princely Court', in: R.G. Asch and A.M. Birke (eds), *Princes, Patronage and the Nobility. The Court at the Beginning of the Modern Age, c. 1450–1650* (Oxford, 1991), 315–27.

——, *Ungleiche Freundschaft. Klientelbeziehungen von der Antike bis zur Gegenwart* (Osnabrück, 2005).

Marcus, K.H., *The Politics of Power. Elites of an Early Modern State in Germany* (Mainz, 2000).

Marshall, S., *The Dutch Gentry, 1500–1650. Family, Faith, and Fortune* (New York, 1987).

Mascuch, M., *The Origins of the Individualist Self. Autobiography and Self-Identity in England 1591–1791* (Cambridge, 1997).

Meer Derval ter, A., 'Namen van de opeenvolgende eigenaars der huizen, staande aan de noord-, west- en oostzijde van het Buitenhof van 1600 tot circa 1830', *Jaarboek Die Haghe* (1941), 123–42.

Meij, J.C.A. de, *De watergeuzen en de Nederlanden, 1568–1572* (Amsterdam, 1972).

Mensonides, H.M., 'De geschiedenis van de huizen op de Lange Vijverberg', *Jaarboek Die Haghe* (1947), 205–33.

Moel, H. de, 'Moet mij voortaen voor stercke bieren wachten, biezonder des avonts. Het dagboek van Willem Frederik van Nassau-Dietz', *Groniek* (2001), 547–57.

Molhuysen, P.C., F.H. Kossmann and P.J. Blok (eds), *Nieuw Nederlandsch Biografisch Woordenboek* (10 vols: Amsterdam, 1911–37).

Mörke, O., 'Sovereignty and Authority. The Role of the Court in the Netherlands in the First Half of the Seventeenth Century', in: R.G. Asch and A.M. Birke (eds), *Princes, Patronage and the Nobility. The Court at the Beginning of the Modern Age, c. 1450–1650* (Oxford, 1991), 455–77.

——, 'De hofcultuur van het huis Oranje-Nassau in de zeventiende eeuw', in: W. Frijhoff, P. Burke and P. te Boekhorst (eds), *Cultuur en maatschappij in Nederland 1500–1850. Een historisch-antropologisch perspectief* (Heerlen, 1992), 39–77.

——, *'Stadtholder' oder 'Staetholder'? Die Funktion des Hauses Oranien und seines Hofes in der politischen Kultur der Republik der Vereinigten Niederlande im 17. Jahrhundert* (Münster, 1997).

Morren, Th., *Het huis Honselaarsdijk* (Alphen aan de Rijn, 1990).

Mousnier, R., *Etat et société sous François Ier et pendant le gouvernement personel de Louis XIV* (Paris, n.d.).

——, 'Les fidélités et les clientèles en France aux XVIe, XVIIe, et XVIIIe siècles', *Histoire Sociale*, 15 (1982), 35–46.

Mulder-Radetzky, R., 'Het hof van Willem en Anna in Leeuwarden', in: J.J. Huizinga (ed.), *Van Leeuwarden naar Den Haag. Rond de verplaatsing van het stadhouderlijk hof in 1747* (Leeuwarden, 1997), 59–72.

——, 'Huizen van Albertine Agnes', in: S. Groenveld, J.J. Huizinga and Y.B. Kuiper (eds), *Nassau uit de schaduw van Oranje* (Franeker, 2003), 99–112.

Nedermeijer ridder van Rosenthal, 'Het strafgeding tegen Johan van Messem en Dirck van Ruyven', *BVGO*, 10 (1856), 195–239.

Neuschel, K.B., *Word of Honor. Interpreting Noble Culture in Sixteenth-Century France* (Ithaca and London, 1989).

——, 'Noblewomen and War in sixteenth-century France', in: M. Wolfe (ed.), *Changing Identities in Early Modern France* (Durham and London, 1997), 124–44.

Nienes, A.P. van, 'Inleiding', in: Idem and M. Bruggeman, *Archieven van de Friese stadhouders* (Leeuwarden and Hilversum, 2003), 13–77.

——, and M. Bruggeman, *Archieven van de Friese stadhouders* (Leeuwarden and Hilversum, 2003).

Nierop, H.F.K. van, 'Willem van Oranje als hoog edelman. Patronage in de Habsburgse Nederlanden?', *BMGN*, 99 (1984), 651–76.

——, *The Nobility of Holland. From Knights to Regents, 1500–1650* (Cambridge, 1993).

Noonan, J.T., *Bribes* (Berkeley, 1984).

Nooten, S.I. van, *Prins Willem II* (The Hague, 1915).

Obreen, H.T., *Harlingen. Inventaris der archieven* (Bolsward, 1968).

Ottenheym, K., 'Van Bouw-lust soo beseten. Frederik Hendrik en de bouwkunst', in: M. Keblusek and J. Zijlmans (eds), *Vorstelijk vertoon. Aan het hof van Frederik Hendrik en Amalia* (Zwolle and The Hague, 1997), 105–25.

Otterspeer, W., *Groepsportret met dame. Het bolwerk van de vrijheid. De Leidse universiteit 1575–1672* (Amsterdam, 2000).

Panhuysen, L., *De ware vrijheid. De levens van Johan en Cornelis de Witt* (Amsterdam, 2005).

Pauw, C., *Strubbelingen in Stad en Lande* (Groningen and Djakarta, 1956).

Peck, L.L., *Court Patronage and Corruption in Early Stuart England* (London, 1990).

——, *Consuming Splendour. Society and Culture in Seventeenth-century England* (Cambridge, 2005).

Perlot, T., *De Staten van Utrecht en Willem III. De houding van de Staten van Utrecht tegenover Willem III tijdens het eerste stadhouderloze tijdperk (1650–1672)* (Utrecht, 2000).

Piattoni, S. (ed.), *Clientelism, Interests, and Democratic Representation. The European Experience in Historical and Comparative Perspective* (Cambridge, 2001).

Plaat, G. van der, 'Lieuwe van Aitzema's kijk op het stadhouderschap', *BMGN*, 103 (1988), 341–72.

——, *Eenheid als opdracht. Lieuwe van Aitzema's bijdrage aan het publieke debat in de Republiek* (Hilversum, 2003).

Ploeg, P. van der and Carola Vermeeren (eds), *Vorstelijk verzameld. De kunstcollectie van Frederik Hendrik en Amalia* (Zwolle and The Hague, 1997).

Poelhekke, J.J., *Geen blijder maer in tachtigh jaer. Verspreide studien over de crisisperiode 1648–1650* (Zutphen, 1973).

——, *Frederik Hendrik. Prins van Oranje. Een biografisch drieluik* (Zutphen, 1978).

—— et al. (eds), *Geschiedenis van Gelderland* (Zutphen, 1975).

Pollmann, J., 'Dienst en wederdienst. Aspecten van patronage in bestuur en samenleving', in: L.H.M. Wessels et al. (eds), *Het ancien régime. Europa in de vroegmoderne tijd* (Heerlen, 1991), 51–74.

——, *Religious Choice in the Dutch Republic. The Reformation of Arnoldus Buchelius (1565–1641)* (Manchester, 1999).

——, 'The Bond of Christian Piety. The Individual Practice of Tolerance and Intolerance in the Dutch Republic', in: R. Hsia and H.F.K. van Nierop (eds), *Calvinism and Religious Toleration in the Dutch Golden Age* (Cambridge, 2002), 53–71.

Porter, R. (ed.), *Rewriting the Self. Histories from the Renaissance to the Present* (New York and London, 1997).

Prak, M.R., 'Republiek en vorst. De stadhouders en het staatsvormingsproces in de Noordelijke Nederlanden, 16ᵉ–18ᵉ eeuw', in: K. Bruin and K. Verrips (eds), *Door het volk gedragen. Koningschap en samenleving* (Groningen, 1989), 28–52.

——, 'The Politics of Intolerance. Citizenship and Religion in the Dutch Republic', in:

R. Hsia and H.F.K. van Nierop (eds), *Calvinism and Religious Toleration in the Dutch Golden Age* (Cambridge, 2002), 159–75.

Price, J.L., *Holland and the Dutch Republic in the Seventeenth Century. The Politics of Particularism* (Oxford, 1994).

——, 'The Dutch Nobility in the Seventeenth and Eighteenth Centuries', in: H.M. Scott (ed.), *The European Nobilities in the Seventeenth and Eighteenth Centuries* (vol. 1, London and New York, 1995), 82–113.

Raa, F.J.G. ten and F. de Bas, *Het Staatsche leger, 1568–1795* (vols 4 and 5: Breda, 1918 and 1921).

Randeraad, N. and D.J. Wolffram, 'Constraints on Clientelism: The Dutch Path to Modern Politics, 1848–1917', in: S. Piattoni (ed.), *Clientelism, Interests, and Democratic Representation. The European Experience in Historical and Comparative Perspective* (Cambridge, 2001), 101–21.

Raptschinsky, B., 'Uit de geschiedenis van den Amsterdamschen handel op Rusland in de XVIIᵉ eeuw. Georg Everhard Clenck', *Jaarboek Amstelodamum*, 34 (1937), 57–83.

——, 'Het gezantschap van Koenraad van Klenck naar Moskou', *Jaarboek Amstelodamum*, 36 (1939), 149–99.

Reinhard, W., 'Oligarchische Verflechtung und Konfession in oberdeutschen Städten', in: A. Mączak (ed.), *Klientelsysteme im Europa der frühen Neuzeit* (Munich, 1988), 47–62.

——, *Power Elites and State Building* (Oxford, 1996).

Rietbergen, P.J.A.N., 'Beeld en zelfbeeld. Nederlandse identiteit in politieke structuur en politieke cultuur tijdens de Republiek', *BMGN*, 107 (1992), 635–56.

Roelevink, J., 'Lobby bij de Staten-Generaal in de vroege zeventiende eeuw', *Jaarboek Die Haghe* (1990), 153–67.

Rogier, L.J., 'Oranje en de Nederlandse staat', in: L.J. Rogier, *Herdenken en herzien. Verzamelde opstellen van L.J. Rogier* (Bilthoven, 1974), 271–92.

Roodhuyzen, T., *De Admiraliteit van Friesland* (Franeker, 2003).

Roorda, D.J., *Partij en factie. De oproeren van 1672 in de steden van Holland en Zeeland. Een krachtmeting tussen partijen en facties* (Groningen, 1961).

——, 'Prosopografie, een onmogelijke mogelijkheid?', in: Idem, *Rond prins en patriciaat. Verspreide opstellen van D.J. Roorda* (Weesp, 1984), 42–52.

——, 'Le Secret du prince. Monarchale tendenties in de Republiek', in: Idem, *Rond prins en patriciaat. Verspreide opstellen van D.J. Roorda* (Weesp, 1984), 172–89.

——, and H. van Dijk, *Het patriciaat van Zierikzee tijdens de Republiek* (n.p., 1979).

Rowen, H.H., *John de Witt, Grand Pensionary of Holland, 1625–1672* (Princeton, 1978).

——, 'Neither Fish nor Fowl. The Stadholderate in the Dutch Republic', in: H.H. Rowen and A. Lossky (eds), *Political Ideas and Institutions in the Dutch Republic* (Los Angeles, 1985), 3–31.

——, *The Princes of Orange. The Stadholders in the Dutch Republic* (Cambridge, 1988).

Rijn, G. van, *Atlas van Stolk. Katalogus der historie-, spot- en zinneprenten betrekkelijk de geschiedenis van Nederland* (10 vols: Rotterdam, 1895–1933).

Salman, J., 'Troebelen en tijdsordening. De actualiteit in zeventiende-eeuwse almanakken', *De zeventiende eeuw*, 17 (2001), 3–17.

Schacht, M. and J. Meiner (eds), *Onder den Oranje boom. Nederlandse kunst en cultuur aan Duitse vorstenhoven in de zeventiende en achttiende eeuw* (Munich, 1999).

Schama, S., *The Embarrassment of Riches. An Interpretation of Dutch Culture in the Golden Age* (London, 1987).

Scherft, P., *Het sterfhuis van Willem van Oranje* (Leiden, 1966).

Schilling, H., 'The Orange Court. The Configuration of the Court in an Old European Republic', in: R.G. Asch and A.M. Birke (eds), *Princes, Patronage and the Nobility. The Court at the Beginning of the Modern Age, c.1450–1650* (Oxford, 1991), 441–54.

Schmidt, S.W. et al. (eds), *Friends, Followers and Factions. A Reader in Political Clientelism* (Berkeley, 1977).

Schöffer, I., 'Naar consolidatie en behoud onder Hollands leiding (1593–1716)', in: S.J. Fockema Andreae and H. Hardenberg (eds), *500 jaren Staten-Generaal in de Nederlanden* (Assen, 1964), 64–98.

Schutte, G., 'Nederland. Een calvinistische natie?', *BMGN*, 107 (1992), 690–702.

Schutte, O., *Repertorium der Nederlandse vertegenwoordigers, residerende in het buitenland 1584–1810* (The Hague, 1976).

Schuurman, A. and P. Spierenburg (eds), *Private Domain, Public Inquiry. Families and Lifestyles in the Netherlands and Europe, 1550 to the Present* (Hilversum, 1996).

Sickenga, J., *Het Hof van Friesland gedurende de zeventiende eeuw* (Leiden, 1856).

Slicher van Bath, B.H. et al. (eds), *Geschiedenis van Overijssel* (Deventer, 1979).

Slothouwer, F.G., 'Een provinciale klerk', *BVGO*, 3rd series, 4 (1888), 88–95.

Smit, F.R.H., 'Jacob Schickhart 1584–1664, raad en landschrijver van de landschap Drenthe', in: P. Brood et al. (eds), *Vergezichten op Drenthe. Opstellen over Drentse geschiedenis* (Meppel, 1983), 206–21.

——, *Bestuursinstellingen en ambtenaren van de landschap Drenthe, 1600–1750* (Assen, 1984).

Smit, J.G., 'De ambtenaren van de centrale overheidsorganen der Republiek in het begin van de zeventiende eeuw', *TvG*, 90 (1977), 378–90.

Spaans, J., *Haarlem na de reformatie. Stedelijke cultuur en kerkelijk leven, 1577–1620* (The Hague, 1989).

——, 'Religious Policies in the Seventeenth-century Dutch Republic', in: R. Hsia and H.F.K. van Nierop (eds), *Calvinism and Religious Toleration in the Dutch Golden Age* (Cambridge, 2002), 72–86.

——, 'Violent Dreams, Peaceful Coexistence. On the Absence of Religious Violence in the Dutch Republic', *De zeventiende eeuw*, 18 (2002), 149–66.

Spanninga, H., 'Patronage in Friesland in de 17ᵉ en 18ᵉ eeuw. Een eerste terreinverkenning', *De Vrije Fries*, 67 (1987), 11–26.

——, 'Ick laet niet met mij gecken. Over beeld en zelfbeeld, macht en invloed van de Friese stadhouder Willem Frederik van Nassau (1613–1664)', *Jaarboek Oranje-Nassau museum* (1997), 55–96.

——, 'Om de vrije magistraatsbestelling. Machtsverhoudingen en politiek in Leeuwarden', in: R. Kunst (ed.), *Leeuwarden 750–2000. Hoofdstad van Friesland* (Franeker, 1999), 128–58.

——, 'Kapitaal en fortuin. Hessel van Sminia (1588–1670) en de opkomst van zijn familie', *De Vrije Fries*, 81 (2001), 9–52.

Stegeman, S., *Patronage and Services in the Republic of Letters. The Network of Theodorus*

Janssonius van Almeloveen (1657–1712) (Amsterdam, 2005).

Stephenson, B., *The Power and Patronage of Marguerite de Navarre* (Aldershot, 2004).

Stern, J., 'The Rhetoric of Popular Orangism, 1650–1672', *Historical Research*, 77 (2004), 202–24.

Stolp, A., *De eerste couranten in Holland. Bijdrage tot de geschiedenis der geschreven nieuwstijdingen* (Haarlem, 1938).

Stone, L., *The Family, Sex, and Marriage in England, 1500–1800* (New York, 1977).

Streng, J.C., *Stemme in staat. De bestuurlijke elite in de stadsrepubliek Zwolle 1579–1795* (Hilversum, 1997).

——, 'Le métier du noble: De Overijsselse Ridderschap tussen 1622 en 1795', in: J.C. Streng, A.J. Mensema and J. Mooijweer, *De ridderschap van Overijssel. Le métier du noble* (Zwolle, 2000), 49–110.

Swann, J., *Provincial Power and Absolute Monarchy. The Estates General of Burgundy, 1661–1790* (Cambridge, 2003).

Swart, K.W., *William of Orange and the Revolt of the Netherlands, 1572–1584* (Aldershot, 2003).

Sypesteyn, J.W. van, *Geschiedkundige bijdragen. Eerste aflevering. Willem Frederik, prins van Nassau en Johan de Witt* (The Hague, 1864).

Tadmor, N., *Family and Friends in Eighteenth-Century England. Household, Kinship, and Patronage* (Cambridge, 2001).

Taylor, Ch., *Sources of the Self. The Making of the Modern Identity* (Cambridge, 1989).

Thoen, I., *Strategic Affection? Gift Exchange in Seventeenth-century Holland* (Amsterdam, 2007).

Tiethoff-Spliethoff, M.E., 'De hofhouding van Frederik Hendrik', *Jaarboek Oranje-Nassau museum* (1989), 41–62.

Tonckens, N., 'Het proces-Schulenborgh (1662) in het licht van de stadhouderlijke politiek in Stad en Lande', *Groningse volksalmanak* (1963), 66–93.

Troost, W., *William III. The Stadholder-king. A Political Biography* (Aldershot, 2004).

Tuinen, P. van, 'Mars en Minerva. De stadhouders en de Franeker Academie', in: S. Groenveld, J.J. Huizinga and Y.B. Kuiper (eds), *Nassau uit de schaduw van Oranje* (Franeker, 2003), 57–70.

Uhlig, C., *Hofkritik im England des Mittelalters und der Renaissance. Studien zu einem Gemeinplatz der europäischen Moralistik* (Berlin, 1973).

Veeze, B.J., *De raad van de prinsen van Oranje tijdens de minderjarigheid van Willem III 1650–1668* (Assen, 1932).

Velema, W.R.E., 'That a Republic is Better than a Monarchy'. Anti-monarchism in Early Modern Dutch Political Thought', in: M. van Gelderen and Q. Skinner (eds), *Republicanism. A Shared European Heritage* (Volume I: Cambridge, 2002), 9–26.

Veluwenkamp, J.W., *Archangel. Nederlandse ondernemers in Rusland, 1550–1785* (Amsterdam, 2000).

Vetter, K., *Am Hofe Wilhelms von Oranien* (Leipzig, 1990).

Visser, J., 'Adel en "Adel" in de Staten van Friesland in de 17ᵉ en 18ᵉ eeuw', *De Nederlandsche Leeuw*, 78 (1961), 430–57.

——, 'Het huwelijk van Willem Frederik en wat er aan vooraf ging', *De Vrije Fries*, 47 (1966), 5–39.

——, 'De Friese stadhouders, De Witt en de Unie', in: J.J. Kalma and K. de Vries (eds), *Friesland in het rampjaar 1672. It jier fan de miste kânsen* (Leeuwarden, 1972), 73–91.

Vries, O., 'Geschapen tot een ieders nut. Een verkennend onderzoek naar de Noordnederlandse ambtenaar in de tijd van het Ancien Régime', *TvG*, 90 (1977), 328–49.

——, 'Friese bureaucratie in Den Haag. Het ambt van klerk wegens Friesland ter griffie van de Generaliteit', *De Vrije Fries*, 58 (1978), 11–29.

——, et al. (eds), *De Heeren van den Raede. Biografieën en groepsportretten van de raadsheren van het Hof van Friesland, 1499–1811* (Leeuwarden and Hilversum, 1999).

Wagenaar, J., *Amsterdam in zyne opkomst, aanwas, geschiedenissen, voorregten, koophandel …* (13 vols: Amsterdam, 1760–68).

Wagenaar, P. and O. van der Meij, 'Een schout in de fout? Fred Riggs' prismatische model toegepast op de zaak Van Banchem', *TSEG*, 2 (2005), 22–46.

Waterbolk, E.H., 'Staatkundige geschiedenis' in: W.J. Formsma (ed.), *Historie van Groningen. Stad en Land* (Groningen, 1976), 235–76.

——, 'Met Willem Lodewijk aan tafel (17.3.1560–13.7.1620)', in: E.H. Waterbolk, *Verspreide opstellen* (Amsterdam, 1981), 296–315.

Weintraub, J., 'The Theory and Politics of the Public-Private Distinction', in: J. Weintraub and K. Kumar (eds), *Public and Private in Thought and Practice. Perspectives on a Grand Dichotomy* (Chicago, 1997), 1–42.

Wheelock A.K. (ed.), *The Public and the Private in the Dutch Golden Age* (New York, 2000).

Wijnne, J.A., *De geschillen over de afdanking van 't krijgsvolk in de vereenigde Nederlanden in de jaren 1649 en 1650* (Utrecht, 1885).

Wijsenbeek-Olthuis, Th. (ed.), *Het Lange Voorhout. Monumenten, mensen en macht* (Zwolle and The Hague, 1998).

Wildeman, M.G., *Elisabeth Musch. Geschiedkundige aantekeningen* (Amersfoort, 1896).

Wolf, E., 'Kinship, Friendship, and Patron-Client Relations in Complex Societies', in: S.W. Schmidt et al. (eds), *Friends, Followers and Factions. A Reader in Political Clientelism* (Berkeley, 1977), 167–77.

Woltjer, J.J., *Friesland in hervormingstijd* (Leiden, 1962).

——, 'De plaats van de calvinisten in de Nederlandse samenleving', *De zeventiende eeuw*, 10 (1994), 3–23.

Woolf, D., *The Social Circulation of the Past. English Historical Culture 1500–1730* (Oxford, 2003).

Wootton, D., 'Francis Bacon. Your Flexible Friend', in: J.H. Elliot and L.W.B. Brockliss (eds), *The World of the Favourite* (New Haven and London, 1999), 184–204.

Zandvliet, K., 'Het hof van een dienaar met vorstelijke allure', in: K. Zandvliet (ed.), *Maurits. Prins van Oranje* (Zwolle and Amsterdam, 2000), 36–63.

——, 'Maurits' Haagse hovelingen', in: K. Zandvliet (ed.), *Maurits. Prins van Oranje* (Zwolle and Amsterdam, 2000), 437–45.

—— (ed.), *Maurits. Prins van Oranje* (Zwolle and Amsterdam, 2000).

Zijlmans, J., 'Aan het Haagse hof', in: J. Zijlmans and M. Keblusek (eds), *Vorstelijk vertoon. Aan het hof van Frederik Hendrik en Amalia* (Zwolle and The Hague, 1997), 30–45.

Zijlstra, S., 'Anabaptism and Tolerance. Possibilities and Limitations', in: R. Hsia and

H.F.K. van Nierop (eds), *Calvinism and Religious Toleration in the Dutch Golden Age* (Cambridge, 2002), 112–31.

Zwitzer, H.L., *De militie van den staat. Het leger van de Republiek der Verenigde Nederlanden* (The Hague, 1991).

Index